Praise for *The Lost History of Ancient America*

"Frank Joseph has in *The Lost History of Ancient America* proven that there were advanced civilizations long before Columbus. Global navigation, trade, agriculture, and major cities existed and thrived. This forgotten, lost history, is amazing when you realize the advancements that were made and lost. This book is meticulously researched and absorbing as Mr. Joseph takes us on an unforgettable journey to our past and perhaps our future."

—Erskine, host of Erskine Overnight

THE LOST HISTORY OF
ANCIENT
AMERICA

HOW OUR CONTINENT WAS SHAPED BY
CONQUERORS, INFLUENCERS, AND OTHER
VISITORS FROM ACROSS THE OCEAN

EDITED BY FRANK JOSEPH

New Page BOOKS

THE LOST HISTORY OF ANCIENT AMERICA
EDITED BY JODI BRANDON
TYPESET BY PERFECTYPE, NASHVILLE, TENNESEE
Cover design by vril8.com
Printed in the U.S.A.

To order this title, please call toll-free 1-800-CAREER-1 (NJ and Canada: 201-848-0310) to order using VISA or MasterCard, or for further information on books from Career Press.

The Career Press, Inc.
12 Parish Drive
Wayne, NJ 07470
www.careerpress.com

Library of Congress Cataloging-in-Publication Data
CIP Data Available Upon Request.

DEDICATION

———————◆●◆———————

John Joseph White III, PhD,
and David John Hoffman,
honored colleagues,
who passed away during the
production of this book.

———————◆●◆———————

CONTENTS

SECTION III: UNDERWATER DISCOVERIES

SECTION IV: ARTIFACTS OF TRANSOCEANIC CONTACT

SECTION V: SITES

SECTION VI: THE FIRST AMERICANS

SECTION VII: GIANTS

SECTION VIII: NORSE

SECTION IX: MAYA

Section X: Pre-Columbian Asians

Section XI: Updates

INTRODUCTION:
COLUMBUS WAS LAST

This book is a breakthrough. Never before and nowhere else has so much valid evidence been assembled on behalf of overseas' visitors in America before Columbus. Presentations offered here are not speculations, exaggerations, or out-of-context half-truths. Instead, they establish beyond question that transoceanic travelers to our continent explored and exploited it hundreds and thousands of years prior to *Santa Maria*'s late-15th-century landfall in the Bahamas.

The Lost History of Ancient America closes the debate between cultural diffusionists—who have always known that our ancient ancestors did not shrink from the sea as an impassable barrier—and cultural isolationists, certain that humans lacked the knowhow and courage for global navigation until little more than 500 years ago.

With publication of this, the fourth in a series of articles from *Ancient American* magazine, skeptics no longer have an academic leg to stand on, but must fall back, as they have always done and surely will do again, on *argumentum ad hominem* and *argumentum ad verecundiam* dismissals of the facts they never address. These up-holders of the Columbus-Was-First paradigm and their textbook denials of our country's prehistory are in the process of being replaced by the truth—the whole truth and nothing but the truth about our origins as a people and a civilization.

Radically innovative as *The Lost History of Ancient America* may seem today, future generations will regard its version of antiquity as self-evident. Rising to the challenge of re-creating it in the face of official disdain, our investigators show how a profusion of plants flourishing throughout the United States and Canada was set in motion more than 20 centuries ago by visitors sailing from Western Europe, Asia, and the Near East. We learn of our country's oldest rock art, and prehistoric oil wells in Pennsylvania. There is Mexico's newly discovered crystal skull, the most beautiful and authentically Aztec example of its kind. It is joined by Lake Michigan's largest island, once the site for a stellar observatory of astonishing complexity; an imperial Chinese sword recovered from a small stream in rural Georgia; Mayan mastery of liquid mercury; a Pharaonic Egyptian cat burial near St. Louis, Missouri. These and numerous other revelations combine to radically rewrite American prehistory, presenting us with a revision more dramatic and engaging than ever before imagined, because it is real.

Even so, *The Lost History of Ancient America* is not a bloodless collection of dry facts narrated in techno-speak only over-seasoned academics and self-satisfied specialists delight in arguing among themselves. They will predictably despise this book, because it is written in concise, comprehensive, clear language for popular audiences—readers intelligent enough to think for themselves and weigh the evidence without being told what to believe on the authority of others. History, we affirm, belongs to anyone who can appreciate it, and is not the exclusive privilege of salaried professionals. But our agenda is not theirs, and we go our way.

Readers need only understand that we have substituted BC ("Before Christ") with BCE ("Before Common Era") and use CE ("Common Era") instead of AD, not "After Death," as is still generally misunderstood, but from the Latin *anno domini*, "in the year of the Lord"—the unknown year in which Jesus was born. As confusingly inadequate as all these terms certainly are, we beg your indulgence and require only a certain open-mindedness for consideration of the heretical information marshaled in the following pages.

SECTION I

FAUNA AND FLORA

———◦•◦•◦———

Perhaps never before has so much incontrovertible evidence been published in so few words establishing beyond question that humans reached and occupied America long before 1492, as in our opening chapters. Their most potent proofs are not pottery shards or ruined cities, but animals and plants. Professor Steven Jones shows that the horse was not introduced to our continent by modern Europeans, but by others long prior to the 16th-century arrival of Spanish conquistadors.

Jones was a full professor of physics at Brigham Young University, where he served for more than 21 years before his early retirement in 2007. He conducted doctoral research at the Stanford Linear Accelerator Center, receiving his PhD in physics from Vanderbilt University, in 1978. Five years earlier, he received his BS degree in physics from Brigham Young University, where he held a David O. McKay Presidential Scholarship. His research interests include studies in fusion, solar energy, and archaeometry. Archaeometry is the application of scientific techniques to the analysis of archaeological materials, to assist in their dating. Jones has published papers in *Nature, Scientific American*, and *Physical Review Letter*s. He taught an advanced class on archaeometry (Physics 513R) and published "Archaeometry Applied to Olmec Iron-ore Beads" in 1997. The radiometric dating he mentions is a method comparing the amount of a naturally occurring, radioactive isotope and its decay products in samples to determine their age.

Jones's pioneering work on pre-Columbian horses is wonderfully complemented by the no less orthodoxy-shattering discoveries made by Carl L. Johannessen, professor emeritus, department of geography, at the University of Oregon (Eugene, Oregon). While there, he conducted research in the United States and Latin America until 1985, when he began studying South Asia and China. Since his retirement as a faculty member of the University's department of geography for 30 years, he conducts research on plants and animals so modified by humans that if they are found away from their region of origin, their presence indicates they had to have been carried across continents and even oceans by subsequent discoverers and collectors.

Born in Bristol, England, Julia Patterson (1931–2015) was a professor of archaeology-anthropology at London College for 16 years before moving to the United States, where her field expeditions in the American Southwest with the University of Illinois (Urbana) unearthed stone tools far older than official versions of the first human habitation sites in the state. Thereafter, she increasingly broadened her research to include overseas' influences in America predating academic opinion. Professor Patterson's analysis of a unique burial near the Illinois River indicates its resemblances to ancient Egyptian funeral practices.

The "Hopewell" she mentions was a populous, relatively sophisticated, mound-building culture that raised elegant ceremonial centers and spread over much of the Middle West and parts of the South from circa 500 BCE to 400 CE. Hopewell origins are controversial, racial differences from Amer-Indian tribal peoples appear in more gracile cranial features, and Hopewell material culture was markedly advanced over that of contemporaneous, indigenous societies.

1

Horses in America Before Columbus

By Dr. Steven E. Jones

Shortly after the turn of the 21st century, I began a project to seek horse bones from sites in North America and Mesoamerica for the purpose of radiocarbon dating them. In this research, I was joined by Professor Wade Miller of the Brigham Young University department of geology, archaeologists Joaquin Arroyo-Cabrales and Shelby Saberon, and Patricia M. Fazio of the Buffalo Bill Historical Center.

We secured horse bones for dating, some directly from the field. Then state-of-the-art radiocarbon dating was performed at Stafford Laboratories in Colorado, the University of California at Riverside, or Beta Analytic in Miami, Florida, employing Accelerator Mass Spectrometer (AMS) dating methods. The reliability of the AMS method of radiocarbon dating of bones is delineated in *Radiocarbon*.[1]

Our goal was to provide radiocarbon dates for samples that appeared from depth or other considerations to be pre-Columbian. The time frame of interest can be expressed in terms of "Before Present" by convention and extends from 10,000 BP (thus, after the last ice age) to 500 BP (when Spaniards brought horses to America). The prevailing paradigm holds that there were no horses in the Americas during this time interval. The samples in our study can be divided into two categories according to their origins: Mexico and the United States. Forty-five *Equus* samples were obtained in Mexico. Based on AMS dating, there was one sample from the Ice Age period and six from the post-Columbus period.

Other samples had insufficient collagen in the bone to permit dating; collagen protein locks in carbon-14, permitting accurate C-14 dating. Thus, the laboratories require a certain minimum amount of collagen in order to proceed with the dating. There were no *Equus* samples found in this study in Mesoamerica for the time interval 14,700 BCE to 1650 CE. By contrast, in North America there are found *Equus* samples, which do indeed appear in the time frame between the last ice age and the arrival of Columbus.

The first of these was found in Pratt Cave, near El Paso, Texas, by Professor Ernest Lundelius of Texas A&M University. Professor Lundelius responded to my inquiries and provided a horse bone from Pratt Cave, which dated to BCE 6020 to 5890 BCE. This date is well since the last ice age into the time frame when all American horses should have been absent according to the prevailing paradigm.

Another *Equus* specimen was identified by Elaine Anderson, an expert on *Equus* identification, at Wolf Spider Cave, Colorado. It dated to 1260 to 1400 CE—again, clearly before Columbus. Note that horses arrived on the New World mainland with Hernan Cortes, in 1519 CE. Dr. Patricia Fazio of the Buffalo Bill Historical Center, in Cody, Wyoming, has joined our network of researchers in this field. Dr. Fazio ([in] private communication) alerted us to a horse bone found at Horsethief Cave, in Wyoming, which dates to approximately 3124 BP (i.e., 1100 BCE) using thermoluminescent methods. We attempted to have this bone re-dated using the AMS methods, which are more accurate, but there proved to be insufficient collagen in the bone to permit AMS dating. The 1100 BCE date (although approximate) still stands.

Dr. Fazio also pointed to a publication, *The Wyoming Archaeologist*, in which results of a horse bone found in Wyoming were dated to 1426 to 1481 CE (one sigma calibrated dates) using AMS methods, long before

Columbus. The authors express difficulty in explaining this early date: "These radiocarbon dates place the horse skeleton at a very early age for modern horses to have been in Wyoming."[2]

A paper by Dr. R. Alison notes evidence for horses in Canada dating 929 hundred years ago, also in the period of interest.[3] However, the complete extirpation of ancestral horse stock in Canada has yet to be completely confirmed, and a bone found near Sutherland, Saskatchewan, at the Riddell archaeological site, suggests some horses might have survived much later. The bone has been tentatively dated at about 2,900 years ago.[4]

Another *Equus sp.* bone found at Hemlock Park Farm, Frontenac County, Ontario, dates to about 900 years ago. Exhaustive confirmation of both bones has yet to be completed, but if they prove to be authentic, they comprise evidence that horses survived in Canada into comparatively modern times.

Thus, there are a half dozen dated *Equus* samples that date in the time frame 6000 BCE to 1481 CE, well since the last ice age and all before Columbus. Note that all of these radiometrically dated *Equus* remains were found in North America.

In addition to this hard physical evidence, a number of researchers are looking seriously into oral histories of Native Americans, which point rather clearly to the existence of horses before the Spanish arrived. In particular, we note that research results have been published by Yuri Kuckinsky.[5] For example, the Appaloosa horse appears to have been in North America before the Spanish brought European horses. A January 2012 publication describes progress in DNA analyses of horses which promises to open new avenues for this research:

> In recent years, many scholars have embraced the hypothesis that the Botai or other inhabitants of the Eurasian Steppes became the first people to tame the wild horse, *Equus ferus*, between four thousand and six thousand years ago. This theory implies that horses were domesticated in a similar manner to other modern livestock, such as cattle, sheep and goats, said Alessandro Achilli, a geneticist at the University of Pavia, in Italy. DNA analyses have revealed little genetic variation among these animals, suggesting that they descended from a small group of ancestors tamed in just a few places, he explained.

But when Achilli and a team of fellow researchers collected maternally inherited mitochondrial genomes from living horses in Asia, Europe, the Middle East, and the Americas, a strikingly different picture emerged. "We found a high number of different lineages that we were able to identify—at least eighteen," said Achilli, a coauthor of a paper outlining the findings in the January 30 issue of the *Proceedings of the National Academy of Sciences*. . . . Why would disparate groups in far-flung corners of the globe hatch similar schemes to forge partnerships with their equine neighbors? "The very fact that many wild mares were independently domesticated in different places testifies to how significant horses have been to humankind," Achilli said. . . . "The latest findings have the potential to open new avenues for further research into horses both modern and ancient," Achilli said. Now that a large number of horse lineages have been defined, they could be easily employed not only to analyze other modern breeds, including thoroughbreds, but also to classify ancient remains, he explained.[6]

In particular, the *Equus* samples that have been identified in North America, anomalous because they date to the "excluded" period between 6000 BCE and 1490 CE, can now be analyzed to determine whether or not the DNA corresponds to domesticated Spanish horses brought over by the conquistadors. My prediction is that the DNA will not so correspond.

In conclusion, using state-of-the-art dating methods, we, along with other researchers, have found radiometrically dated evidence for the existence of horses in North America long after the last ice age and before the arrival of Columbus. These data challenge the existing paradigm. Further DNA analyses will provide additional data and insights.

2

Plants Connect the Old and New Worlds

By Dr. Carl L. Johannessen

Evidence from 14 plants indicates their presence in both the Old World and America before 1492 CE. We found that drugs and medicinals, such as tobacco, coca, marijuana, datura, and prickly pear, were probably the moneymakers for seafarers connecting both sides of the Atlantic Ocean even millennia ago. The carbohydrates corn and amaranth would also have been attractive, as they were transported after being harvested and dried. The technological benefit of *agave*, a succulent plant with rosettes of narrow spiny leaves and tall flower spikes, as fiber for caulking ships made it a very attractive commercial product. For instance, the fruit of the *Annona* that may have been loaded originally to resist scurvy could have had its seeds dried and carried home as an additional rationale. *Annona* is a plant having a permanently woody main stem or trunk, ordinarily growing to a considerable height, and usually developing branches at some distance from the ground.

The peanut, kidney bean, lima bean, and phasey bean were especially useful to the pre-Columbian sailors, because they are dry and are a reasonable source of concentrated protein and carbohydrates for onboard food. Basil must have interested the ancient voyagers, due to its light weight and high trade value. Many contacts between people of cultures on both sides of all Earth's oceans took place before Columbus first sailed to America. Until the advent of radiocarbon dating and DNA analysis, there was really no definitive way to prove an alternative theory of contact between people from civilizations separated by distant seas in different hemispheres.

But new evidence of dated discoveries demonstrate tropical sailors from both sides of the world did indeed exchange plants, diseases, and animals. Emphasis here is on certain plants that were moved and whose remains have been discovered in archaeological excavation horizons and radiocarbon dated to the period prior to the turn of the 15th century CE. Under discussion are those pieces of evidence for which there can be no dissent, because the physical remains of the plants involved were discovered on foreign shores, not their continent of origin, and distributed throughout the new continents into their own proper ecological niches.

Although we describe research focusing on tropical sailors and cultures, we fully acknowledge the important evidence and contribution of Norse mariners of the pre-Columbian era. The fact that there is acknowledged genetic, artistic, cultural, and biological evidence for regular and repeated contact between these Nordic peoples and populations of the northeastern region of North America simply strengthens the hypothesis we are proposing about the tropical sailors of southeast Asia, India, Africa, and the Middle East. The northeast American region supplied relatively few plant exchanges.

Certain rules of evidence have been accepted as a definitive way of ascertaining the quality of the data studied. American paleontologist and evolutionary biologist Stephen J. Gould (1941–2002) once observed that the chances of a living species evolving in two places continents apart independently were so astronomically low as to be an impossible occurrence. The process of evolution is so complex and depends on so many specific conditions that no two places on the planet would ever compare closely enough on another continent for a long enough period of time to allow a species to develop identically in both continents without the presence of the wild ancestral species.

Therefore, hard evidence for early interaction between cultures separated by the vast stretches of ocean between the Americas and the Old World would have to come from showing that living species somehow were taken between hemispheres prior to the historically accepted Voyages of Discovery and after the time of the earliest human migrations to the Americas from East Asia, Europe, or Africa.

Discovery, settlement, and trade are the most obvious reasons for how the transfer of plants and some animals took place, but this report will deal only with the plants.

When people travel to a far land to trade, capture, or settle, they bring things from their homeland as reminders of their roots, and they discover new items, some of which are taken back to the home country. Humans inadvertently carried micro-organisms, parasites, seeds, and small animals on their persons and in their ships long ago, when they went exploring. On returning home, if they had found plants or animals that would be useful to them, they could have packed them up and delivered them to their homelands. With new organisms, the returning mariners could be expected to have known the ecological niches from which they came, and supplied them to their homeland's appropriate niches. Evidence shows that the sailors did, in fact, have this information, on the basis of where the plant remains were found archaeologically.

In the 1970s and 1980s, John Sorenson, professor of anthropology at Brigham Young University, began a massive, annotated bibliography of the available literature published in professional books and journals relevant to demonstrating whether there was sufficient evidence of pre-Columbian transoceanic diffusion to warrant a new look at this theory. After the first two volumes were released in 1990 in the affirmative, a second edition was published in 1996, improving his selections and adding new sources. His two volumes of bibliographies detail hundreds of articles that either infer or directly state that biological species and cultural traits were transferred prior to 1492 CE. If only one or two plants or animals could be discovered as having been transferred, the previously accepted explanations could still explain a few exceptional, accidental travels.

However, Sorenson found indications of a sizable number of organisms and asked me if I would cooperate with him in the production of a report on species of interest for further research. We collaborated and have now positively identified 124 species. These included 97 plant species that have decisive evidence of pre-Columbian transoceanic diffusion. Eighty-four of these 97 plant species originated in the Americas and were transported across the oceans to various locations in the Old World. Fifty of these plants were taken from America to their proper ecological niches in India.

We researched and indexed a large number of these plants to decide how strong the evidence was. We found archaeological evidence of the plants or their biochemical signatures in hemispheres where they did not originate. The archaeological data that had been published in scientific literature contained sufficient information about 15 species that we present now in an attempt to stimulate scientific study of the data. We present the evidence by species for your evaluation.

Drugs, Tobacco, Coca, and Marijuana

Tobacco (*Nicotiana tabacum*) and the coca plant (*Erythroxylon novagranatense*) are both native plants of the Americas, whereas marijuana (*Cannabis sativa*) is a native plant of the Middle East. These three plants have been used for millennia in the Middle East, Egypt, and Peru. Taken together, these three plants are strong evidence of trade among early transoceanic cultures. Each plant would have been used for medicinal or religious purposes, and therefore would have a high sales value for the sailors trying to maximize their profits and still fit the cargo into their relatively small ships. Archeological data disagree with the extant academic Post-Columbian Diffusion Hypothesis. Many of the natural mummies found in Peru have been tested and demonstrate their long use of the native tobacco and coca plant leaves. In the process of these tests, the mummies were also tested for THC, the active ingredient in *Cannabis sativa*, as well as the residue of presumed nicotine/coca chemicals.

In many of the mummies—60 of the 70 studied—one or more of these chemical traces were discovered. The chemicals were discovered inside the hair, teeth, and tissues of the mummies. In 20 of the mummies, researchers discovered the chemicals to which THC breaks down upon ingestion. This indicates that the people who were later mummified were using the Middle Eastern marijuana prior to their deaths. These mummies have been accurately dated to between 115 CE and 1500 CE, in Peru.

Moreover, several researchers studying ancient Indian and Chinese peoples have found metabolized nicotine in the bodies of many pre-Columbian populations. Although there is a remote possibility that another plant may have been responsible for the buildup of the metabolized chemicals from tobacco, it is not likely considering the concentrations they found; and the most rational and economical explanation was that the tobacco leaf was present in Southern China from 3750 BCE!

Marijuana is postulated to have been brought over to the Americas in trade for other plants, animals, and products.

The discovery of metabolically processed chemicals in the Peruvian mummies, enough to indicate sustained use, allows researchers to infer an active and robust trade between the Americas and the Mediterranean Basin and the Middle East. The chemicals related to coca and nicotine found in several Egyptian mummies, dating over a period of 1,400 years, is reciprocal proof of the trade in medicinal plants that existed between the Old World, specifically the Mediterranean Basin, and the Americas, specifically the Peruvian peoples, before Columbus. German forensic researchers discovered the chemicals from digested residue of tobacco and coca, and even pieces of tobacco leaf, in the back of the mummified abdominal cavity of Pharaoh Ramesses II (1303 BCE to 1213 BCE).

The relevant chemicals associated with the ingestion and use of the coca plant have been found in numerous Egyptian mummies of the New Kingdom that date from approximately 1070 BCE to 395 CE. This could not have been contamination, as the metabolites were found inside the body tissues of the radiocarbon-dated mummies, showing that the living person (including children) partook of the plants prior for a significant period of time until their deaths. The presence of the coca products in the Egyptian mummies makes it highly likely, given *cotenien* (metabolized nicotine) in the mummies as well, that both products were traded at the same time from the Americas to Egypt. The three plants all show marked use in the highest levels of Peruvian and Egyptian societies, a steady supply, and understanding of the effects of the plants on the persons using them.

Datura

The thorn apple, datura plant, and Jimsom weed (all datura species) are definitely of American origin. However, they have been used from ancient times in the Eurasian region as a drug, medication, and as hallucinogenic compounds. There are also reports of the use of datura by the Greeks and Romans in their oracles. The earliest archeological evidence of datura appearing in India is from an excavation in the Punjab at the site of Sanghol, where archaeological researchers discovered a fragment of a datura plant among the ruins.

Prickle Poppy

The Mexican or Prickle Poppy (*Argemone Mexicana*) is indigenous and native to the Americas. However, it is so common in India that it is considered a natural wild weed. The introduction of this weed, however, is easy to date, as it has traditionally been used in medical treatments and as part of funeral ceremonies in earlier sub-continent Indian societies. Charred seeds of this plant have been found in India and accurately dated to 1300 to 800 BCE and 1100 BCE to 1060 BCE.

These seeds could have been charred as a result of medicinal treatments or the tradition of cremating the dead with important items. Further evidence of an early transoceanic diffusion is the traditional medical uses for the plant in both the Americas and the Old World; they are very similar in many respects, including their use as hallucinogens. Drugs of this type seem to have attracted many of the tropical mariners to transport their seeds. A little goes a long way; therefore, seeds were easier to pack on the small ships of the time.

Carbohydrate Sources

Corn

Zea mays—corn, for our purposes here—originated in the Americas, where it has been cultivated for several thousands of years. Although there is already a vast amount of literature written about this particular species, it is important to quickly summarize the main archeological evidence for its early diffusion across the oceans to Asia. In archeological excavations on the island of Timor, a researcher has discovered evidence of the corn stalk and seeds dating from 1000 CE. As pointed out earlier, in the same set of caves where annona and peanut were also discovered, peanut was from a slightly earlier levels (800 CE) in the caves.

Representations of corn in the bas-relief sculptures of Hindu temples are dated to the year the temples were constructed during the 11th to 13th Centuries CE by epigraphic written messages on the stelas within the front of the Indian temples. The corn ears being held by consorts to the Hindu gods show more than 35 morphological variations, all specifically related to the distribution of the kernels on maize ears and their shapes in about 100 temples. The depiction is positively corn, as the top left side of the ear shows a parallel seed distribution while the lower right side of the ear reveals the distinctive tessellate distribution.

The varieties of corn ear morphology were recognized as well by corn breeders at the U.S. Department of Agriculture, Ohio Agricultural Research and Development Center, Ohio State University. Wheat and corn breeders in Wooster, Ohio, laughed when told that the photos of maize had been rejected by some "experts" in India. The corn breeders are the real corn experts. Recognize that we, in addition, found maize sculptures in Hindu temples dated in the fifth and eighth centuries CE in Karnataka Pradesh, India.

In addition to maize sculptures, further evidence is given in the use by the Maya Indians of Central America of a written symbol of a "J" on corn plants and ears in their drawings; they wrote the "J" on corn plants on their codices to clarify that the image was in fact a maize plant. The "J" is also used in India in their temples when the stone statues were sculpted with maize ears in their husks held in the corn maiden's hands.

Amaranths

Grain amaranths (*Amaranthus hypochondriacus* and *Amaranthus caudatus*, specifically) are natives to the Americas, yet there is a vast region where these same species are grown that stretches from Eastern China, through the Himalayas as far as ancient Persia (Iran). The vast amount of grain amaranth grown across the Southern Asian region supports the suggestion that the genus has been there since very early times. A review of very complete and extensive official literature from the many empires and states within the region confirms their likely introduction from America. An early-15th-century author, Zhou Ding Wang (d. 1425 CE), definitely includes grain amaranths among his writings, in which he quotes an even older (ninth-century) text on amaranths.

Grain amaranths are well established among some of the most remote peoples of the region. However, the diversity of grain amaranth species in the Old World is miniscule compared to the diversity of grain amaranths in the Americas, solidly placing the origin of the genus in America. It is also important to note that the uses of the plant in food processes are very similar within the cultures of the Americas and the cultures of the Old World, indicating that there was at least some communication between the farmers/consumers in the Americas with those of China at the beginning of the process of transfer. In a final piece of evidence suggesting pre-Colombian diffusion of these species into Asia, archeologists have discovered the seeds of *A. caudatus* and another amaranth, *A. spinosus*, a spiny, weedy amaranth that was also widely distributed in the Americas, in the temple complexes of India. These seeds date from the eighth to 10th centuries CE at excavation sites in Narhan, India.

Fiber: Agave

Historically, the agave plant (*genus Agave*) was important for caulking and waterproofing in early wood shipbuilding. This was done by soaking the agave fibers in a resin of pine pitch and other ingredients, then stuffing this mixture into cracks between boards of the hull. Because the *agave genus* is most definitely a plant of American origin, it would have seemed highly unlikely that any European ships would have used this technology prior to the Voyages of Discovery and the beginning of trade by the Spaniards. Even with the diffusion of the *agave genus* in India being so widespread, a traveler there at the end of the 17th century CE noted that it was almost impossible to believe that the agave plants came to India only after Columbus's voyages. As the traveler's report could not be firmly established, it did not constitute anything more than anecdotal evidence.

However, over the last hundred years, there have been several shipwrecks of European or African origin and ship design that have been excavated by maritime archaeologists. To date, one researcher, Richard Steffy, has announced the discovery of agave fibers found on a ship he was excavating on the bottom of the Mediterranean Sea, north of Cyprus.[1] Other marine archeologists are soon expected to release similar findings, although they must go against conventional wisdom in the process, and Steffy says they have been afraid to publish heretical data.

Archaeologists have found ships close to European and African coasts that had been caulked with the agave fiber/pitch mixture. Steffy's ship used the fiber and pine pitch to seal a lead covering onto the bottom of his ship to reduce Toredo worm damage and make the ship more seaworthy. These sunken ships are of Greek, Phoenician, and Roman design. The Steffy ship is of Greek design, and has been dated accurately to the fourth century BCE.

Some researchers insist that there was a source of agave in the Mediterranean Basin, and it is possible agave had been brought over and planted, although there is no archaeological/botanical evidence of agave plant remains in the ground to be dated so far. Optimistic researchers may find agave plants that grew in the Mediterranean Basin in future investigation. I have seen pictures of what I consider to be agave painted on inside house walls at Pompeii. This location would be a good place to start to hunt for the remains in ash deposits. More likely, the agave-caulked ships were either freighters that were repaired and refurbished in the Americas before a return voyage, or vessels that had been sent to the Americas specifically to undergo this treatment, or to obtain the materials and expertise to bring back to Europe.

By checking the type of pine pitch on the resurrected craft, it should be possible to determine from where the pine resin came. Such laboratory work has not been done as yet. Botanists with high-grade microscopes at London's Kew Gardens, the world's largest collection of living plants, informed Steffy that the fibers were definitely from agave plants, though they could not discern the species; this could be done with DNA analysis. If the pine species were American, it would add another species to the list, which can be discerned by their terpines, any of a large group of volatile, unsaturated hydrocarbons found in the essential oils of plants, especially conifers and citrus trees.

Fruit: *Annona*

The custard apple (*Annona* squamosal) is another plant that originated in the Americas and was transferred across the ocean as far as India and Turkey. Seeds of the *Annona* have been found in caves on the island Timor and radiocarbon dated to between 800 and 1000 CE, when these caves ceased to be inhabited by human populations. In India, seeds of the *Annona* have also been found in archaeological strata dated by radiocarbon dating to 700 BCE among the iron-using culture at Raja Nal-Ka-tila, in the Sonbhadra District of Uttar Pradesh. The inferred route of introduction, supported by the Asian dates and other evidence, suggests the *Annona* was transported across the ocean to India and to Indonesia. I have also seen stone sculptures of the annona fruit in other countries, such as on stone sarcophagi, in Turkey.

Protein Sources

Peanut

The peanut (*Arachis hypogaea*) is another American species that has been extensively discovered in East and South Asia. It was found in the same cave sites as the *Annona* (*Annona squamosal*) and corn (*Zea mays*) on the island of Timor, in Indonesia, by archaeo-botanist Ian Glover, in 1977. This peanut is definitely of American origin, as shown in very early archeological data from Peru and other South American sites. The archeological evidence of the peanut in China is vast and difficult to ignore. Radiocarbon dating of peanuts found in Chinese tombs shows that peanuts were harvested by at least 2000 BCE. The peanuts in Timor were left prior to 800–1000 CE, when the caves became unoccupied. Furthermore, the peanuts found in ancient tombs and archeological sites in Peru look the same as those still harvested to this day, not in Peru, but in South China.

Kidney and Lima Beans

The kidney bean and lima bean (*Phaseolus vulgaris* and *Phaseolus lunatus*) are native to the Americas and had been taken to India at some time before the second millennium BCE. *Phaseolus vulgaris*, *P. lunatus*, and the phasey bean (*Macroptilium lathyroides*) have all been discovered in multiple archaeological sites in India of the second millennium BCE. *P. vulgaris* was recorded from the pre-Prabhas and Prabhas cultures at Prabhas Patan, Junagadh District, Gujarat, dated from 1800 BCE to 600 CE; from Chalcolithic Inamgaon (about 1600 BCE), Pune District, Maharashtra; and from Neolithic Tekkalkota, Bellary District, Karnataka, with a radiocarbon date of 1620 BCE. *P. vulgaris*, *P. lunatus*, and the phasey bean have been recorded in deposits of the Malwa and

Jorwe cultures (1600–1000 BCE) at Diamabad, in Ahmednagar District, Maharashtra. The phasey bean was also found at the Sanghol site, dated in early CE times.

Phasey Bean

The phasey bean (*Macroptilium lathyroides*) is a leguminous plant of American origin. It is the result of the renaming of a species once known as *Phaseolus lathyroides* and is similar in many respects to the members of the *genus Phaseolus*. It has been found in numerous archeological sites around India, dating from as far back as 1800 BCE, and forward through 600 CE. It is known to have been present (perhaps as a weed) and may have been used as food on the Indian subcontinent throughout many empires.

Spice Basil

The basil plant (*Ocimum sp.*) is likely a species of the Old World, native to the Indian subcontinent. There are three species of basil that we are interested in: *O. americanum*, *O. basilum*, and *O. sanctum*. Evidence shows that the sweet basil (*O. sanctum*) was growing widely in the Americas when the Spanish arrived. A carbonized branch (species undetermined) was excavated from the Sanghol site in each of Periods I and II (1300–800 BCE and 800–600 BCE, respectively).

--- * ---

With the 15 plant species described above showing decisive archeological evidence of having been grown on islands and continents separated from their sources by either the Atlantic or Pacific Ocean, it seems impossible that there was no contact between the early cultures of the Old World and the Americas. Because four of the 15 plants we have considered are not foodstuff, but rather those used as medications in religious rituals or for recreational use, it follows that these four were plants that would have been utilized specifically for trade.

Fifteen plants were cited, but coconut, bottle gourd, and sweet potato could have been added, as all are represented by strong archeological evidence in both the Old World and the Americas long before the 16th-century Voyages of Discovery, had space allowed. If only one or two plants showed this early transference, then we might conclude that contact between the cultures of the Old World and the Americas was accidental or occasional, at best. With these plants, plus the numerous other plants and animals for which there is firm but slightly less conclusive than hardcore archaeological evidence, it is unlikely that there was anything less than regular, sustained medicinal and religious drug trade and open contact between the many cultures of these two hemispheres.

Indisputable evidence of archaeological finds across the oceans in, for example, Asia, these numbers demonstrate that sailors traveling between the tropical regions of the hemispheres were not Caucasians. The tropical sailors and crews doing the trading had to have made enough voyages to get to know the habitats of tropical America and Asia (especially tropical India), Africa, and Oceania. The sailors transported plant elements from many ecological niches, so they had to know both continents' habitats, where they were collected, and were subsequently planted. In the process of doing so, the tropical sailors surely exchanged many other cultural traits, as well as biota.

Roff Smith and photographer S. Alvarez for *National Geographic* have pointed out that Polynesians successfully navigated the Pacific to America; however, their view is that these exchanges did not occur until 1000 CE, instead of our suggested date of more than 5,700 years ago, in the case of tobacco to China.[2] Smith simply did not have the archaeological data we have found. The National Geographic Society also could have helped Smith and Alvarez to be reminded that the winds blowing from the west on the Pacific are always blowing as the Roaring 40s on the latitudes poleward of the mid-Pacific high-pressure zones.

The high pressure of the winds, or their lack, are referred to as the Doldrums. The easterly winds, normally blowing in the tropical zones, are known as the trade winds and were counted in the course of America-to-Asia voyages. The vagaries of wind direction during El Niño could have been nearly ignored by the early navigators had they depended on the normal events on the Pacific Ocean. El Niño, "the Child," refers to an irregularly occurring and complex series of climatic changes affecting the equatorial Pacific region and beyond, every few years. This meteorological condition is characterized by the appearance of unusually warm, nutrient-poor water off northern Peru and

Ecuador, typically in late December. Smith simply did not recognize the extent of the movement of plants, and so forth, across the Pacific in earlier times.

Henceforth, we in science will have to accept that the civilizations of the world were in contact with each other and exchanged thousands of traits. Scholars John Sorenson and Martin Raish, director of the David O. McKay Library at Brigham Young University-Idaho, have documented this contact. In the future, scholars working in the field of pre-Columbian diffusion will have Occam's razor on their side of the theory, while others who deny transoceanic diffusion in pre-Columbian times will have an insurmountable task trying to prove that contact did not occur.

3

Egyptian-Style Cat Burial in Illinois

By Professor Julia Patterson

More than 30 years ago, before highway construction engineers could obliterate a prehistoric burial ground, archaeologists excavated its 14 earthworks of various sizes. The structures were perched atop a bluff overlooking the Illinois River in the western part of the Prairie State, less than 50 miles north of St. Louis, Missouri. The largest dome of configured soil measured 92 feet across and stood 8 feet high, as part of a Hopewell Culture complex some 2,000 years old.

The Hopewell were a mound-builder people of far-flung traders and skilled artisans who flourished from circa 600 BCE to their extermination at the hands of Native American tribes by 400 CE. The Illinois site's foremost tomb was found to contain the bones of 22 human adults evenly laid out in a ring formation around the central sepulcher of a male infant skeleton. Nearby the child, carefully interred in its own grave, paws respectfully placed together, were the remains of a bobcat wearing a necklace of drilled, carved bear teeth and the shells of marine animals.

"No other wild cat has been buried by humans in the entire archaeological record," researchers claimed in a study published recently by the *Mid-Continental Journal of Archaeology*.[1] But this supposedly unique discovery went unrecognized until 2011, when Angela Perri, then a PhD student at Britain's University of Durham, re-examined the bobcat's bones, originally misidentified as those of a puppy. She and her colleagues surmised that the Hopewell had tamed the creature, and its revelation is therefore insightful into the human domestication of animals. Perhaps, but the Illinois find might be significant of something else.

The interred bobcat was only between four and seven months old when it died of natural causes. "There were no cut marks or signs of trauma," writes David Grimm, in *Science*, "suggesting that the animal had not been sacrificed . . . The pomp and circumstance of the burial, she [Perri] says, 'suggest this animal had a very special place in the life of these people.' "[2]

Though no other ceremonial internments of the kind have been found in a pre-Columbian setting, many hundreds of thousands of ritualized feline graves are known in Egypt, where Bast, the famous cat-goddess, was worshipped from at least the Late First Dynasty (circa 2900 BCE), probably during earlier, pre-dynastic times. Bubastis (Greek for the original *Per-Bast*, "House of Bast") was a huge city, the capital of its own state (*nome*), located on the Lower Nile, where 20th-century excavation of its chief temple yielded in excess of 300,000 thousand mummified cats.

Previously, during 1888, a farmer accidentally uncovered 700,000 in Beni Hasan, Middle Egypt. These million feline mummies testify to the high veneration with which the ancient Egyptians accorded the creature, which they protected with animal rights legislation. Killing a cat was a capital offense, punishable by death. Whenever a household cat passed away, mourning residents traditionally shaved their hair and eyebrows as expressions of respect and grief. Something of this reverence for the animal seems suggested by the Illinois River's prehistoric gravesite. Another intriguing parallel is Bast's function as the goddess of childbirth, *vis-à-vis* the large mound's infant burial in close proximity to the bobcat. It had been adorned with a necklace, reminiscent of ancient Egyptian representations of Bast.

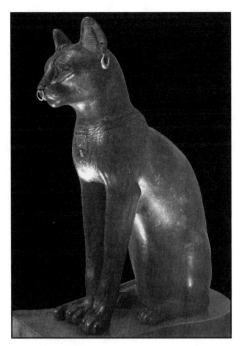

*Late Saite Period Egyptian bronze statue of
Bast, circa 525 BCE.*

These comparisons join a vast body of complementary evidence accumulated on behalf of Pharaonic influences at work in pre-Columbian America. At very least, they suggest that, although the Hopewell were not themselves transplanted Egyptians, they were nonetheless inheritors of cultural legacies left behind by visitors from the Nile Valley to our Continent during prehistory.

4

Eyewitness Engravings of Ancient American Mammoths

By Frank Joseph

During 2009, James Kennedy was cleaning a small animal bone fragment he found two or three years before at Vero Beach, in east-central coastal Florida, when he noticed for the first time that it was engraved with the faint likeness of a wooly mammoth. Intrigued, the fossil hunter innocently showed it to local scholars for their reaction. He did not realize that when approached by lowly amateurs with untypical finds, professional archaeologists routinely condemn such discoveries out of hand as "fakes," often ruining the discoverer's reputation by calling him a "fraud."

For whatever reason, Kennedy was treated differently, and his Vero Beach bone was sent to the Smithsonian's National Museum of Natural History (department of North American archaeology) in Washington, D.C. There, it languished unnoticed for two more years, and, like many other artifacts swallowed up by that enigmatic establishment since the late 19th century, might have been negligently lost or deliberately discarded. This is no baseless accusation. According to Randolf E. Schmid, a science writer for the Associated Press, another bone bearing the image of a mammoth "came from Mexico in 1959, but questions were raised about that object, and it subsequently disappeared."[1]

Kennedy's own discovery was no less in jeopardy. "There was considerable skepticism expressed about the authenticity of the incising on the bone," said University of Florida's Barbara Purdy, even though Kennedy found it within an archaeological zone known as the Old Vero Site.[2] As far back as the early 20th century, human bones began emerging here side by side with those of extinct Ice Age animals during extensive excavations from 1913 to 1916. Unimpressed by such an obviously appropriate setting, Purdy was instead suspicious of alleged evidence contrary to official views of the past until someone finally got around to cursory testing the 3-inch-long, 3/4-inch high image.

Follow-up investigations by forensic anthropologists, materials science engineers, and artists compared it with other particles recovered from the Old Vero Site. These showed no differences in coloration between the carved grooves and surrounding substances, indicating that both surfaces had aged together. Neither were there any indications that the bone fragment had been carved recently, while markings that form the image were not etched with a modern, metal tool. According to anthropologist Christopher J. Ellis at the University of Western Ontario, "all indications are that the carving is the same age as the bone."[3] It is heavily mineralized, which prevents standard dating, but if the engraving was made from life, it can date back no later than 13,000 years ago, when the last mammoth died out in North America.

Anthropologist David J. Meltzer of Southern Methodist University (University Park, Dallas, Texas) said he doesn't "for a moment, think the specimen begs any questions about the larger issue of the peopling of the Americas. It's just one specimen—albeit an interesting one—of uncertain age and provenance, so one should not get too carried away."[4]

But the engraving does indeed call into question mainstream academic belief that the first human occupation of what is now the United

States occurred in New Mexico with the so-called "Clovis Culture," circa 13,500 years ago. The Florida bone fragment is at least as old and probably much older. "It could be quite early," admitted Dennis J. Stanford, Smithsonian curator and coauthor of a report about Kennedy's find in the *Journal of Archaeological Science*, published June 22, 2012.[5]

"It's pretty exciting," he went on to say. "We haven't found anything like this in North America," and he was seconded by Schmid, who said, "This may be the first in the Western Hemisphere," and Melzer, who said, "It does appear to be the first American depiction of a mammoth or mastodon."[6]

The artifact's discovery simultaneously shines a glaring spotlight on the benighted condition of modern American anthropologists. In imagining primacy for the Vero Beach image, they are blissfully ignorant of at least five similarly prehistoric portrayals found as long ago as the late 19th century and as recently as the early 20th and 21st centuries, finds that cultural diffusionists have known about, in some cases, for generations.

The first example of its kind was removed from a peat bog near a railroad station in Holly Oak, northern Delaware, during 1864. A 1976 issue of Science Magazine (192:756-761) described it as "a pendant carved from a fossil whelk shell, into which was incised the image of a wooly mammoth."[7] The roughly delta-shaped object is about 2 inches on its wide side and 4 inches long. Science writers John C. Craft and Ronald A. Thomas reported, "Clifford Irving and his colleagues at the Smithsonian Institution re-examined the carving on the surface of the shell and reached the conclusion that the incisions show the same stages of weathering as the shell surface itself. Most who have examined the Holly Oak specimen indicated that they think this object is legitimate and do not see any possibility of even suggesting the remote conception that it is a fake."[8]

Eight years after the Holly Oak artifact came to light, a small stone covered with strange symbols on one side was accidentally plowed up by a farm boy working his fields near Doylestown, Pennsylvania. On the reverse side of the object was "a scene that could only be interpreted as a pictographic account of an Indian encounter with a mammoth," as described in a 1972 NEARA Newsletter article, by Richard L. Greene.[9] He wrote that the Lenape Stone, named "after a local branch of the Delaware Indians," was investigated and deemed authentic by the Buck

County Historical Society spokesman, Henry C. Mercer. "His reputation as a researcher is well established today for his studies on colonial fire-backs on Ancient Carpenters' Tools (the standard work in this field), and various subjects related in early American architecture."[10]

Currently displayed at the Mercer Museum in Doylestown, the Lenape Stone is about 4.5 inches (11.4 cm) long and was configured into a *gorget*, an ornamental necklace of unknown significance worn by various prehistoric Americans. As such, two holes drilled in the Lenape Stone enabled it to be worn about the neck. An anonymous skeptic at Wikipedia rightly points out that "the type of gorget the Lenape Stone resembles is known to have been popular no earlier than 1000 BCE— thousands of years after the mammoth was extinct."[11]

The implication here is that the Lenape Stone must be fake, because its style came into being millennia following the last glacial epoch. To be sure, gorgets were unknown until nine or 10 centuries later. Scientific testing of the object to determine its age was long ago rendered impossible because its surface has been thoroughly cleaned more than once. If not a hoax, either the artifact is an engraving executed during the Ice Age on a common stone very much later fashioned into a gorget, or it was originally conceived within the last 3,000 years as an adornment illustrating surviving Native American folk memories of ancestral encounters with wooly mammoths.

The latter possibility is suggested in oral traditions of the *Big Quis-quis*, a monster remembered from the ancient past when "a herd of these tremendous animals . . . began a universal destruction" that "so enraged . . . the Great Man above, that he seized his lightning . . . and hurled his bolts among them till the whole were slaughtered," according to a Delaware chief quoted by Mercer, "except the big bull, who, presenting his forehead to the shafts, shook them off as he fell; but missing one at length, it wounded him in the side, whereon, springing around, he bounded" away.[12]

This is the same story illustrated on the Lenape Stone, which represents a mammoth, an arrow in its side, confronting spear-armed men; two of them lay trampled, while lightning bolts thunder from out of the sky at the Big Quis-quis. It would seem then, that the Lenape Stone is not itself an Ice Age artifact, but a much-later commemorative gorget depicting tribal memories of mega fauna confrontations many thousands of years before it was made. Needless to add, although important to point out, a simple farm boy would not have been capable of perpetuating a hoax by portraying such an obscure, complex account.

"Most evidence suggests that modern humans did not co-exist with mammoths in North America," argues the Wikipedia critic, an assumption negated by the latest Florida find and contradicted by Naskapi Indian folk memories of an extinct beast referred to as the *Katcheetohuskw*.[13] This traditionally nomadic "people beyond the horizon" have lived north of the Gulf of Saint Lawrence in eastern Quebec for time out of mind. Writing in *American Anthropology*, W.D. Strong was told by a Naskapi informant that the extinct Katcheetohuskw of long ago "was very large, had a big head, large ears and teeth, and a long nose with which he hit people. His tracks in the snow were described in their stories as large and round . . . the older Indians questioned were unanimous in declaring that such had always been the description of Katcheetohuskw, so far as they had any knowledge."[14]

Naskapi oral traditions of the Katcheetohuskw were borne out by a profusion of mammoth bones antiquarians and farmers alike stumbled upon throughout Hopewell Culture country and described in *Archaeology of Ohio*, by M.C. Read: "Placing such bones side by side and bearing in mind the places from which they were exhumed, one cannot resist the conclusion that the human remains are quite as old as those of these extinct animals." Read even concluded that the abundance of such bones "proves the co-existence of the mound builders with the extinct American pachyderms."[15]

"There is much evidence against the authenticity of the Lenape Stone," Wikipedia's skeptic continues. "The stone is unique in the fact that there are no other carvings depicting mammoths that have been found in North America."[16] On the contrary, four other prehistoric representations of North American mammoths, as cited, are known to exist (five, if the lost Texas example is included), and now Florida's inscribed bone fragment.

Sometime during the early 1920s, a deer bone incised with the rudimentary but unmistakable representation of a mammoth or mastodon was found in Jacobs Cavern, Pineville, Missouri. Ludwell H. Johnson, III wrote in *Scientific Monthly*:

The authenticity of this bone was vigorously challenged by N.C. Nelson, who felt that the carving was a recent forgery. His detailed allegations were answered fully, and, it must be said, convincingly, by V.C. Allison, who subjected the bone to a number of exhaustive tests. . . . On the basis of his chemical investigations (the bone was heavily mineralized), Allison conjectured a minimum age of fourteen thousand years, but, at best, this is only a guess.[17]

Yet another mammoth engraving in Utah was found by a resident of Moab "some three miles down the Colorado Canyon from that town," according to a 1935 article in *Scientific Monthly*: "That this carving is designed to be an elephant or mastodon is evident. It represents a good deal of work on the part of the primitive artist, for the figure, from the end of his very 'pachydermous' tail to the tip of his trunk, is almost two feet long, and appears to have been made by a painstaking method of chipping the whole figure from the solid rock wall with a blunt pick, chisel, or similar tool. It is a recessed or etched figure, composed of closely spaced pock marks."[18] A precise date for the Moab pictoglyph proved elusive, but its ancient authenticity is probable.

Perhaps the most dramatic discovery of its kind took place in 2007, as a pair of scuba divers was gliding over the bottom of Lake Michigan, scouting for a series of old boat wrecks. Assisting them was Dr. Mark Holley, a professor of underwater archaeology at Northwestern Michigan College (Traverse City). He was joined by Greg MacMaster, president of the Grand Traverse Bay Underwater Preserve Council. During their work in the lake together, Dr. Holly happened to observe an apparently deliberate formation of large, similar boulders apparently laid out in a distinct circle on the flat, sandy bottom otherwise strewn with algae and zebra mussels, about 40 feet beneath the surface. Not far from the formation, laid out in a straight line, was a row of smaller stones.

"It appears the rocks have been manipulated by man," Dr. Holley declared. But a particular granite rock about 38 inches tall and 54 inches long located outside the circle attracted MacMaster's attention. Its exterior was emblazoned with a man-made image. "We couldn't believe what we were looking at," he remembered. On a second dive, they returned with a professional underwater photographer, Chris Doyal, who documented their discovery. It was the representation of a massive back, hump, head, trunk, tusk, triangular shaped ear, and stumpy legs of a great beast with a spear in its side. The figure was virtually identical to Pennsylvania's Lenape Stone illustration and the Delaware Indians' Big Quis-quis. "It wasn't until Mark stared at the photos," Doyal recalled, "that the mastodon image came to him."[18]

All these prehistoric images—some discovered only a few years ago, others decades and even centuries earlier—are utterly unknown to today's scholars delighted with what they imagine is the first depiction of a mammoth. They are neither aware of nor care about the Holly Oak shell engraving, the Lenape Stone, the Jacobs Cavern bone, or the Moab pictoglyph, because their like-minded predecessors dismissed the ancient illustrations as "fakes," thereby condemning them to obscurity. On Dr. Holley's more recent discovery of Lake Michigan's sunken petroglyph, his conventional colleagues are mute or sullenly skeptical. Accordingly, modern American anthropologists are as fossilized as the bones they purport to explain for the rest of us.

SECTION II

NATURAL WEALTH

———◆•◆•◆———

Even researchers familiar with the extraordinary achievements of ancient America will be surprised to learn about the Keystone State's 2,000 oil pits used by prehistoric Pennsylvanians, 16 centuries ago. The generally unknown and certainly underappreciated mystery is described by Thomas Anderton, whose own family background in petroleum runs over several generations. In 1885, his great-grandfather founded Oil City's Continental Oil Refining Company. Later, Thomas's grandfather and two great uncles perpetuated the family business until bankrupted by Rockefeller during the early 1930s.

No less surprising was the application of quicksilver at Mesoamerica's greatest city, Teotihuacán, which means "the place where men become gods." What possible employment could the Mayas or their predecessors have made of mercury in such large quantities?

But liquid riches were not our continent's only natural resources sought after on a grand scale by unknown exploiters. The greatest mystery of American archaeology is the Copper Question. More than 5,000 years ago—when pharaonic Egypt was new and only tiny populations of primitive paleo-Indians inhabited our continent—someone launched a colossal mining enterprise across the Upper Great Lake Region. Over the next 19 centuries, at least 125,000 tons of the world's highest-grade copper were excavated. Compounding the mystery, none of the numerous workshops required for processing the metal was found until nearly

60 years ago by an amateur archaeologist, whose forgotten discovery has only recently come to light.

Another misplaced clue to unraveling ancient America's copper enigma is revealed for the first time anywhere by Rick Osmon, host of a popular Internet program *The Oopa Loopa Café*, devoted to the discussion of American prehistory. After earning his associate's degree of science in laser and electro-optics technology at Vincennes University (Indiana), he worked for the U.S. Navy as a civilian specializing in radar, night vision, and laser equipment for surveillance and munitions guidance. Osmon is the author of *The Graves of the Golden Bear: Ancient Fortresses and Monuments of the Ohio Valley*.[1] He identifies the missing piece in the copper mining puzzle as *fluorspar*, the mineral form of calcium fluoride, used as a flux—a chemical cleaning or purifying agent—for smelting metals, purging them of their imperfections that would otherwise weaken them for the production of tools and weapons.

5

Who Were the Oil Tycoons of Pre-Columbian Pennsylvania?

By Thomas Anderton

Literally thousands of pits excavated by unknown human hands and used to mine oil many hundreds, perhaps thousands of years ago are spread some 20 miles across Pennsylvania's Oil Creek Valley, between Crawford County's historic city of Titusville and Oil City, in Venango County. More recently, in 1859, Colonel Edwin Laurentine Drake was historically the first man to successfully drill for oil by sinking his premiere well in the middle of one of the primeval wells.

"These ancient oil pits reach far back of the historic period," according to 1890's *History of Venango County* (Vol. 1), which described them as

> very numerous and bear the mark of antiquity. They are generally oblong in form, about four by six feet in depth, notwithstanding the wear and tear of centuries and the accumulation

of extraneous matter. The deeper and larger ones have been cribbed with timber at the sides to preserve their form. This cribbing was roughly done: the logs were split in halves, stripped of their bark, and safely adjusted at the corners.

The walls seem to be so thoroughly saturated with oil as to be preserved almost entire to this day. These pits are on the west side of Oil Creek, about two miles below Titusville, in Venango County. They cover perhaps five hundred acres of land and there may be in all *two thousand* [author's italics] pits. In some cases, large trees grow in the pits, and on the septa [a partition separating two chambers] that divide them showing their antiquity.[1]

The pits were operated by letting them fill with water overnight, then skimming the lighter oil on the surface into containers. Some had a door at the bottom that could be opened to drain out the water. The larger ones had ladders and rafts that the laborers used to extract oil from the pits. These pits were operated over time at varying degrees of intensity. The oil from these pits was unlike the thick, black tar depicted in Hollywood movies. It is golden-olive and sweet smelling. The "first sand" (i.e., oil that would have been seeping out of the ground) was the most pure. It had a very high gas and paraffin content, and was used unrefined by some 19th-century settlers for lighting. The "third sand" drilled today is darker, but still the best unrefined oil on Earth. Local old timers relate burning it in their Model T's.

When the French arrived, the Seneca Indians were gathering and using this oil, as told by Sherman Day in *Historical Collections of the State of Pennsylvania*:

> The Seneca oil from the oil springs on Oil Creek was used by the Seneca Indians as an unguent . . . the other use made of the oil was for religious worship. Here, I cannot better describe it than in the imaginative language of the commandant of Fort Duquesne to his Excellency General Montcalm, the unfortunate hero of Québec. "I would desire," says the Commandant, "to assure your Excellency that this is a most delightful land. Some of the most astonishing natural wonders have been discovered by our people. While descending the Allegheny, fifteen leagues below the mouth of the Conewango, and three above

Fort Venango [above Franklin, at current Oil City], we were invited by the chief of the Senecas to attend a religious ceremony of his tribe.

We landed and drew up our canoes on a point where a small stream [Oil Creek] entered the river. The tribe appeared unusually solemn. We marched up the stream about half a league, where the company, a large band it appeared, had arrived some days before us. Gigantic hills begirt us on every side. The scene was really sublime. The great chief then recited the conquests and heroism of their ancestors. The surface of the stream was covered with a thick scum, which burst into a complete conflagration. The oil had been gathered and lighted with a torch. At the sight of the flames, the Indians gave forth a triumphant shout that made the hills and valley re-echo again! Here then is revived the ancient fire-worship of the East. Here then are the Children of the Sun."[2]

In an article for the *Oil Field Journal*, J.E. Thomas tells how Professor J. S. Newberry, when visiting Titusville, "noticed that the bottom-lands on Oil Creek below the town . . . were pitted in a peculiar way: that is, the surface was occupied by a series of contiguous depressions ten or fifteen feet in diameter and from one to three feet deep [indicating their depth at the surface]. They were circular and symmetrical, in that respect differing from the pits formed by the uprooted trees."[3]

The strange depressions long predated the arrival of modern Europeans in the region, to say nothing of the first pits excavated there by Colonel Drake. Newberry was then taken to a new well being dug, noting:

As it chanced, this well was sunk in one of the pits referred to. It was carried to the depth of about twenty-five feet in the earth when the rock was reached and the drilling began. Throughout this depth, it followed the course of an old well, which had been cribbed up with timber, and in it was a ladder such as was commonly used in the copper mines of Lake Superior by perhaps the same people who worked the oil well. This ladder was a portion of a small tree of which the trunk was thickly set with branches.

These were cut off four or five feet from the trunk. And thus formed steps by which the well owner could go down and gather the oil as it accumulated on the surface of the water, just as was done by the old oil producers on the banks of the Caspian and Irrawaddy. Some of the trees which grew over the pits which marked the sites of oil wells were three and even four feet in diameter, thus proving that the wells had been abandoned at least four hundred for five hundred years ago."[4]

My research shows that many of these pits go down 25 feet or more below the surface. How long would it take for a 25-foot-deep pit, ten or fifteen feet wide, to fill with leaves and detritus? But the site described by Newberry was not the only location where the ancient oil pits were found. They appear to have spread into the State's natural oil fields across the northeast, where the oil was near the surface, including some as distant as Canada.

"On an extensive plain," reported Sherman Day in *Historical Collections of the State of Pennsylvania*:

> there is a vast mound of stones containing several hundred thousand cart loads. This pyramid has stood through so many ages, that it has become covered with soil, and from the top raises a noble pine-tree, the roots of which, running down the sides, fasten themselves in the earth below. The stones are many of them so large that two men can only move them with difficulty, and yet they are unlike any others in the neighborhood. Indeed, there are not in the neighborhood any quarries from which so large a quantity could ever have been taken.
>
> This artificial curiosity is on the borders of Oil Creek, a name derived from a natural curiosity no less remarkable than the foregoing. Springs exist on its margin from which there is a constant flow of oil, floating on the surface of the water and running into the creek, which may be seen for a great distance down the stream. The oil is burned in lamps and used in various ways, but is particularly valued for its medicinal qualities. Considerable quantities are annually brought to this city and sold to the apothecaries.[5]

Although the stone pyramid was long ago dismantled for building material, its former proximity to the oil springs indicates a prehistoric relationship between members of a relatively high culture and local petroleum. Another, if entirely different, stone structure situated on the highest bluff overlooking Franklin, directly above a Native American village, is described by 1890's *History of Venango County*: "There was first a pit in form like an inverted cone, or like the den of the ant lion. It was regularly formed, some eight feet in diameter, and six to eight feet in depth, and lined with stones neatly laid and forming a symmetrical wall. These stones were brought from a distance, and were nearly uniform in size."[6]

Like the Oil Creek pyramid, Venango County's conical pit did not survive the 19th century. Faded rock art depicting a sailing ship closely resembling a European Bronze Age vessel was found along the old Venango Path near a tributary of and close to the Allegheny River not many miles south of Franklin was documented by Jim Leslie and Tom Anderton in the *Midwestern Epigraphic Society Newsletter*.[7]

Thomas concluded:

> Although the documentary evidence clearly establishes that the Seneca collected and used petroleum from the oil springs, there is, surprisingly, no oral tradition of this phenomenon according to the Seneca ethnographer Elizabeth Tooker. . . . The implications that Native Americans were actively extracting petroleum as early as the late Woodland (100 C.E.-500) are striking. To date, there are no known references of oil or oil residue found in any local or regional archaeological contexts. It must be assumed, however, by the number of pits found on Oil Creek, that the practice of oil mining and its use took place over an extended period of time. This, In turn, indicates that the 'path' that would ultimately lead to the protean discovery at Drake Well, in 1859, was first walked by Native Americans hundreds and perhaps thousands of years earlier.[8]

Did Pennsylvania crude oil light the homes and streets of the ancient Old World? If so, that would explain the more than 2,000 wells sunk by prehistoric oil-men in the Keystone State. The Roberts report gave figures showing that each one of the ancient wells yielded 15 barrels per season. A single barrel of oil is 41 gallons. This number multiplied by 15 seasons equals 615 gallons, times 2,000 pits results in 1,230,000 gallons per year.

One of prehistoric Pennsylvania's several thousand oil pits.

Thomas reported attempts at carbon dating several smaller pits from which a time frame of 1,415 to 1,445 Years Before Present was obtained. This would mean that at least a few of the lesser wells were being worked from circa 570 CE to 600. The period is particularly cogent to our discussion, because a famous European wonder weapon took to the field of battle shortly thereafter. "Greek fire" was a super flame-thrower used by Byzantine warriors against Muslim hordes advancing on the Eastern Roman Empire.

Successfully deployed in decisive naval engagements, it contin-ued burning while floating on water, suggesting an oil base. Emperor Constantine Porphyrogennetos (reigned 945–959 CE), in his book, *De Administrando Imperio,* admonished his son and heir, Romanos II (reigned 959–963 CE), to never reveal any information about his mir-acle weapon.[9] So strict was secrecy surrounding it that its composition was lost forever and remains a source of speculation to this day.

Byzantine military authorities did not invent "Greek fire," but intro-duced the improved version of an established weapon. Its first fully recorded operational use was described by the late-5th-century BCE historian Thucydides, who told how a large bellows blew flames through a long tube mounted on wheels during the bloody siege of Delium, in 424 BCE, when about one thousand of his fellow Athenians died. More fragmentary sources suggest a similar device saw action against Persian forces at 539 BCE's Fall of Babylon, as dramatized by D.W. Griffith in his 1916 motion picture of the same name. In any case, the oil likely required to operate these flame-throwing cannons extended further back in time than surviving records are able to document, although a surge in need coincided with Byzantine reliance on "Greek fire" and contemporaneous oil extraction in 7th-century Pennsylvania.

At Titusville's Drake Well Museum and Park—located where the Colonel "discovered" oil 157 years ago—depicted in a recreation are Native Americans gathering oil, the only such portrayal anywhere. Outside, at the edge of the Park, and within view of the Museum building itself, are several acres of ancient oil pits their ancestors worked. But no marker stands to identify them.

6

An Ancient Mexican Pyramid's Liquid Mercury

By Frank Joseph

In November 2014, "large quantities" of mercury were discovered in a chamber 60 feet beneath the Temple of the Feathered Serpent, located thirty miles outside Mexico City. This third-largest structure in Teotihuacán belongs to pre-Columbian America's largest ceremonial city, where an estimated 100,000 residents lived in "The Place Where Gods Became Men," located at the southern end of the Avenue of the Dead, the site's main thoroughfare. Dated between 150 and 200 CE, the Temple of the Feathered Serpent is so-called after its exterior representations of an overseas' culture-bearer, who arrived in the distant past from his homeland across the Atlantic.

On each terrace of the six-level step pyramid's outside edges are sculpted heads of the Feathered Serpent alternating with those of another snake-like signifying Teotihuacán's symbol for war. Although now missing, their eyes were made of carved obsidian glass that glimmered menacingly in reflected light. Until the massive urban center's inexplicable abandonment about 700 CE, the building's entire exterior was painted in blue, pink, and white pigments, and adorned with carved seashells, symbols of its namesake's oceanic origins. Under each row of heads are bas-reliefs of the Feathered Serpent in profile, together with depictions of other gods and more seashells along panels on either side of the grand staircase.

The discovery of liquid mercury under Mexico's Temple of the Feathered Serpent has shocked some cultural diffusionists into comparisons with Qín Shi Huáng Dì, the first emperor of China, whose massive tomb is believed to likewise contain prodigious amounts of quicksilver. Han Dynasty historian Sima Qian wrote about 100 years after the Emperor's death, in 210 BCE, that the mausoleum contained the large, scale model—including 100 rivers flowing with mercury—of all the lands ruled by Qín Shi Huáng Dì. The tomb has been identified at the foot of Li Mountain, less than 20 miles away from Xi'an, capital of Shaanxi province, in the northwest of China, but the Communist authorities forbid its excavation. Modern archaeologists have been restricted to inserting probes deep into the subterranean structure, revealing abnormally high quantities of mercury, some 100 times the naturally occurring rate.

Knowledge and use of quicksilver was not restricted to the ancient Chinese nor pre-Columbian Teotihuacáns, however. According to Rosemary Joyce, a professor of anthropology at the University of California, Berkeley, liquid mercury has been found at other archaeological sites in Mexico. Among the ruins of Lamanai—a Pre-Classic Maya ceremonial center that flourished in northern Belize from the fourth century BCE—a pool of mercury was found under a marker at the center of its ritual ball court.

"Quantities of liquid mercury ranging from ninety to six hundred grams (3.2 to 21.2 oz)," according to Wikipedia, "have been recovered from elite Maya tombs or ritual caches at six sites. This mercury may have been used in bowls as mirrors for divinatory purposes. Five of these date to the Classic Period of Maya Civilization (circa 250–900 C.E.), but one example predated this."[1]

The Maya produced liquid mercury by heating cinnabar, a bright red mineral consisting of mercury sulfide. Europeans were manufacturing liquid mercury long before either the Chinese or Mesoamericans discovered it. Traces of mining operations in Spain at Almadén, Monte Amiata in Italy, and Slovenia's Idrija date back 2,500 years. The earliest known manufactured quicksilver has been found in the Upper Nile Valley in XVIII Dynasty tombs from 1500 BCE.

Liquid mercury's real mystery does not lie in its manufacture by various peoples during ancient times, but why they used it.

Some Classical Era Greeks and Romans applied quicksilver as makeup—a kind of facial beauty aid—usually with tragic epidermal consequences caused by such a toxic element. But the cosmetic needs of a few aristocrats could have hardly justified the large-scale mining and production of mercury, which, some scholars speculate, may have been sought out for imagined medicinal or alchemical purposes. These demands, too, would have been insufficiently compelling to prompt the widespread use of quicksilver over so many centuries and by so many disparate peoples.

Larry Brian Radka, a retired broadcast engineer, offers abundant, well-documented, credible evidence on behalf of the application of electricity during Classical and Pre-Classical Times, among various civilizations, especially Ptolemaic Egypt.[2] Could our ancestors' extensive, abiding interest in quicksilver have stemmed from their determination to light up the Ancient World?

According to Wikipedia, liquid mercury "is used in lighting: electricity passed through mercury vapor in a fluorescent lamp produces short-wave ultraviolet light, which then causes the phosphor in the tube to fluoresce, making visible light. Mercury is a fair conductor of electricity used primarily for . . . electrical and electronic applications in fluorescent lamps. . . . The mercury battery is a non-rechargeable electrochemical battery, a primary cell that was common throughout the middle of the 20th Century."[3]

Did the Ancients recognize quicksilver's electrical properties and employ them in ways we might find astonishing? In at least Teotihuacán's case, that question was underscored not only by the recent discovery of liquid mercury beneath the Temple of the Feathered Serpent, but by an earlier find made just across the Avenue of the Dead. About 35 years ago, archaeologists investigating a newly found chamber beneath the Pyramid of the Sun, discovered a stone shelf containing several

The Pyramid of the Sun's cross-section indicating internal passage for liquid mercury.

out-sized flakes of wafer-thin mica that had been imported nearly two thousand years before from Brazil—4,615 airline-miles away!

Why would the Teotihuacános have gone to the immense trouble of bringing such delicate materials from so far away, only to conceal them deep underground where they would never be seen? Like liquid mercury, mica has important electrical properties. Perhaps both were employed in tandem to power "The Place Where Gods Became Men."

7

First Copper
Workshop
Discovered

By Wayne N. May

During the early 1960s, Greg Perino found the first known copper work-shop of its kind in North America. It went back to the Mississippian Culture, a vast, sophisticated society of astronomer-priests, pyramid-builders, and transcontinental traders that ranged from the Gulf of Mexico to Wisconsin, beginning around 900 AD. Less than four centu-ries later, its dozens of ceremonial cities were mostly abandoned or in steep decline, like its foremost urban center across the Mississippi River from St. Louis, Missouri, Cahokia, the Detroit of its day—formerly a splendid metropolis of cultural significance, now a ruined caricature of itself. But professional archaeologists were not interested in Perino or his claims, because he was, after all, only an amateur.

When he died at 91 years of age in 2005, his terrific discovery was mostly forgotten and certainly not credited by the snobbish technicians, who never made such a find themselves. Nor did they deign to glance at the surviving map he left them of the copper workshop's location, until the details he sketched began to coincide seven years later with surface features at a structure some 200 yards east of Cahokia's Monks Mound, named after some French Trappist monks who briefly occupied its immediate vicinity in the early 19th century. Almost within the shadow of this 100-foot-high pyramid, larger at its base than Egypt's Great Pyramid, a graduate student in metallurgy (God forbid, another outsider!) noticed pieces of flat copper sheets atop 10-foot-tall "Mound 34."

He observed through an electron microscope that their molecular structure had been annealed, or heated and allowed to cool slowly, in order to remove internal stresses, and toughen them. The young man had rediscovered Greg Perino's copper workshop. The metal did not merely adorn Mississippian Culture, but spiritually empowered it. A royal burial site excavated within Cahokia's sacred precinct entombed its privileged dead with long sheets of beaten copper. There were no sources available in the Central Middle West, but lay only in the Great Lakes Region, specifically Michigan's Upper Peninsula, more than 700 miles by river route—the fastest way—northward from Monks Mound to the copper-laden shores of Lake Superior and its especially rich Isle Royale.

Marking the precise midpoint between both points once lay a colossal cross of landscaped soil and clay 420 feet in diameter and 4 feet thick at all four arms, with a 44-foot spread at its midpoint near Lake Sinissippi, in southern Wisconsin. The monumental exactness of its construction at right angles and perfect orientation to the four cardinal directions made it resemble a compass, a suggestion that belied its function half way between Cahokia and Isle Royale, and underscored by its Algonquian name, which means "Serpent Ore," a reference to copper not found anywhere in the area of the structure, which lies between Monks Mound and Lake Superior's copper deposits. Its design was unique among the many thousands of other earthworks surveyed in the 19th century before most of them, like the Sinissippi Cross, were meticulously surveyed before their obliteration by farmers' plows.

Expanding on the graduate student's find of Cahokia's lost, copper workshop, professional archaeologists from Northwestern University (Evanston, Illinois) and Washington University (St. Louis, Missouri) discerned dark, circular stains in the soil of the 1-by-2-yard area, where the copper remnants were found at the ceremonial center, together with the remains of tree stumps. These served as anvils for pre-Columbian craftsmen, who placed a flat stone on a leveled off stump. A palm-sized piece of very hard basalt, a volcanic rock, was used to pound raw copper flat. This method accounts for the immense rolls of copper sheets interred as treasured grave goods in the city's royal burial.

Because no practical associations have been made for copper among the Mississippians, investigators conclude the copper workshop functioned entirely for religious purposes, producing ornaments for participants in ritual activities atop and around the mounds. Cahokia's copper figures appear to depict otherworldly beings similarly portrayed on painted pottery and decorated shells, such as a conch shell found at the top of Mound 34, where the copper workshop was situated. The exterior of the shell—a trade good from the far-off Gulf of Mexico—has been incised by a copper stylus or pin with a very distinctive symbol first discovered at other distant locations: rock shelters in Wisconsin and east central Missouri dated to circa 1000 CE, a century after Cahokia was founded. Mound 34's conch shell design is an arrow-like logo with a circle in the arrowhead. Although its meaning is unknown, the symbol is at least emblematic of ancient Cahokia's far-flung influence over thousands of miles from the Upper Middle West to the Gulf Coast and beyond.

The mysterious arrow-sign likewise signifies the enigma of Cahokia Mounds State Historic Site itself: Less than 1 percent of its 2,200 acres has been excavated. According to Wikipedia, "the ancient city was actually much larger. In its heyday, Cahokia covered about six square miles, and included about one hundred twenty human-made earthen mounds in a wide range of sizes, shapes, and functions."[1]

When someday they are more fully investigated and their contents disclosed, the story of this once-mighty capital of a lost culture would be far more amazing than anything we presently imagine.

8

Michigan's Copper Barons Left Their Fingerprints on Greenland Ice

By Rick Osmon

In May 1835, a cavern cemetery was discovered on the banks of the Ohio River, opposite Steubenville. It was thirty or forty feet in circumference and filled with human bones. They were of all ages, and had been thrown in indiscriminately after the removal of the flesh. They seemed to have been deposited at different periods of time, those on the top alone being in a good state of preservation. Dr. Morton regards these remains as "of no great age" and as "undoubtedly belonging to individuals of the barbarous tribes."

A similar cave was discovered some years ago at Golconda on the Ohio River, Illinois. It contained many skeletons. Henry, in his travels, mentions a cave in the island of Mackinaw, in Lake Huron, the floor of which was covered with human bones. He expresses the opinion that it was formerly filled with them. The Indians knew nothing concerning the deposit; our author, nevertheless, ventures the conjecture that the cave was an ancient receptacle of the bones of prisoners sacrificed at the Indian war-feasts.[1]

These passages from E.G. Squire's 1851 *Antiquities of the State of New York*, transcribed from Dr. Samuel George Morton's *Crania Americana*, illustrate how much attention was trained on the bones of the ancients. But let's concentrate here first on the locations, starting with Golconda, after the ancient city of Golkonda, in India. The proximity of southern Illinois' Golconda to Cave-In-Rock may have much to do with both a pile of skeletal remains and the copper trade.

Cave-in-Rock.

Today a state park, Cave-in-Rock is a striking, 55-foot-wide riverside cave that, until half of its roof collapsed in the 1950s, was partially decorated with painted rock art portraying men and women "clothed not as Indians, but in the costume of Greece and Rome," according to Josiah Priest, a highly educated and respected antiquarian, who personally observed the cave paintings:

> The dress of these figures consisted of a *carbasus*, or rich cloak; a *sabucala,* or waistcoat or shirt; a *supparum*, or breeches open at the knees; *solea*, or sandals tied across the toes and heels; the head embraced by a *bandeau* [a narrow band worn around the head to hold the hair in position] crowned with flowers.
>
> The dress of the females carved in this cave have a Grecian cast, the hair encircled by the crown and confined by a *bodkin* [a blunt, thick needle with a large eye used especially for drawing tape or cord through a hem]. The remaining part of this costume was Roman. The garments, called *stolla*, or perhaps the *toga pura*, flounced from the shoulders to the ground. An *indusium* [a thin, membranous covering] appeared underneath. The indusium was confined under the breast by a *zone* or *cestue*. Sandals were worn in the manner of those of the men.[2]

The area around Cave-in-Rock and on both sides of the Ohio River is rich in a mineral known as fluorspar among metallurgists and chemists, or among gemologists as fluorite. When used in industry, fluorspar is a high-efficiency flux when purifying metal ores for smelting, separating mineral ores, and in preparing alloys. Fluorspar mining concerns in the Cave-in-Rock quadrangle and surrounding area were capable of producing something more than 4,000 tons per day as recently as 1974. This production fell off sharply with the decline of the U.S. steel industry later that decade. Fluorite is one of those "magical" minerals, like quartz, that glows when mechanical stress is applied to its crystalline matrix.

However, it is also a comparatively soft crystal, and flakes and fractures under impact, so it is far less durable for magical glowing rattles (*triboluminescence* or *mechanoluminescence*) than are quartz crystals. Fluorite usually glows green instead of quartz's white, bluish white, or pink. The fluorescent light color of any crystal, as well as the apparent crystal color, is dependent on the types and amounts of "contaminant" trace elements in the crystal. Fluorite gave its name to *fluorescence*, rather than vice versa. It is often found with another mineral called *Smithsonite*, discovered by British chemist, mineralogist, and mining engineer, James Smithson, who financially underwrote the Institution that still bears his name: the Smithsonian.

Fluorspar is nearly as magical in metallurgy as fluorite is in ceremonies. Its use as a flux helped drive the industrial revolution; and all the iron, steel, bronze, copper, brass, gold, silver, and so forth, that were produced in the U.S. from its formation until the present day depended on the use of a flux, sometimes limestone, sometimes calcium from bones, sometimes glass or even diamond dust for some more exotic alloys—and even different types or colors of glass for different desired characteristics in the final alloy. The natural crystalline structure in fluorspar helps bond to specific molecules in the molten ore that forms a slag or dross, a froth on top of the molten and purified molten metal. That slag is then removed and carries away undesirable constituents of the ore.

Imagine a scene in which a metal smith pulverizes some fluorspar to use as part of a flux. Each hammer blow creates a flash of light. Other minerals and materials would be processed and mixed to the flux before use based on the smith's experience with ores and their properties. Then, when the metal smith added the flux to the molten ore and the pot frothed and spit and bubbled, it might have seemed somewhat magical to the uninitiated in its powers to make good metal out of dirty ore. It may have been the inspiration for Tinkerbell's glowing fairy dust. "Fluorspar can serve as a flux that removes impurities such as sulfur and phosphorous from molten metal and improves the fluidity of slag. Between twenty and sixty pounds of fluorspar is used for every ton of metal produced. In the United States many metal producers use fluorspar that exceeds metallurgical grade."[3]

In order for any of this metal smelting magic to occur, something has to burn. Peat, soft or hard wood, buffalo chips, grasses can all be used as heating fuels. Charcoal can achieve higher temperatures at a higher cost of production than the preceding fuels, but only coal was an economical, industrial-strength fuel for smelting until the very end of the 20th century, when resistant electricity, natural gas, solar furnaces, and induction furnaces became viable alternatives (just in time for the U.S. steel industry to go belly up). Some of the best coal for metallurgical use is anthracite type, and sometimes that resource underwent its own improvement cycle and requisite cost increase before being brought to market. Anthracite coal is the first stage of the coke used by smiths and industrial steel makers alike.

Drift mining—digs following an outcropping bed of coal—extracted fluorspar from some of the Cave-in-Rock mines. Some of the ancient drift mines of the Superior region have yielded charcoal in their tailings that carbon dates as early as 4500 BCE. Both the Cave-in-Rock fluorspar district and the Steubenville coal districts were reported to have ancient drift mines when White settlers first arrived, but no dating techniques were ever carried out for these.

According to Dartmouth Toxic Metals:

> Scientists in the 1990s discovered that copper contamination is present in seven thousand-year-old layers of ice in the Greenland glacial caps. As copper smelting became widespread at the beginning of the Bronze Age, enough copper was released into the air to contaminate ice thousands of miles away. Peaks in copper concentrations in ice layers correspond to the era of the Roman Empire, the height of the Sung dynasty in China (circa 900–1100 CE), and the Industrial Revolution, with decreased concentrations found in ice deposited immediately after the fall of the Roman Empire and during the later Middle Ages of Europe when copper and bronze use was lower.[4]

I would offer a counter to the Dartmouth statement that copper and bronze use was lower after the fall of the Roman Empire. The production waned, but the use of existing implements continued. Also, if the only "treatment" of native copper seven thousand years ago was annealing and hammering, and that just in amounts sufficient to outfit small hunting bands, how did sufficient copper particulates enter the atmosphere to contaminate ice thousands of miles away? Wouldn't that indicate a more significant amount and more advanced methods using higher processing temperatures? Or could there be some unexplored, undetermined natural source of atmospheric copper?

> The first evidence of copper production in the Southern Levant goes back as early as the 5th millennium BCE and corresponds with the period of metallurgical innovation throughout

the ancient Near East [e.g., Avner, 2002; Rothenberg, 1990; Hauptmann, 1989; Levy and Shalev,1989]. For the first time humankind learned to produce metallic copper from ore, an elaborate process that signifies a notable change in the archae-ological records. The art of smelting requires pyrotechnologi-cal skills such as furnace construction to achieve temperatures above 1100°C. The basic technique involved preparation of the smelting mixture (copper ores and other minerals which are used as fluxes), charcoal manufacture, and construction of high-temperature furnaces. These probably made use of a bellows system including tuyères (a nozzle through which air is forced into a smelter, furnace, or forge) and/or bellows pipes from the beginning.[5]

Thus, the ice record of atmospheric copper is ahead of the archeo-logical record by some 500 years. And the assumption that they used charcoal is based on what again? The supposition that they used bel-lows or blowpipes is just that; there is no extant evidence of it. Have we missed some important clue? Judging by the ice record, did copper smelting actually predate the Levantine copper smelting industry by 500 years somewhere else in the world? Most importantly, with regard to the Levantine slag piles, what did they use for a flux? Shouldn't the trace element analysis of that slag contain the answer? What did they use for fuel? What did they use for bellows or blowpipes, if anything? We may never know the answers to all these questions, but the clues are fascinating, nevertheless. Most archeologists still contend that they used charcoal as fuel without benefit of evidence to that effect.

Though it is possible to achieve the necessary temperatures using charcoal and bellows, the fuel usage rate is extremely high, and so is the thermal constant of copper and copper ore—meaning, it takes much more time at temperature to melt copper ore than some ores with a lower thermal constant. And it takes more flux to make the slag flow easily. It's not just about getting it to temperature: It's also about *hold-ing* [emphasis added] that temperature long enough to get a good melt and to process the ore with flux. Why do they stick to this ill-founded hypothesis? Because if they find that the ancient Levantines used coal or coke, it would have had to come from somewhere else very far away from where it was used. The slag could potentially show what fuel was used, as well as what flux was employed.

None of that, even with possession of the elusive answers to those burning questions above, addresses directly why there were piles and deposits of human bones found in proximity to many of these potentially important mineral deposits. The Golconda bone deposit was close to both the Cave-in-Rock fluorspar mining area and historic Fort Massac. Local legend holds that Massac got its name from some ancient pile of bones that resulted from a huge massacre. Historians instead cite the surname of the French officer who built the first (historic) fort on the site.

However, there is a truly ancient fortress in the adjoining county to the north of Golconda, Saline County. At least 10 and possibly as many as 20 other ancient fortresses once existed across the southern portion of present-day Illinois. One of the very early French colonial maps, the Delisle map of 1716, depicts and notes an ancient fortress that could still be seen at present-day Cairo, Illinois, not far downriver from Fort Massac.

The Steubenville, Ohio, burial cave was actually on the present-day West Virginia side of the river (Virginia at the time of Squier's writing) and less than 5 miles from the Pennsylvania line. Ancient fortresses and signal points lined that river on both sides every few miles, usually no more than 5 miles from one to the next from headwaters of the Monongahela and Allegany, to confluence with the Mississippi. Many historic period coal mines and perhaps a few ancient ones operated in the area with some of the best coal for metallurgy that the planet offers. Numerous other human bone deposits were reported by antiquarians and officials in proximity to the Ohio and other waterways. Sand Island, now submerged, was near present-day Louisville, Kentucky, said to cover some 12 acres, and the bones were waist deep.[6]

A similar story is told for the first White settlers in Mobile Bay:

The Le Moyne brothers' first excursion to the Gulf Coast came in 1698, when they set sail from Brest, France, with the intent of establishing a military post and colonial capitol in the Mississippi River Delta. The two were accompanied by French soldiers and somewhere around two hundred potential colonists in an attempt to settle the region in the name of the French king. In January 1699, the Le Moynes entered Pensacola Bay, but left soon after, due to the presence of the Spanish already at work building their community. The first landing in Mobile Bay came on February 1, 1699, near the site of present-day Fort Morgan. The French, under the command of Iberville, explored the peninsula and rowed across the bay to examine Dauphin Island which they named *Ile du Massacre* ("Massacre Island") after locating several skeletons there.[7]

Other accounts indicate there were far more than "several" skeletons. One report described the sight as "a mountain of bones." The peninsula offered both a natural breakwater and a deep port, so that was the first spot chosen to fortify out of the approximately eight hundred twenty-seven thousand square miles of La Louisiane. Some one hundred twenty years later, the United States would build Fort Gaines less than a mile from the original French site, and name it for the officer who arrested Aaron Burr, in 1805. The bone cave on Mackinaw Island mentioned by Squier was, of course, isolated from the shores of Lake Huron by several miles. It is also only a few miles from the eastern outlet of Lake Superior, where the world's best copper was mined for some 2,000 years.

Odd and massive collections of human remains, whether on remote islands or hidden in caves, are all associated with major water routes of prehistoric or truly ancient times. They also echo in strong local traditions of massacres. Many are in proximity to potentially valuable natural resources. We don't know why large numbers of human remains were gathered in these places. We have no extant evidence that might tell us who they were, how or where they died, or how or where they lived. However, it is tempting to speculate that they may have been slaves of the ore traders, who were simply no longer needed, and were simply liquidated.

UNDERWATER DISCOVERIES

———•◆•———

Our pursuit of Upper Michigan's copper barons leads beneath the waves of a Wisconsin lake to the discovery of prehistoric tools and enigmatic stone structures. Five years ago, their finder published photographs of the site and told his story for the first time anywhere in an *Ancient American* exclusive.

Likewise unprecedented was the observation of a keen-eyed reader of our magazine, who spotted traces resembling the ruins of an urban center sprawling across the floor of the Pacific Ocean off the northwest coast of the United States.

More definite are massive walls at the bottom of a Minnesota lake, monuments to unknown construction engineers at a time, long ago, when the North Star State's topography was radically different than it appears today. They are described by Rhode Island's Andrew E. Rothovious (1919–2009), the Sage of Providence, a writer as prolific as he was insightful; still revered by his followers as a master of Lovecraft-style fiction, but highly valued for his serious, highly significant and beautifully written research of ancient stone chambers throughout New England.

9

Drowned Village of the Ancient Copper Miners

By Wayne N. May

Three thousand two hundred years ago, Upper Michigan's enigmatic copper miners left behind some 5,000 pits and in excess of one million stone tools, but no trace of their towns has ever been found until the discovery of a village site 10 fathoms beneath the surface of a Wisconsin lake. Due to the site's untouched, if presently unguarded condition, its exact position is concealed, as some measure of protection. The ruins were found in June 2011 by Scott Mitchim, owner of the Superior Water-Logged Company, operating in Wisconsin, Canada, and Brazil.[1]

Mitchim said:

> I had never looked in deep water off the island point, but knew the rocky shore gradually sloped down, but previously only covered the first twenty to thirty feet around the island, not in depth. As I got closer, I slowed to an idle and waited until I

Apparently, the stone foundations for separate rooms on the lake bottom about 30 feet beneath the surface.

could see the bottom. I knew I had extra visibility, so I would be able to view greater depths. As the rocky bottom started to appear, something immediately caught my eye: a formation of piled rocks. I got the mask, put it on, and dunked my face overboard to see mounds and circles of stone, perfectly stacked.

I quickly returned to shore, tied up the boat, and put on my diving suit. The sun was already down, so I didn't have much time. I swam back to where the boat had been hovering earlier, and could faintly make out dark structures lining the bottom in every direction, but declining light conditions terminated my dive. The next day, June 23rd, I arrived back at the site around 2:30 in the afternoon. Conditions were windy, with lots of pollen on the water, so visibility was not the greatest. I put on my scuba gear and dove with camera in hand. As I swam down to the largest mound, I could see a dark, long pile of rocks, its vicinity littered with hammers and other stone tools, including what appeared to be a wood planer made from some sort of marble-like, non-local stone. I logged the site via my global positioning system.

A sunken circle with a small, triangular monolith at its center. The same type of three-pointed stone was found inside a Wisconsin earthen mound at Aztalan, a 13th-century CE ceremonial center, less than 200 miles south of Scott Mitchim's underwater find. The significance of these triangle stones is unknown.

Mitchim went on to find what he described as "workbenches used for pounding and grinding. At one of them, two tools were left on top: a hammer and a grinder." The surrounding lake bottom was profuse with stone arrowheads, but an awl and fishhook were made of copper. Another fishhook he found was "much bigger, four-sided," and likewise copper.

Mitchim's most remarkable encounter was with "a mini-pyramid about four feet wide and approximately four feet high."

Because all his dives occurred between depths of approximately 30 and 60 feet, the materials he found can be dated back from 4,100 to 3,200 years ago, when water tables in the Upper Middle West began to rise from previously lower levels. In other words, the structures and implements he observed were on dry land prior the circa 2100 BCE, after which they were progressively covered by rising waters. This period tends to affirm their identification with the Great Lakes Region's ancient copper barons, who were busily engaged in large-scale mining operations just then.

Elegantly laid out, enigmatic stone structure on the lake floor, approximately 60 feet down.

Because, in its present, pristine condition, the site is extremely vulnerable to vandalism and theft, it must await the final installation of security systems before its precise location is publicized. Until then, the ancient copper miners' workshop is concealed in a murky darkness that has preserved it for more than 40 centuries.

10

Sunken Civilization Found off Oregon?

By Professor Julia Patterson

Ancient American reader Tamara Szalewski writes:

> I have recently come across an anomaly on the Juan De Fuca plate that I am unable to find information on. Every map I go to, from Google Earth, NOAA [National Oceanic and Atmospheric Administration] topographical ocean maps and USGS [U.S. Geological Survey] Live Earthquake maps, show the same topographical anomaly. It isn't natural in my estimation.
>
> Because Frank Joseph wrote about the lost continents of Lemuria and Atlantis, I am wondering if these anomalies are recorded already. I know with the current satellite imagery available new under-ocean civilizations are being found on the boarders of continents the world over.[1] The area in question is off the Oregon Coast on the Juan De Fuca Plate in the Cascadia Subduction Zone. As some of the lines and configurations

re-appear on the southwest side of the plate fracture, I believe these anomalies to have been in place before the plate itself fractured in that area.[2]

The discovery Szalewski refers to lies approximately 12 miles off the Oregon coast parallel to and north of Coos Bay and south of Winchester Bay, at a depth of about 200 feet. The image is composed of 22 interconnected, elongated ovals, mostly running north and south, but one pair is laid out on an east-west alignment, and four others lie at contrary angles. The overall length of the feature appears to be some 20 miles. Although its artificial configuration is self-evident, what purpose it may have served, who was responsible for its creation, and when are enigmas beyond speculation. The Juan De Fuca Plate structure is not alone, however. Following along perhaps 50 miles due north on the same Cascadia Subduction Zone, another underwater site approximately 270 miles off the coast of Washington State yielded physical evidence of a sunken civilization.

Discovered in 1950, the Cobb Seamount is part of a chain of sunken mountains extending into the Gulf of Alaska. Relatively easy exploration of its 23-square-acre flat top has been afforded by comparatively shallow, 120-foot depths, making it one of the most thoroughly studied *guyots* in the Pacific Ocean, and, in the words of David Hatcher Childress, "a star program of the University of Washington for years."[3] Named after A.H. Guyot (1807–84), a Swiss geographer and geologist, guyots are flat-topped submarine mountains, common in the Pacific Ocean, usually extinct volcanoes, whose summits do not reach above the sea surface. Their flat tops are believed to have been formed by the erosion of wave action when they were initially above sea level.

Childress cites a September 10, 1987 issue of the *Seattle Times* describing man-made artifacts retrieved from the Cobb Seamount. They included pottery dated to 18,000 Years Before Present, plus the mummified remains of porpoises and whales. Little more has been published about these finds since they were made, probably because they contradict academic doctrine purporting that North America was uninhabited until just 13,000 years ago. Perhaps Washington State's Cobb Seamount treasure trove of ancient materials is related to Oregon's underwater feature, which suggests the layout of a huge population center. If so, both sites belong to a high culture that flourished on formerly dry territories, until melting glaciers at the end of the last

The Pacific Ocean off the northwest coast of the United States appears to conceal the ruins of a sunken civilization.

ice age unleashed catastrophic flooding that elevated sea levels world-wide by 390 feet.

As such, geology is in accord with archaeology when dating the Cobb Seamount artifacts to 18,000 years ago. They belong to an unknown civilization that flourished off America's Pacific Northwest Coast millennia before textbook versions of the past claim man invented the first cities in Mesopotamia, little more than 5,000 years ago.

11

The Walls in the Lake

By Andrew E. Rothovious

During late October 1984, workers were startled to behold what appeared to be a pair of stone walls rising through the murky waters of a Minnesota lake. Located in the town of Willmar, about 60 miles west of Minneapolis, Foot Lake was the focus of a Kandiyohi County dredging project initiated 11 years earlier. Before the mysterious structures could be investigated, a late-autumn ice-storm struck Minnesota, freezing over the lake, and the underwater site was not examined until the following summer.

On July 10, 1985, a research team composed of George Couleur, Kandiyohi County Water Safety Officer, Virgil Olson, County Commissioner, and Edwin Bredson, dredge operator, relocated the precise position of one of the submerged targets. Equipped with a searchlight, steel pipe and measuring line, Michael Roe, Kandiyohi County Sheriff's Deputy and a professional scuba diver, dove following their directions. He soon found the top of the two walls under just 10 feet of water.

Both were completely concealed beneath superimposed layers of mud and silt, which the diver painstakingly removed before completing his examination. The walls are laid out on an east-west axis, "parallel to Ella Avenue, about two hundred yards out," he said, from the south shore at that street. Roe told J.D. Horning, a staff reporter from Willmar's *West Central Tribune* that the rampart nearest the shore appeared to have been made of "granite, smooth on one side with rounded corners."[1] He described it as "chest high, about four feet tall," and approximately 3 feet in diameter. He determined its overall length at almost exactly 100 feet, because "it went as far as my rope on either side, and it was pitch black down there."

Roe found the slightly larger second wall about 100 feet away from the first. Standing a foot taller, it was likewise nearly 100 feet long, with a diameter of 2 feet. Using his steel pipe, he pried a sample from its exterior. Brought to the surface while still wet, the specimen was a deep blue color. After it dried, however, it changed into "a chalky white," according to Roe. "It looks like plaster of Paris." The whole wall itself resembles "a plaster board once it gets wet, real soft and mushy, kind of a pasty material. I could dig right into it."

Referring to its composition, he commented, "We're not sure of the materials, but it seems like some kind of masonry wall." As he was chiseling samples, he observed numerous tiny fossils, "almost like snails," embedded in the wall. He speculated that the structure might be the result of "some type of accumulation of lake animals" that had become fossilized over time. "But I'm no biologist, and I'm only guessing. We wondered if it (the wall) could be the foundation of a fort or some other building. But who would put something there?"[2]

The Kandiyohi County investigative team next looked for help from state archaeologists. But the academics dismissed Foot Lake's "walls" sight unseen as nothing more than "glacial remnants." Critics point out, however, that all glacial til alignments are north-south, whereas the underwater structures run east-west, and very roughly, at that. Moreover, Roe's physical, first-hand description of the ramparts clearly define their non-glacial provenance.

Even so, scientific officials expressed no interest in the site, presumably because they were not the first to discover it. Their lack of enthusiasm aside, County Commissioner Olson wondered about the age of the sunken walls. "I'm sure they date back a ways," he said, "maybe over one hundred forty years. They could even be centuries old, for all we know. And if they were built by somebody, it had to have been before Willmar was here." The town was established in 1850.

Foot Lake's dynamic geology may be a clue to the origins of its anomalous structures. Olson went on to recount that in 1934 it "was completely dried up. You could walk across it. Of course, there was nothing there, but these walls would probably have been about seven feet down in the mud."[3] Around that same time, a much younger Olson met an old-timer who was among the first settlers in the area. "I remember him telling me that this was all dry then, no water anywhere. He said he drove wagons across" the ground now covered by the lake.

Donald Miller, president of the Kandiyohi County Historical Society, added that the Foot Lake area was reportedly dry twice within the previous 150 years, the earlier period falling in the 1850s, just as Olson's source recounted. Miller stated that an examination of county records document early settlers "building roads across the dry lake bottom and digging wells" during the drought, but nothing resembling 100-foot-long stone bulwarks is mentioned. Perhaps, as Olson surmised, they were, even then in the mid-19th century, buried under at least several feet of earth, attesting to their pre-modern origins. During a second dry period, in the early 1930s, Miller said the walls would have probably been concealed "in about six feet of mud."

Olson collected local stories about Foot Lake, but they did not prove particularly enlightening. "Everybody has got a different version, either from their grandparents or somebody else." Suggestions included an old sunken ice-house, an abandoned farm, and a tower built in the center of the lake bottom 80 years ago, when the area was dry. None of the explanations panned out. In view of the walls' location in the middle of the water, far from shore, Olson said, "to me, it almost prohibits any type of construction outside of when Foot Lake was dry." The ramparts "could possibly have come from the Indians or some other race," he wondered. "I'm sure I don't know, but it would be very interesting to find out."[4] Apparently, the archaeology authorities do not share his interest, especially since the drowned walls of Foot Lake might challenge their dogmatic paradigm of no overseas visitors in pre-Columbian America.

Minnesota's underwater palisades appear to be the ruins of a man-made construction built long before the earliest arrival of modern European settlers, just 170 years ago. The structures were obviously completed in one of the dry periods that afflict Foot Lake. During the only such periods known in the 1850s and 1930s, they were already buried under at least 6 feet of mud. Hydrological studies show that the state's next previous drought took place during a climate phase known as the Little Ice Age, from the late 13th to early 14th centuries CE. Foot Lake would have been dried up then, but who was around to build its massive stone walls?

Indian tribes scattered across south-central Minnesota at the time did not engage in any significant public works programs, and tended, moreover, to avoid permanent settlement, as they followed and hunted migrating animal herds. Interestingly, a Little Ice Age date appears to allow the most likely time-parameter for construction of the Foot Lake walls. Previous to that period, the Upper Midwest was far wetter than it has been since. All its lakes were broader and deeper, and its river systems far more powerful and extensive than today or in the last thousand years.

Given the historically unstable water conditions and levels at Foot Lake, its ramparts may have been originally built as flood-gates or dikes to regulate ebb and flow, or even performed as a kind of reservoir for a materially sophisticated community, of which nothing else remains.

Who might have created such a project around the turn of the 14th century seems beyond knowing. But another surprisingly advanced culture did flourish in the Midwest at the same time, and its people were likewise skilled in irrigation. These were the inhabitants of Aztalan, who raised a 45-acre, Maya-like ceremonial center on either side of the Crawfish River, in southern Wisconsin, located between Milwaukee and the state capitol, Madison. Regarded by native Ho Chunk (Winnebago) Indians as "foreigners," the Aztalaners built a stone canal more than 3 miles long from the Crawfish River to Rock Lake, whose shores they ringed with many hundreds of burial mounds.

Coincidentally (?), this anciently occupied body of water is likewise known for the masonry structures, which lie under its surface. Some of them resemble great stone ramparts about 100 feet long, approximately the same lengths of wall scuba diver Michael Roe found in Foot Lake. Rock Lake is some 320 airline miles away. Could there nonetheless have been a connection of some kind? Actually, the Aztalaners were known to travel much further: They imported mollusk shells (probably chiefly for ornamentation) from Key West, Florida, and as far as the West Indies.

They established direct relations with another outstanding ceremonial center even more distant than Willmar, Spiro Mounds, in northeast Oklahoma. Perhaps Wisconsin's Aztalaners had something to do with pre-Columbian events in Minnesota, too. The "walls" in both Foot and Rock Lakes may have suffered a common watery fate through the same or similar geologic changes that affected the whole Upper Midwest region of North America, about seven centuries ago. Whatever the cause, the sunken structures in Foot Lake cry out for modern investigation.

In 2010, attempts at locating the structures with an underwater television camera lowered from a pontoon boat at the positions indicated by Miller, Olson, et al., were frustrated due to turbid conditions limiting sub-surface visibility within one foot. Repeated exploratory efforts were consistently hampered, even in relatively dry seasons, by unrelieved lack of sufficient clarity. Sonar expeditions to Foot Lake were no less ineffective, because increased silting since the 1980s could have entirely buried the walls under muddy deposition (impenetrable to sonar signals), and/or the structures location in a depression difficult for sonar imagery to distinguish from the lake floor. They will remain cloaked within the murky depths until improved underwater research technologies finally reveal their sunken hiding place.

ARTIFACTS OF TRANSOCEANIC CONTACT

———•◆•———

The appearance of a newly disclosed crystal skull four years ago was a particularly memorable occasion, especially for the object's unusually high standard of execution and undoubted Aztec provenance, making it the best-authenticated specimen of its kind.

Our cover illustration of an ancient Old World coin lost in a North American setting is no visual fantasy, but comes to life with the real-life discovery of a 2,200-year-old coin found near the banks of the Missouri River. The story is recounted by Dr. Cyclone Covey (1922–2013), professor emeritus of history, Wake Forest University (Winston-Salem), North Carolina, and author of *Calalus: A Roman Jewish Colony in America From the Time of Charlemagne Through Alfred the Great* (Vantage Press, 1975). One of cultural diffusion's hardest hitting intellectuals, Dr. Covey's personal contribution to alternative research is as valued today as it will continue to be in the future.

From the early 19th century until just after World War One, 3,000 or more slate tablets inscribed with ancient Old World illustrations and a mysterious written language were excavated, sometimes under scientifically controlled conditions, from Native American mounds across the state of Michigan. Although investigators have consistently failed to understand these intriguing artifacts, Steven A. Wilden may have found the key that unlocks their secret.

An architect and project manager, the former USMC Captain was president of Idaho's Twin Falls County Museum from 2004 to 2006. Wilden demonstrates that the Michigan tablets were engraved by foreign followers of Gnosticism, a prominent heretical movement of the sixth century, partly of pre-Christian origin. Gnostic doctrine taught that the world was created and ruled by a lesser divinity, the demiurge, of which Christ was the divine intermediary to God. "Gnostic" derived from the Greek gnosis for esoteric knowledge. The Pistis Sophia, or "Faith in Wisdom," he mentions is a Gnostic text written between the third and fourth centuries CE.

Professor of Tribal Art History, M.T. Bussey is the leading authority on discoveries coming to light at Lake Michigan's largest island, among them, a beautifully engraved stone suggesting the handiwork of a Keltic visitor during antiquity. Her important book, *Aube Na Bing: A Pictorial History of Michigan Indians*, was released by Michigan Indian Press in 1988.

An experienced mariner, Jay Stuart Wakefield was educated at Dartmouth and the University of Washington in biology, but his passion for investigating ancient connections between Neolithic or Bronze Age Europe and pre-Columbian America shines through his two books and more than 25 magazine articles devoted to the subject. Here, his fresh evidence for prehistoric axe-heads from either side of the Atlantic Ocean is no less brilliant, insightful, and inescapably convincing.

12

Mexico's "New" Crystal Skull

By Frank Joseph

An unusual event took place December 13–17, 2012, aboard a gigantic vessel steaming round trip from Fort Lauderdale, Florida, to Cozumel ("Island of Sparrows" in the original Mayan). At more than one thousand 111 feet long, the third largest cruise ship afloat became headquarters for a collection of more than a dozen crystal skulls in a "Return to Atlantis" Conference aboard the 154,407-ton *Liberty of the Seas*. Some internationally renowned experts on the subject assembled in a large meeting room on her second deck where the translucent objects were displayed to discuss the pros and cons of these alleged artifacts.

Despite occasionally fervent claims for ancient authenticity on behalf of sculpted skulls by their enthusiastic owners, each gleaming curiosity appeared well-made, most likely in 21st-century China where a growing appreciation for foreign markets in such ready-made "New Age" goods is being translated these days into brisk sales, mostly for American customers able to afford them. Historically questionable as such attractive items may be, one specimen stood out among them all.

The Conference's final lecturer Dr. Benjamin Passmore told of a remarkable object never before described in public and entirely unknown to even the crystal skull experts on board.

"During early 1992," Dr. Passmore explained, "I started treating a young man in his thirties for what appeared to be endogenous depression,"[1] an atypical sub-class of clinical depression. When no particular source of this mood disorder is found, it is considered endogenous; in other words, resulting from conditions within the organism rather than externally caused. Because of patient confidentiality, Dr. Passmore was unwilling to provide the real names of those involved in his acquisition of a relatively small, if exceptionally beautiful, crystal skull perched before him on his lectern from which it leered fixedly at the attentive audience.

He referred to his patient only as "Mark," who, previous to the onset of an unfortunately terminal condition, had been employed in Mexico by a company manufacturing batteries. Gradually, it became apparent that Mark was growing increasingly demented with loss of ability to communicate and twitching of the face, extremities, and eventually his entire trunk. Neurologic consultation gave a presumptive diagnosis of Creutzfeldt–Jakob disease, a degenerative neurological disorder, an incurable invariably fatal brain illness. Following his death a few months later, I made frequent home visits to his grieving parents.

"On one occasion when the mother was not at home, his step-father surprised me by bringing out two crystal skulls as unalike from each other as such things could be. He claimed to have bought them around 1960 in Mexico City. He also showed me their color photograph that had been published in some periodical, I forget which. Frank confessed that he had been a pot-hunter in Mexico for many years. He claimed both skulls had been 'stolen' long ago by the Mexican despot Díaz from a museum in Oaxaca and kept on El Presidente's desk, along with another skull made of amethyst."

Dictator Porfirio Díaz (1830–1915) was born in Oaxaca (pronounced "Wha-haka") in southwestern Mexico. During 1865, he was captured by his enemies in that state, but went on to win an important battle there one year later. He built his home in Oaxaca from which he launched a rebellion in 1876. Clearly, Oaxaca played an important role in the life of this man, lending at least some credence to connections linking him with the crystal skull through Oaxaca.

A possible relationship was reinforced in 1932, when an equally magnificently carved though entirely different sort of ritual object was found, likewise in Oaxaca at "Tomb 7," a Monte Alban site. State University of New York (Albany) archaeologists Jill Leslie Furst and Peter T. Furst describe the object as a "small pedestal cup, carved and polished to absolute perfection from a block of rock crystal. . . . Rock crystal carving reached its greatest height in the Late Post-Classic, particularly among the Tarascans of Michoacan, the Aztecs, and the Mixtecs."[2]

Of these three contemporaneous peoples, the Mixtecs are most identified with the crystal cup because they occupied Oaxaca. As such, the crystal skull in question may indeed have originated among the same skilled craftsmen in southwestern Mexico and been carved there sometime between the 13th through 15th centuries CE.

Dr. Passmore continued:

After Mark passed away I began treating his father for grief and depression when Frank brought the two skulls to my office and asked me to keep them as prevention against their destruction by his wife. She blamed her son's illness and death on them, convinced they were evil. Frank shot himself to death a few weeks later. His widow requested I return the skulls for their disposal, but I managed to convince her that they should be preserved and studied by university-trained experts as possible archaeological treasures.

I must mention here that until I acquired the crystal skulls, I took neither stock nor interest in claims on behalf of anything 'paranormal.' For the previous three decades, I led the life of a practicing professional schooled in and dedicated to the scientific method, which I felt sure was capable of explaining everything in terms of natural phenomena. Unaccountably, however, and by slow degrees I gradually came to loathe the larger of Frank's crystal skulls without reasonable cause until, in late 1992, I packed it off as an anonymous donation to Washington, D.C.'s Smithsonian Institution."

Curators there dismissed the oversized hollow and crudely executed object as a modern fabrication when they allegedly found traces on its surface of carborundum, a silicon carbide powder mass-produced since 1893 for use as an abrasive. Assigned Catalogue Number A562841-0 in the collections of the department of anthropology, it is the largest of all crystal skulls, weighing 31 pounds and standing 15 inches high.

"It has been displayed as a modern fake at the National Museum of Natural History," according to Wikipedia. "The skull was meant to be owned by a Mexican-American named Eduard Aguayo."[3] All attempts to identify this person have come to nothing. In the 21 years Dr. Passmore has had custodianship of the crystal skull, he never discussed it in public, and its existence was unknown to the outside world—until 2012's "Return to Atlantis" Conference aboard *Liberty of the Seas*—nor published until his exclusive report for *Ancient American.*

He has been recently aided in researching the object by his grandson, a senior-year art major at New Mexico State University-Las Cruces. After a three-year investigation, Deret Roberts determined that a bas relief design covering the cranium—in itself a unique feature not found on any other crystal skull—is a stylized representation of the Aztec deity Coatlicue, "the One with the Skirt of Serpents," also known as Cihuacoatl, "the Lady of the Serpent," or Teteoinan, "the Mother of Gods," divine patroness of women who die during childbirth.

She was revered as the "Mother Goddess of the Earth who gives birth to all celestial things," "Goddess of Fire and Fertility," and "Goddess of Life, Death and Rebirth." As the Earth goddess, she was envisioned as

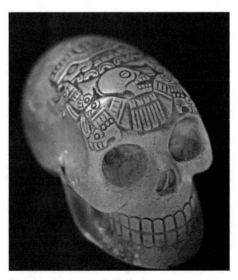

The Coatlicue crystal skull.

both a nurturing mother from which all life springs and an insatiable monster that consumes everything that lives—simultaneously the womb and tomb of Creation. Aztec myth stated that, at the beginning of time, death did not exist because Coatlicue continued to nurture life. But after she was beheaded by a rebellious daughter, the Earth Mother's de-fleshed skull henceforward signified the mortality of organic life for the rest of eternity.

Coatlicue is represented in Aztec temple art as a woman wearing a skirt of writhing snakes and a necklace made of human hearts, hands, and skulls, her feet and hands adorned with claws. Her face is formed by two facing serpents representing blood spurting forth from her neck at the moment of decapitation. These motifs are clearly featured in bas relief atop Dr. Passmore's artifact. While it could have been made by Aztec craftsmen, its origins are more probably Mixtec, owing to the object's alleged, if credible, discovery in Oaxaca where a version of Coatlicue was likewise revered as Toci, "Our Grandmother," and local artisans specialized in the carving of rock crystal. As such, the Skull is between 600 and 800 years old.

In light of Roberts's research, he refers to it as the "Coatlicue Crystal Skull," a designation seconded by Dr. Passmore. Despite an utter lack of any information about the circumstances of its discovery, internal evidence more than adequately affirms Coatlicue's pre-Columbian authenticity. All the shipboard experts who personally scrutinized the object were unanimous in their assessment of its late Mesoamerican identity. They were struck by its overall fine workmanship, far surpassing all other crystal skulls, especially in the delicate incising of the dentition—an area almost invariably botched by modern fakes—but particularly the subtle carving of the bas relief atop the cranium, an expressionist-like rendering of the Mother Earth goddess only a master sculptor could have executed with such flare and finesse.

"Rock crystal is one of the hardest and most difficult minerals to work with," the Fursts point out, "harder even than jade. . . . The difficulties of working so hard a mineral with simple tools must have been enormous" and therefore beyond the purview of late 19th- or 20th-century fakers. Although the surface of the skull is at ambient temperature," Dr. Passmore said, "it feels cold. Temperature measurements in the eye sockets and under the jaw are slightly higher or (on the ship) slightly lower."[4]

Top of the crystal skull.

He went on to describe its peculiar optical traits:

Laser light in the eye sockets illuminates the opposite occipital area. What appear to be tubes or "tunnels" at the jaw line are visible in some of the photographs. Laser light, but not white light, directed to the top of Coatlicue creates a hemispheric "constellation" of lights sharply focused at two to three feet. Moving the input light moves the pattern but doesn't change it, suggesting this is not coming from the glyph but from the interior. The Skull appears to light up with an ambient light—blue on the outside shots, yellow indoors. There are areas primarily at the angle of the jaw on the left and under the mandible, which fluoresce under ultra-violet light. These areas look gray in daylight, but appear yellow in photographs taken by artificial light. They are obviously inclusions in the quartz and occur throughout the Skull in smaller amounts. With UV light, they glow yellow with a slight green tinge. From what I have read, fluorite is rarely found as an inclusion in quartz.

According to Deret Roberts, the Coatlicue Crystal Skull measures 5 5/8 inches long, 4 inches tall, 3 1/2 inches wide, with a circumference of 14 ¾ inches and weight of 4.06 pounds. Beyond such fundamental data, scientific testing of the artifact is urged to possibly learn more about its origins, provenance, optical effects, and perhaps energetic qualities that were locked within its crystalline matrix some eight centuries ago by the unknown master or masters of artistic and other techniques rivaling or perhaps surpassing anything we know today.

13

Ancient Greek Coin Found in Western Missouri

By Dr. Cyclone Covey

Shortly before World War Two, a man working his field within sight of the Missouri River's south bank, just outside the city of Independence, plowed up an unusual coin about the size of a dime, but much thicker and heavier. This was nothing minted in the United States, however. Badly worn, the shiny piece seemed very old to the farmer, who kept it as a curiosity. After he died many years later, his daughter inherited it and contacted *Ancient American* publisher Wayne May, who photographed the find in January 2011.

The coin is as anciently authentic as it is identifiable. Its obverse is mostly occupied by the rightward-facing profile of a woman made recognizable by the reverse representation of a goat standing over the Classical Greek letters, Eta-Sigma-Kappa, signifying sacred affection, nurturing, helper, and so on. Four letters over the animal's body are an abbreviation of Amaltheia, the mother of Zeus, commonly represented as a goat that suckled the infant-god. From her derives the English word *nanny*, a term for anyone entrusted with caring for infants or young children when their parents are absent.

The goat's proud stance, long neck and gracefully curved horns demonstrate that the coin is a *Didrachm* from the southern Aegean island of Paros—only 77 square miles, but far-famed for its white marble—in the Eastern Mediterranean, dated to circa 230–200 BCE. The Didrachm was a standard unit of silver coinage valued at the daily wage of a skilled worker—a stonecutter, sailor, bureaucrat, etc.—during the Classical Epoch.

Although the coin is authentically ancient, its out-of-place discovery in western Missouri is less certain. When confronted by such finds— and there have been many throughout the United States, from Colonial days (as mentioned below) into the present century—mainstream archaeologists invariably ascribe their anomalous appearance to careless collectors. The basis for this baseless assumption rests on another unwarranted supposition: Because ancient Greeks never visited Missouri, a Paros coin found by the farmer must have been accidentally dropped there in modern times, certainly no earlier than 1673, when Father Jacques Marquette and Louis Joliet were the first Europeans to set foot on land that would later become the "Show Me" State.

Although it seems unlikely that either of these explorers or generations of settlers who came after them during the next several centuries would have had rare and valuable ancient spare change rattling around in their pockets, cultural diffusionists are nonetheless open-minded

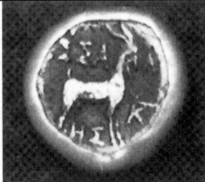

The Missouri River coin.

enough to allow, all things being possible, that some nameless numismatist traveling through the backwaters of western Missouri was absent-minded enough to lose a rare and valuable *Didrachm* before World War Two. That speculation, as improbable as it seems, can be neither confirmed nor disproved. It diminishes into absurdity, however, when we learn something of similar finds that came to light elsewhere in North America.

During 1882, for example, another farmer, this one in Cass County, west-central Illinois, likewise plowed up a bronze coin emblazoned with the image of Antiochus IV, a Hellenistic Greek king who lived from 215 BCE to 164 BCE. In 1957, a small boy playing in a field near Phenix City, northeastern Alabama, picked up a coin issued by Greek colonists at Syracuse, on the Mediterranean island of Sicily, circa 490 BCE.

These three discoveries share more in common than their Classical identity. All were found near or at major river systems, the chief means of inland travel from prehistoric until modern times. The Illinois find seems especially credible, because a Maccabean Revolt broke out during the reign of Antiochus IV. Seven bloody years of insurrection displaced many Jews, of which only the wealthiest could afford escape by ship, taking them far away from murderous upheavals in the Near East. Some refugees may have gone as far as North America, where one of them accidentally lost or hatefully discarded the contemporaneous coin with its profile of his Hellenic enemy.

But more than ancient coins testify to Classical Greek contact with pre-Columbian America. Two thousand years ago, writes Dr. Gunnar Thompson, in his 1992 book, *American Discovery* (WA Misty Isles Press), a Greek sailor named Euhemus claimed to have sailed westward across the Atlantic Ocean until he reached landfall on the other side, where red-skinned natives wore horses' tails. His account was seconded by the second-century Greek geographer, Pausanias. "He described their hair as being fashioned after the mane of a horse. Indeed, [North American] natives of several Eastern Woodland tribes wore their hair in such fashion. It was called a *roach*." [1]

The ancient Greeks appear to have contributed more than scattered coins to the prehistory of America. Pat Morgan writes in *Ancient American*:

> The constellation of the Great Bear was distinguished by various Mediterranean peoples of the Bronze Age, among them the Greeks, who called it *Arctos*, and the Romans, who knew it

as *Ursa Major*, both signifying *the Bear*, though there is nothing about the star group to suggest why they were given that name . . . when Cotton Mather (New England's infamous and influential Puritan minister) inquired of the Natick Indians in Boston as to what knowledge they had of the motions of the stars, he wrote in a letter addressed to London's Royal Society, "It has been surprising unto me to find that they have always called Charles' Wain [a 17th-century reference to the constellation Ursa Major] by the name *Paukunnawaw*, or 'the Bear,' which is the name whereby Europeans also have distinguished it."

Algonquians know the biggest star in the Big Dipper as *Maskwa*—the "Great Bear." An Algonquian tribal society enacts a ritual each year "when the Great Bear in the Sky comes down to Earth."[2]

John Johnston, an agent of the Shawnee, described them in his Indian Tribes of *North America*:

The people of this nation have a tradition that their ancestors crossed the sea. They are the only tribe with which I am acquainted which admit to a foreign origin. Until lately [1819], they kept yearly sacrifices for their safe arrival in this country. From where they came, or at what period they arrived in America, they do not know. It is a prevailing opinion among them that Florida had been inhabited by white people, who had the use of iron tools. Blackhoof [a Shawnee chief] affirms that he has often heard it spoken of by old people, that stumps of trees covering the earth were frequently found, which had been cut down by edged tools.[3]

The Greeks mastered iron metallurgy, a technology unknown to Native Americans, who nonetheless appear to at least have learned from their overseas' visitors an enduring name for the stars.

14

A Gnostic Presence in Prehistoric Michigan

By Steven A. Wilden

In the 2004 foreword to the *Ancient American* edition of Henriette Mertz's book, *The Mystic Symbol: Mark of the Michigan Mound Builders,* David Deal wrote, "In arcane religious doctrine of these early Gnostic, Christian Egyptians called 'Copts,' spelled out in the Pistis Sophia, we see that the doctrine portrayed there in words, is exactly the same as that which is graphically portrayed on the Michigan tablets."[1] Standing on the shoulders of the late Henriette Mertz and David Deal, I will review the three primary deities of Gnostic religious doctrine and then identify the "serpent savior" and "rooster archon" alternate or sub-deities found on five ancient Michigan Tablets. Following the Gnostic teachings further, it becomes apparent that the presence of Gnostic deities and doctrines within the Michigan Mound Builder culture point to an almost unavoidable cultural conflict and division similar to that which took place in the Old World. The Gnostic doctrine that apparently caused the most problems held the belief that Lucifer or the "son of the left hand" was coequal with or even pre-eminent to Christ, and therefore a worshipped deity in the Gnostic Mound Builder's godhead. The inscriptions on the tablets suggest that the outcome of the Gnostic experience led to warfare and the eventual fall of the Michigan Mound Builder civilization.

Discovery of Gnostic symbols on the Michigan Tablets provides strong evidence for the historical authenticity of these artifacts, and further confirms the doctrine of Cultural Diffusion from the Old World to North America before Columbus. The presence of Gnostic inscriptions corroborates the previous dating of the Michigan relics to the third and fourth centuries CE by Henriette Mertz and David Deal. It also confirms their proposed origin and ethnic background of the Coptic and Gnostic, Egyptian and Mediterranean-based Christians, who fled religious persecutions to ancient North America. It should be pointed out

The Gnostic serpentine "demiurge" on a Michigan artifact.

that not all Copts were Gnostics. However, the Christians who came to Michigan and produced these remarkable tablets in clay, copper, and slate were Hopewell by location, Caucasian by race and, from their own inscriptions, their religion was predominately Gnostic-Christian.

Their predecessors and surrounding neighbors were either Judeo-Christian or pagan. Inscriptions found in central North America already attest to the Judeo-Christian and pagan presence among the Mound Builders—the first-century Hebrew Bat Creek Stone of Tennessee, Phoenician Baal inscriptions from Canada to Ecuador, and the Ohio Decalogue Stone, also Hebrew, are good examples.

Underlying the Gnostic controversy, some immigrants who arrived in prehistoric Michigan preferred a more orthodox belief and practice than tenets espoused by the radically unorthodox Gnostics. Not all Michigan Mound Builders were willing to embrace the worship of Lucifer and the divergent lifestyle of the Gnostic philosophers and teachers we know about from contemporaneous Old World writers. Gnosticism is the historical key to understanding the cultural division and strategic crisis that overtook the Michigan Mound Builders by the end of the fourth century.

David Deal pointed out that these Michigan Gnostics believed in the three principal deities that they inscribed on their tablets, that of the "Greater Yahweh" (God the Father), the "Lesser Yahweh" (Jesus Christ, the Messiah), and the "Sama-el" Lucifer).[2] This belief was dissimilar from the Catholic Trinity of the fourth-century Orthodox Church, and, of course, would have caused problems for the Michigan Mound Builders, just as it did for the Gnostic Copts of Egypt, leading to the latter's expulsion and eventual immigration to the New World. At least two cross and serpent tablets were unearthed in Michigan between circa 1900 and 1910. Golden Barton and Wayne May described the first in the February 2000 issue of *Ancient American*, and suggested that the narrow, rectangular cross and serpent slate tablet with hieroglyphics below could be a New World reminder of the "fiery serpent" of brass placed upon a "pole" by Moses in Numbers 21:8–9.[3]

Further searching in 2 Kings 18:4, the reformer King Hezekiah of eighth century BCE Judah "brake in pieces the brass serpent that Moses had made," because the people worshipped the serpent instead of Yahweh. Then, in John 3:14, Jesus says he will be "lifted up" like the serpent Moses made. Now consider Genesis 3:1–5, in which Lucifer is represented by the serpent hanging in the Tree of Knowledge, where he beguiles Eve in the Garden of Eden, as if he were God. Following the primitive Christian era, where the serpent symbol was never worshipped, the Ophite Gnostics secretly replaced Christ with Lucifer, representing the latter as a serpent, and even made Lucifer pre-eminent. The Ophite-Gnostics preferred the serpent to Christ in symbolism and ritual. According to several early Christian writers— Hippolytus, Tertullian, Epiphanius, and Irenaeus of the second and third centuries—the Ophite-Gnostics re-interpreted the meanings of the biblical accounts to reflect their belief that the "serpent" was a type for Lucifer, who was the savior, rather than Jesus Christ.

Several inscriptions on the narrow slate tablet mentioned above have been interpreted. First, the *IH I*, or Mystic Symbol, is dominant on nearly all the Michigan artifacts. Its meaning is said by both Mertz and Deal to be *YHW*, or Yahweh. The Hebrew letters *YAH*, and Greek letter *PI*, as in the first letter of the word *Pater*, both refer to Yahweh and Father, or a supreme God. We also see the "son of the right hand"—*Aberamentho* in Coptic— who was referred to in both Christian and Gnostic writings as the "right hand of God." The third textual symbol of the primary deities, or the "son of the left hand" symbol," in Gnostic teaching, Lucifer, the older brother of Jesus Christ, is not found on the narrow slate serpent tablet.

A fourth symbol, newly interpreted in this article, is the forward or backward S-shaped serpent symbol seen on the narrow cross and serpent slate tablet as a serpent wrapped over and down the cross and also seen below in the text next to a symbol ostensibly signifying the serpent overcoming the "son of the right hand," or son of God. This S-shaped Egyptian hieroglyphic *tch* means "serpent," according to Budge's *Egyptian Hieroglyphic Dictionary*, and appears to signify the Ophite-Gnostic savior as the serpent, or Lucifer, who claims the heirship position at the crucifixion, as in the Garden of Eden, instead of Christ.

This means that by the fourth century, the Michigan Gnostics appear to have worshipped Yahweh the Father, Jesus, and Lucifer, the latter two interchangeably. The second and similar slate cross and serpent tablet has a notch at the top, plus four holes drilled through the tablet apparently prior to its inscription. A single glyph appears at the top of the cross, the Mystic Symbol, or *IH I*. There are also two profiled heads, both Caucasian-like, of what appears to be a bearded leader on the left and another beardless leader on the right. Each is faced away from the other with the cross between their heads, ostensibly representing a significant theological dispute.

It is proposed that both fourth-century Michigan slate serpent tablets depict a Gnostic inscription in which the serpent discreetly represents Lucifer and is elevated upon the cross to be the Messiah in the place of Christ.[4]

We also note the Michigan clay tablet depicting the crucifixion of Jesus Christ in bodily form, not as a serpent, on the wooden cross, as described by the New Testament writers, which may be of a significantly earlier date than the Gnostic serpent slate tablets. The only comprehensive explanation is that there was significant theological conflict among the Michigan Mound Builders culminating in the fourth century as the more radical Gnostic element gained ground. As it was in the Old World, certainly the Gnostic godhead would be a huge impetus for societal conflict and division for the Michigan Mound Builders and the entire Hopewell culture.

Two symbolic rooster-like heads and two goat-like portraits embellish a Coptic-Gnostic funerary or slate tablet found in the mounds of Michigan. The rooster archon and pagan goat head are recognizable symbols in the iconography of Gnostic worship and practice. What we see on these Gnostic Michigan Tablets is the mixing of Christian and pagan symbols, including crosses, serpents, roosters, goats and altars. In the case of this funerary tablet, it is done very discreetly. The two decorated Coptic coffins with crosses appear on either side of the center section of the tablet.

Between the two coffins of this tablet rooster-like heads rise above a circular seven-day Sabbath calendar of observance, with goat-like heads below the circle. There is also, in the lower section of the tablet, a priestly altar with a vase emitting engraved lines of mystical power, identifiably Gnostic, in contrast to primitive or fourth-century Orthodox Christian symbolism. A very unique clay tablet made with impressed objects and letter dies, rather than by tooled fonts, portrays the original Tower of Babel scene from Genesis chapter 11.

We see a partial Mystic Symbol, or *IH I* at the top-center of the tablet with a man standing to the right of the symbol as the final letter, as if he were God Himself. We see the "son of the right hand" on the upper right of the tablet, in the opposite location from its usual place on the right side of *IH I*, or Yahweh. We don't see the symbol for Lucifer or the "son of the left hand." This omission of the "son of the left hand" is insightful, as in accordance with Gnostic doctrine, Lucifer had nothing to do with the scene depicted here. Instead, we see at the bottom left of the tablet, the Gnostic rooster deity, or servant of the Demiurge, identified as *Yaldabaoth* (Yahweh), spewing out confusion to the people, who are depicted with their arms raised in the attitude of worshiping the rooster as God.

The Demiurge was considered a heavenly entity, subordinate to the Supreme Being, the controller of the material world, and antagonistic to all that is purely spiritual. Here, he is a negative Gnostic term for Yahweh and his servants, who were said to be saviors of only material world. In other words, the Gnostics attributed to the rooster archon the role of servant to the creator of the material world, Yaldabaoth (Yahweh), and condemned the servant rooster and Yaldabaoth in favor of the rebellious and immaterial spirit, Lucifer, who has no physical body.

The rooster archon or sub-deity in this clay tablet is similar to the *sidicus* bird that speaks all the human languages and presides over the confusion of tongues on Earth following the construction of the tower of Babel, which is shown on another Michigan tablet referred to by Henriette Mertz as "plate 7" in her book. These two rooster sub-deities do not have the serpentine legs as the rooster deities of the Oslo Papyrus, first published in 1925, or of the Michigan slate flood tablet discussed below; however, the inscription is clear that the rooster archon or demiurge, servant of Yaldabaoth of Gnostic origin is present.

Perhaps the most striking and now obvious Gnostic sub-deity symbol is inscribed on a two-sided Great Flood and Tower of Babel tablet. It represents the rooster archon found on the Tower of Babel side of this slate tablet, spewing out teachings of confusion to the people at the bottom left, under the image of the biblical tower. This Gnostic archon figure is recognized by its upper rooster body and head with lower, serpentine leg or legs, being adored by worshippers to the right of the rooster image, similar to the clay Tower of Babel tablet described above. The Gnostic Christians called their supreme God Abraxas or Yaldabaoth, and represented his earthly archon or power as a rooster.

Above the head of the rooster archon on Tablet 17 is a combination of two symbols: the Egyptian shepherd's crook and a symbol for the people, interpreted as the rooster archon's power and authority over the people. The upper portion of Tower-Rooster tablet indicates the mercy of God after the Great Flood, showing the mystic symbol *IH I* with the all-seeing eye and the "son of the right hand" symbol in its proper place at left above the rainbow sign or covenant by God to not entirely inundate the Earth again. The "son of the left hand" symbol appears in the top-right scene of the tablet also, above the zigzag water symbol representing the power of Lucifer over the waters of the world.

The physical resurrection of Christ and of humanity in general is curiously absent from the Michigan Tablets. Gnostics would not, in any case, teach the bodily resurrection as found in the New Testament. In Gnostic doctrine, Lucifer competes with Christ for all the honors, including resurrection, even if it makes no sense, as Lucifer, being a spirit, has no physical body to resurrect. The Gnostics' denial of the physical resurrection of Christ and the human family further strengthens the historicity and doctrinal accuracy of the Michigan Tablets.

The Gnostics, according to the *Pistis Sophia*, believed that Christ remained with his disciples and taught them for 11 years after He arose from the dead, as a spiritual, not a physical being. The Gnostics deemphasized the physical body in favor of the spiritual body. According to Irenaeus, the Bishop of Lyon, France (died circa 202 CE), the Gnostics rejected all physical existence and assumed a higher spiritual realm

A Michigan cask decorated with Gnostic imagery, including the sidicus bird.

than other Christians, regardless of their conduct. This gave the Gnostic teachers a certain sense of superior knowledge, or *gnosis*, and, presumably, social status. They also claimed that special knowledge was given to the Gnostic teachers after the apostles passed away.

The Old World Gnostics were accused of attending pagan feasts, human sacrifices, and wearing elaborate clothing. Contemporaneous Christians, fearful of competition, accused Gnostics of immorality and sexual transgressions among their leaders and adherents without any conscience, while claiming to be Christians. In Egypt and Eurasia, Gnosticism developed a theological synthesis from philosophies of the Persians (Marcion, circa 85–circa 160 CE), Greeks (Plato, 428–347 BCE), and Christians (Valentinus, died circa 150 CE), constructing a separate body of knowledge and doctrine outside the biblical canon. *Gnosis* was the Gnostics' secret knowledge. In addition to alleged worship of sub-deities and immoral practices, their biggest and most malevolent Gnostic secret was worship of "the serpent," or Lucifer of Genesis in the Garden of Eden—the rebellious son of Yaldabaoth (Coptic for "God"), and the supposed true liberator of the children of Adam and Eve, the "real hero," not Jesus Christ.

Evidence indicates that the powerful influence of the Gnostics was widespread not only in the Old World, but also in at least two Hopewell regions of North America as well. It would be naive not to assume that most if not all of these Gnostic doctrines and practices followed the Old World Gnostic immigrants to Michigan. It has been proposed that the arrival of these doctrines and practices in the Middle West of prehistoric North America caused division and civil strife between the Gnostics and the more orthodox Judeo-Christian Mound Builders. The presence of the Gnostic "serpent savior" and "rooster archon" deities and the worship of Lucifer would guarantee conflict.

Numerous records exist of conflicts and wars inscribed on the Michigan Tablets. The existence of these Gnostic records in a correct historical setting confirm the authenticity of the Michigan Tablets, and give us strong and unique clues concerning the cause of internal strife and eventual destruction of the Michigan Mound Builders. This internal conflict would have weakened the Mound Builders against outside attack from the rising Algonquin Nation, ancestors of the Ojibwa and Delaware, or Lenni-Lenape tribes who would eventually kill off all the white immigrants they called the Allegewi, or Alleghany.

15

Ancient Kelts in Lake Michigan?

By M.T. Bussey

In June 2010, a high school student walking the north end of Beaver Island noticed a pile of leaves that might hide a morel mushroom. When young McCauley brushed them aside, he was surprised to uncover instead a small, flat stone—5 inches long, 2 inches wide, and 3 inches thick—beautifully engraved on one side with the likeness of a bird and other, stylized images. The boy temporarily loaned his discovery to the local Historical Museum, where it was professionally photographed before being returned to its finder. Before any legitimate research could be completed on the object, he and his family left the island, taking the "McCauley Stone" with them, leaving behind only prints and negatives with which to further any investigation.

Even so, detailed enlargements and microscopic analysis of its imagery revealed aspects of a lithic artwork that could not have been created or altered by some high school student or any carver of our time. The portrayed beak belongs to a water bird, its heavy form suggesting a goose. The Greyleg Goose, often called "the first wild goose," is the original foundation breed for all later, domesticated geese. They are bulky birds, weighing from 6 to 10 pounds. Their migration loops through the northern latitudes of the Arctic Circle from Northern Europe to Greenland, returning en route to the British Isles for winter.

As a distinction among other geese, these birds have black, vertical lines running from head to shoulders. Lines deliberately carved along the bird's neck act as an identifier for the Greyleg Goose. This wild bird is a clan totem animal of the Algonquin tribal groups of northeastern America, but also of Scotland's Iron Age Picts and later Kelts in the Orkney Islands. Algonquin oral history claims the symbol of the wild goose is associated with the medicine wheel or the calendrical circle of the year.

The swan constellation, Cygnus, placed on Lakota medicine wheels in their early star knowledge, is often referred to as "the goose," a symbol of protection and defense—the same qualities associated with the wild goose in Pictish/Celtic myth. Geese have always been known to defend themselves, their flocks, and their territory, as would a warrior. The Kelts and other members of Arctic Circle cultures revered wild geese as spiritual guides.

The Picts were a Keltic people who occupied most of Alba, the White Kingdom, their name for most of Scotland, from circa 200 BCE until the 19th century CE. Their so-called "King's Stone, among the largest examples of the Rollright Stone Circle, stands at the borderline between Oxford and Warwickshire, in the English Midlands. The carved boulder is adorned with the Picts' totem birds: the goose and the eagle. Near them is a zigzag line of stars in the constellation Cassiopeia. The same alignment of stars appears on a zigzag line that connects with circles extending from the foot of the frontal humanoid figure on the goose of the McCauley Stone.

"The Way of the Wild Geese" (*El Camino de las Ocas Salvajes*) is an ancient trail in Spain also known as "the Way of the Stars." As its pilgrims parallel the migration of wild geese, they are guided by stone markers incised with the trident "goose foot," a glyph also in the Upper Peninsula of Michigan. Two humanoid figures accompany the Greyleg goose on the McCauley Stone. The larger, primary figure appears to be actually riding the bird, arms stretched apart, raised high over his head forming a V. In Tengrianism, a Central Asian religion with roots going back to the last ice age, a holy man was often portrayed in Mongolian

The McCauley Stone.

and Magyar folk art riding a bird, signifying "the flight of the shaman," a euphemism for his out-of-body experiences and altered states of consciousness that allowed him to visit and retrieve important information for his tribe from visits to the spirit realm.

Rays emanate from the head of the McCauley Stone's anthropomorphic figure, as though from a bright sun. Facial features exhibit a uni-brow, nose line, and slightly smiling mouth. The uni-brow and sunray hair also appear on stone-carved images of the Keltic sun-god, Bel, found throughout the Iberian Peninsula. The interior form of the McCauley Stone figure is laced abstractly with linear carved marks that seem to intend action and movement. They are not smoothed, nor do they conform to the organic curvature of the body.

The raised lines of the figure give us a clue to the carving technique of negative space. The left leg of this figure projects at an angle lengthening from in front of the bird's breast, while the foot forms a Pythagorean Triangle. Extending from the toe of this foot is a zigzag line that connects five sun circles, three of which have carved ray lines. This zigzag line, found on stones all over Beaver Island, is emblematic of the thunderbird of Algonquin legend. The island's Stone Circle claims the most zigzag lines.

A second humanoid figure, leaning slightly forward with out-stretched arms also raised overhead in the V shape, seems to sit on the tail of the bird. Its head too, streams with vertical lines, possibly indicating wavy hair. There are two stippled spots for eyes, one larger stippled spot for a nose, and a smile line for the mouth. The torso is a mass of angular, carved lines, which allow the background of the stone to show through. A pair of carved circles indicating placement of the hip and the knee of the leg are joined by a rectangle-shaped thigh.

Its configuration mimics the Double Disk symbol often found on Pictish standing stones. The indicated V-shapes made by both figure form a dominant sign reflected by the Picts' iconic V-rods adorning many of their surviving material objects. Their megaliths typically display the V depicted beneath a crescent. Together, they compose an alignment scheme for the rising and setting of the sun on the Summer Solstice, additionally found on North American medicine wheels in the West and at Beaver Island, as described in "Lake Michigan Stonehenge" (Chapter 21).

Microscopic analysis of the McCauley Stone reveals color within its images. The seemingly black lines of the bird configuration, parts of the anthropomorphic figures and the thousands of color filled stippled dots are an indigo blue. In fact, three colors are represented on its exterior: turquoise blue, indigo blue, and red sienna brown. Turquoise blue (in light and dark hues) appears in front of the first figure's leg on the bird's breast, in a carved rectangle on the side of the bird, and a small spot on the bird's tail. Indigo blue fills in tiny, stippled holes, plus all the extended dark lines of the entire image. Sienna reddish brown is visible on the two circles that make up the hip and knee of the figure on the bird's tail and the bird's eye.

The stone itself is white calcium carbonate and therefore allows for easy tool carving. The bird image is completely surrounded by sun circles with rays and central spots, spirals and intentionally placed circles, some having "cup and ring" qualities. Above the two figures are three, large circles with indigo blue spot centers and carved rays. There are two more circles under the bird's beak showing sunrays, but they are spirals within circles. Five circles connect with the zigzag line off the front foot of the figure.

An important carving methodology emerged with photo enlargement, which revealed that the entire lithic illustration is composed of stippled, indigo-blue holes. Stippling in stone carving is the technique of creating tiny holes on the surface with a small awl or needle. Soft calcium carbonate rock is a good choice for this approach. These holes can be filled in with color, resulting in the image. Stippling forms the lines which fill in holes on McCauley's Stone, spreading chosen colors from one hole to the next, resulting in dark lines. Close scrutiny of the bird's head reveals stippled holes connected by a blue line to render the back of the bird's head and neck. Spirals and a circle begin as stippled holes.

The artisans of Arctic cultures were noted for their stippled images on wood, bone, leather and stone. They used plants for coloring, as well as for their tattoos; indigo blue was a common hue from a flowering plant identified as *Isatis Tinctoria*. Tattooing is a common practice of many peoples residing within the Arctic Circle. Stippling the skin with tiny holes filled in with color creates the lines for a desired image on the skin. This same process for tattooing was used on the McCauley Stone. Roman legionnaires of the first century referred to the Keltic tribesmen of northern Britain as the *Picti*, the "painted people," for their ornate tattooing. They employed negative space imagery and stippling in their stone carvings, which were quite visually involved; raised, twisted lines often protrude in images that are linear and arranged next to blocks of negative space.

This carving style acts as hidden imagery for a great source of information. It was a method often used by tribal societies with the intent of concealing certain truths, and practiced by Circumpolar peoples, such as the northern tribes of the Algonquin, whose shared culture and root language extended across North America from coast to coast. Even today, tribal elders understand how the extensive history of their folk is preserved within art imagery. The Picts were especially known for their spirals, double circles and "cup and ring" designs, all of which crowd the McCauley Stone.

It would be highly unlikely for a teenager from Beaver Island to have known about the symbolic, ancient origins of designs on the stone named after him. Similarly, the time expended and the carving dexterity used to produce the stippling technique and the involved negative space carving found on the object is an unrecognized choice of a

modern carver. That it surfaced on Beaver Island, where there are identified stone circles with solar and lunar astronomical alignments, stone
carvings of bulls and carved ligature of a handful of ancient scripts,
including Early Ogham, may be all the explanation necessary.

16

Ancient Old World Axes in Pre-Columbian America

By J.S. Wakefield

Side by side at the University of London's Petrie Museum are paired two ancient axe-heads that puzzled Flinders Petrie nearly 100 years ago. As the first English archaeologist granted permission to dig in the Nile Valley, he was allowed to remove any small, relatively insignificant items he might find. Among them was a so-called "lugged" axe-head. Although similar examples were common enough throughout Dynastic Egypt, he could not avoid its close comparison with a specimen from pre-Conquest Peru.

In his *Tools and Weapons*, Petrie states that a

type peculiar to Egypt was that with broad lugs by which to secure the blade to the handle . . . Strange to say, this method of handling is totally absent from the rest of the Mediterranean lands, North Europe, and Asia. It seems almost incredible that a type characteristic of Egypt for thousands of years could never be established elsewhere. Yet, this type recurs as the regular form in Peru and Central America. The Egyptians, like the Peruvians . . . went on the natural lines of lengthening the blade along the handle to give a larger bearing and a means of firm lashing. The entire absence of it in many intermediate lands must preclude our supposing a case of borrowing. It is one of the strong examples of independent invention.[1]

Or is there another explanation?

In another source addressing the subject (*Catalogue of Egyptian Antiquities in the British Museum* Vol. VII, by W.V. Davies), a stone axe from Valdivia, Ecuador, resembles Dynastic Egyptian examples collected by Petrie. Valdivia lies on the north side of the Gulf of Guayaquil, near several natural harbors and a river mouth used by Inca sailing rafts, and later the landfall for the Spaniards' conquest of South America. Like nearby San Agustin, up the Magdalena River, in Columbia, these rivers provided easy access for visitors arriving by sea. Davies offers photographs of other axes from Colombia and eastern Ecuador, plus two more from Tiahuanaco on the Bolivian Antiplano, around Lake Titicaca. All appear to have been modeled after Egyptian lugged axes—unless the Egyptian axes themselves were South American exports, or copies of them.

In any case, such tool components would have been useful for extracting the 125,000 tons of pure copper mined in Michigan's Upper Peninsula—particularly at Isle Royale, in the northwest of Lake Superior—from circa 3100 BCE to 1200 BCE. This tonnage comprised the world's first industrial metal product that fueled a Bronze Age in Europe, as described in *Rocks and Rows*.[2] The same mining procedures were common in Europe during the Bronze Age, when the ground was heated with huge wood fires, followed by quenching the hot rock-face with cold water, then beating the metal out of the cracked rock with stone hammers.

Davies publishes the photograph of a stone hammer with lugs "found with two others" on Isle Royale by the seller's great-grandfather, who worked in the mines there, long before the island became a national park in 1937. These lugged hammers were considered unusual by the miner, or he would not have collected them. They illustrate

Photo 6

Neolithic stone axehead, "found on Isle Royale by the
collector's great-grandfather, who lived in
Keweenaw County, and was a miner on Isle
Royale"

*Stone axe-head found during the late 19th
century on Isle Royale by a Keewanee County
miner, who was a great-grandfather of the
collector.*

the diffusion of ideas through replicating tool designs during Bronze
Age times, when mining engineers sailed from the Near East and the
Mediterranean World to the western shores of Lake Superior for copper
wealth. Close similarities between later Egyptian and South American
bronze axe designs were likewise apparent.

"Double-edged knives start with the great expansion of copper
tools at the rise of the dynastic people," writes Petrie. "The later metal
lugged axes were sharply square with the blade. . . . As no trace of this
type is found in Roman remains, it probably died out about 400 BC,
killed by the advance of socketing."[3]

A preponderance of socketing among American "copper culture"
artifacts is evidence for the major involvement of European ("Bell
Beaker Pottery") people in the prehistoric mining of Michigan copper.
In his discussion of chisels, Petrie observes, "the socketed chisel was
also developed in Peru." When discussing "straight-backed knives," he
notes, "this form was nearly arrived at in the independent copper work

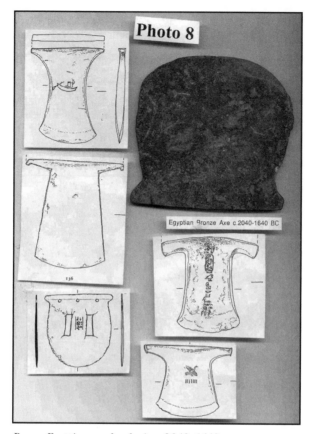

Bronze Egyptian axe-head, circa 2040–1640 BCE.

of America. . . . The halberd arose independently in America, as seen by two from Wisconsin, one curiously like the Coptic form."[4]

Lugged axe-heads were far from universal use during antiquity. They were, after all, limited to so few cultures on either side of the Atlantic Ocean, that their simultaneous appearance among Dynastic Egyptians in the Nile Valley and prehistoric copper miners of Michigan's Upper Peninsula can only signify, as Flinders Petrie described it, a most remarkable instance of "independent invention," or evidence of contact between America and the ancient Old World.

SECTION V

SITES

———◆————

The recent discovery of petrogylphs near Nevada's Pyramid Lake is unprecedented, not only for their age as the oldest examples of North American rock art, but because they are stylistically related to Neolithic patterns found in Ireland.

Effigy mounds are raised piles of earth formed into the shapes of stylized animals, symbols, men, or other figures, sometimes containing one or more human burials. These structures were built primarily as sacred centers by shamans of the Hopewell Culture, from the fifth century BCE to about 400 CE. Surviving examples in Wisconsin's Richland County are among the most obscure, but finest of their kind.

Easter Island is far more famous, but less well-known for its natives' recently established genetic connection to Native Peruvians, separated by 2,300 miles of Pacific Ocean. Also from Peru comes one of the greatest mysteries of ancient America—the huge, stone imagery of Markuwasi—formed by either erosional forces or the hand of man. In Chapter 15, M.T. Bussey described what appears to be a stone inscribed by visitors from the ancient Old World and found on Lake Michigan's Beaver Island. That identification is powerfully underscored here with her analysis of a lithic observatory uncovered not far from the same location.

Another mysterious island off the Georgia coast features an abandoned city made mostly of marine animal shells, more than 4,000 years ago. This unique site is investigated by Gary C. Daniels, who authored the *Mayan Calendar Prophecies* series and founded LostWorlds.org. While studying for his master's degree in communications at Georgia State University, he received a Roger K. Warlick Best Media Project award from the Georgia Historical Society.

Keltic mariners sailed across the sea to escape their Roman conquerors, even as far as Middle America, where one of their iconic crosses still stands monumentally in San Angel. It would have remained unrecognized by the outside world without the attention of Dr. Cisco Drake, professor of education at the University of Mexico City.

17

America's Oldest Rock Art

By Wayne N. May

The recent discovery of North America's oldest rock art potentially threatens textbook versions of our country's prehistory. The petroglyphs were found in August 2014 along a dry waterbed on limestone boulders in a Paiute tribe's reservation, near Pyramid Lake, in northern Nevada's high desert, and are utterly unlike anything known to archaeologists. All other examples are mostly lightly incised depictions of animals, human figures, weapons or geometric designs. These are dissimilar from the Pyramid Lake specimens, which are deeply cut and tightly clustered in linear, curved and circular geometrical designs, together with tree-forms or ferns, series of evenly spaced, vertically oriented V shapes bisected by a vertical line, lozenges, and solar or flower patterns.

Although not duplicated anywhere else in North America, related etchings came to light earlier at Winnemucca Lake, in Oregon, evidence that the culture responsible for the Pyramid Lake rock art was not confined to a single site in Nevada. If its carvings seem otherwise unique,

Pyramid Lake petroglyphs.

their mirror image is found on the other side of the word, across the Atlantic Ocean, at a Neolithic passage grave perched atop an overlook at the Boyne Valley, in Ireland. New Grange, or "New Light," signifies its orientation to sunrise of the winter solstice, an annual event engraved into surrounding curbstones, decorated with solar or flower patterns and stings of diamond designs, or lozenges.

The construction of New Grange has been radiocarbon dated to circa 3200 BCE. But that period is far later than the age of Pyramid Lake's petroglyphs. They were dated by radiocarbon testing of a carbonate layer underlying them to roughly 12,800 BCE. This time-signature was supported by geochemical data and sediment and rock samples from adjacent Pyramid Lake, which show they were exposed to air from 13,200 to 14,800 years ago.

The find therefore conflicts with current archaeological dogma, which insists that Nevada was uninhabited then, because humans only began crossing over a hypothetical "land bridge" more than 1,000 years later, from Siberia to Alaska, where they unaccountably lingered for perhaps another 2,000 or more years. This standard explanation for the peopling of America was debunked as long ago as 2006, when geological surveys proved that any glaciers that could have connected Siberia with Alaska had melted before 13,000 years ago, making migrations from one continent to the next impossible. Ignoring this inconvenient revelation, mainstream scholars continue to argue that the earliest humans to arrive here did not enter what is today the continental United States in time to have carved Pyramid Lake's rock art. Yet, there it is.

Despite conventional scientists' official versions of prehistory, they are being radically dismantled by more recent discoveries proving our land was occupied by outside visitors long before we have been led to believe.

18

Wisconsin Effigy Mounds

By Andrew E. Rothovious

Effigy mounds are earthworks prehistoric artists landscaped into specific designs. "Zooglyphs" are the images of animals, whereas "bioglyphs" depict animals and humans, together with the images of various plants. Both classes are also known as "geoglyphs," which also include abstract or geometric patterns. Effigy mounds range in size from a few yards across to more than 1,000 feet in overall length. The largest effigy mound in North America—Ohio Valley's famous Great Serpent Mound at Locust Grove, Adams County—is 1,348 feet long. Mainstream scholars teach that a majority of representational earthworks found above the Rio Grande River belonged to the Hopewell, a convenient name archaeologists use to define an otherwise unknown people and high culture that flourished primarily in the Middle West from roughly 300 BCE to 400 CE. But some of the effigy mounds clearly portray animals that went extinct long before the Hopewell appeared.

The great surveyor T.H. Lewis spent decades making accurate line drawings of these pre-Columbian structures before they were mostly obliterated by the farmer's plow. Among hundreds of his original illustrations preserved at the Minnesota Historical Museum in St. Paul are the unmistakable images of elephants, virtually all of them victims of agricultural, industrial, and residential development. According to Ho Chunk Indian scholar Larry Johns, nine elephant mounds still exist along the Wisconsin banks of the Mississippi River from Lake Pepin to La Crosse. Ho Chunk means "people of the sacred language," a reference to their belief that Wisconsin has been their homeland for time out of mind.

Accordingly, *Ancient American* publisher Wayne May hypothesizes that the elephant mounds probably precede the Hopewell time frame assigned to them by conventional archaeologists because mastodons are supposed to have died out in North America at the close of the last ice age. Or, did they? The earthwork landscapers depicted animals with which they were familiar, so it does not seem likely that the Hopewell would have portrayed a creature that had not existed for several thousand years. Indeed, oral traditions among the Ho Chunk and other tribal peoples preserve folkish memories of a great beast long extinct that very closely resembled a pachyderm. As such, at least some of the effigy mounds, May argues, might have been constructed by post-ice age artists who personally experienced mastodons centuries ago.

Although these geoglyphs occur from the Mississippi Valley to the Ohio Valley, most were concentrated in the Upper Middle West where Wisconsin embraced more than 10,000 examples. The finest surviving specimens are perfectly preserved atop a hill in southern Richland County, located on both sides of Highway 193 just north of the intersection with Highway 60 west of Muscoda (pronounced "muss-co-day"), a small town in the southeast corner of the state near the Wisconsin River.

The four effigies represent a turtle, bison, and eagle led by an anthropomorphic bird. This figure may possibly memorialize a precursor to our version of Corn Woman cited in Cheyenne myth as a compassionate goddess of agricultural abundance. In most Native American oral traditions, the eagle was associated with spiritual power; the bison meant physical strength, endurance, and protection; the turtle—because of its ability to hibernate throughout the winter underwater and return to the land each spring—signified regeneration, rebirth. The very presence of these holy images defines the ground on which they are located as a sacred site.

They form a line approximately 120 feet long by 35 feet wide and officially referred to as the Elder Group, but more commonly known as the Shadewald Mound Group at the summit of Frank's Hill named after Frank Shadewald. A retired farmer and engineering instructor at Southwest Technical College in Fennimore, Shadewald in 1998 bought the land on which the effigies sit from a neighbor. That same year, adjacent property his family owned became the Ho-Chunk Bison Ranch, which includes several other earthworks. Both ridges were added to the National Register of Historic Places in 2008.

A ridge across the road from Frank's Hill is surmounted by one dozen conical mounds, each one standing 5 feet tall in an almost perfect linear formation within an equal distance from one another. Their astronomical significance is revealed in their number. Twelve is universally the embodiment of cosmic order. We know it in Western civilization as the 12 houses of the Zodiac, the 12 hours of the day, the 12 months of the solar year, the 12 Olympian gods, the 12 Norse gods (the Easier), the Etruscan League of 12 sacred cities, the 12 apostles of Jesus Christ, the human body's 12 pairs of ribs and thoracic vertebrae in the human spine, and so forth.

The first Roman code of law was written on 12 tablets. In the closing chapters of the book of Revelation, the celestial city of divine perfection has 12 gates, each guarded by 12 angels and inscribed with the names of the 12 tribes of Israel. Twelve foundation stones bearing the names of the 12 apostles and encrusted with 12 jewels support the walls. They surround the tree of life with its 12 kinds of fruit. The city itself is a cube 12,000 *stadia* (1,400 miles) high, broad, and long.

When traveling through the wilderness toward the Promised Land with the Ark of the Covenant, the Israelites formed their camp to represent the celestial city. In Exodus (chapter 28), the "breast-plate of judgment" worn by the Old Testament high priest was set with 12 stones: carnelian, topaz, carbuncle, emerald, sapphire, diamond, jacinth, agate, amethyst, beryl, onyx, and jasper.

In Plato's dialogue, the *Timaeus*, 12 is the number of the structure of the universe. That it may have had at least a similar meaning to the ancient Wisconsinites who carefully placed their uniformly dozen, equally spaced conical mounds outside Muscoda is implicit in the astronomical alignments incorporated into them, particularly their various orientations to several lunar cycles, such as the rising of the Moon at its most northerly point, where it appears biggest at the horizon. Modern investigators have discovered that these prehistoric cones were built to function in conjunction with the nearby Shadewald Group.

"Sky-watchers have long gathered at this hill where the effigy mounds align with celestial events," according to archaeo-astronomer John Heasley of Cultural Landscape Legacies, Inc.[1] To be sure, the ancients would not have sculpted their finest earthworks here unless the ground was of special importance to them. Before Merlin Redcloud, a leading authority on the Ho Chunk, passed away in 2007, he told Wayne May that the Muscoda region and particularly the area including the effigies with their adjacent conical mounds long ago comprised a kind of "capital" or major urban center for large numbers of his people in the deep past.

If so, then the presence of the state's foremost earthworks is an enduring monument to that time. Indeed, Frank Shadewald regularly led fellow enthusiasts to the mound site, where they observed the structures align with sunrise on the summer and winter solstices. After a long lifetime of generous service to the preservation of Wisconsin's foremost effigy mound site, he died of a heart attack at eighty years of age on November 9, 2013. But the hill bearing his name will continue to stand as a monument to Frank Shadewald's living contribution to American prehistory.

19

Ancient Americans to Easter Island

By Professor Julia Patterson

In fall 2014, results were released of the first, comprehensive genetic testing of Easter Island's native population. The remote, 63.2-square-mile island is most famous for its colossal statues, called *moai*. Though most archaeologists have long held that civilization at Easter Island, originally referred to as Rapanui—the same name by which their 21st-century inhabitants are known—was an entirely Polynesian affair, Norwegian ethnographer Dr. Thor Heyerdahl (1914–2002) found so many valid comparisons with Andean kingdoms, he concluded that culture-bearers sailed the nearly 2,500 miles of open ocean from South America to establish an advanced society in the South Central Pacific.

Even after the success in 1947 of his *Kon-Tiki* Expedition, which showed that prehistoric Peruvian mariners possessed the wherewithal to make round-trip voyages to Easter Island, his achievement was dismissed as "a pointless stunt" by mainstream scholars, who went back to teaching the next three generations of their students that only Polynesians paddling from the west settled in Easter Island.

On October 26th, 2014, however, *Current Biology* magazine announced that researchers

> generated genome-wide data for twenty-seven Rapanui. We found a mostly Polynesian ancestry among Rapanui, and detected genome-wide patterns consistent with Native American and European admixture. By considering the distribution of local ancestry tracts of eight unrelated Rapanui, we found statistical support for Native American admixture dating to AD 1280–1495, and European admixture dating to AD 1850–1895.
>
> Rapanui bear Polynesian (76%), Native American (8%), and European (16%) ancestry. The Native American admixture event was dated from nineteen to twenty-three generations ago. Our genome-wide data can be explained by pre-European trans-Pacific contact(s) . . . [These findings indicate] an ancient ocean migration route between Polynesia and the Americas.[1]

Science writer Elizabeth Armstrong Moore went on to point out that a separate study, also published in *Current Biology*, "details the genetic makeup of two ancient human skulls from Brazil's indigenous Botocudo tribe. The skulls were genetically Polynesian without any Native American mixing, further suggesting that islanders traveled to the Americas."[2]

The genetic time parameters defined by these investigations coincide with Peru's Late Intermediate Period, which was dominated by the white-skinned Chachapoyas from their stone cities high in the Andes Mountains, and on the coast by the megalopolis of Chan Chan, the mud-brick capital of a pre-Inca Chimu. Either or both of these advanced peoples left their surviving genetic mark on the modern inhabitants of Easter Island. Heyerdahl's professional skeptics likewise insisted that Rapanui influence never ventured beyond their obscure island, because they failed to ever make a single boat.

But the October 9, 2014, edition of the *News World Daily Report* told how a "recent landslide on Henderson Island has unearthed the first ever *moai* statue to be found outside of Easter Island."[3]

Moai distribution is no longer confined to Easter Island.

Henderson is an uninhabited, raised coral atoll, 6 miles long and 3.2 miles wide, with an area of 14.4 square miles, lying more than 1,300 miles west of Easter Island. Henderson is part of the Pitcairn Islands, a group of four volcanic islands in the southern Pacific Ocean that form the last British Overseas Territory in the Pacific. Henderson's *moai* was accidentally discovered by University of Chile biologists at the island during their study of its fauna and flora. They notified department of archeology professor Juan DeSilva, who verified the authenticity of their find as the first *moai* recovered outside Easter Island, physical proof that the prehistoric Rapanui did indeed sail far from home.

"Perhaps there are more of these *moai* statues on other islands," DeSilva wondered, "and possibly underwater. Has a great catastrophe submerged these islands at one time in history and covered them with heaps of mud and stones?"[4]

In any case, the "great catastrophe" of benighted archaeological dogma that has "submerged" the truth for too long is sunk.

20

The Great Stone Faces of Peru

By Frank Joseph

Fifty miles northeast from the modern city of Lima stands a desolate plateau in remote central Peru. One mile across and less than 2 miles long, its flat top is populated by human and animal forms frozen in stone on a colossal scale, ranging from 10 to 30 feet high. They represent full-faced human heads, some of them wearing bizarre turbans or caps, and animals, such as dogs—all of them randomly scattered in no apparent order or deliberate arrangement. And each one shows varying degrees of severe erosion, indicating their deep antiquity. But these same weathering forces on the rocky outcroppings may have been responsible for their appearance. Were they actually made by men long ago, or fortuitously formed by Nature? Are they statues or *simulacra*?

These are some of the questions film-maker Bill Cote poses in his latest DVD, *The Mysterious Stone Monuments of Markuwasi, Peru*. In Quechua, an Inca language still spoken throughout the Andes, *Markuwasi* means "Road in the Sky," an apparent reference to the plateau's 12,500-foot elevation. It was here that Cote brought his cameras to document the

An ancient Egyptian-like profile at Markuwasi.

strange structures, and, in so doing, created a fully professional production, as original as it is intriguing.

For example, his employment of time-lapse photography to capture the lengthening or fore-shortening of shadows probably brings the figures to life more effectively than even a personal visit might provide. He also outlines the features to deftly highlight their alleged identities, without distorting them—an important technique, because some of the supposed "heads" or "animals" are otherwise difficult to discern. As such, Cote offers a well-balanced presentation, allowing viewers to make up their own minds about this undeniably evocative location, regardless of its real origins.

That Markuwasi alone of all other plateaus throughout the entire region possesses this remarkable collection of structures underscores their artificial creation to some investigators. The figurers first came to the attention of the outside world as recently as 1952, when Peruvian archaeologist Daniel Ruzo (1900–1993) began his eight-year-long research of the "Road in the Sky" after seeing an earlier, black-and-white photograph of the so-called "Head of Humanity." It is the site's largest effigy, the supposed depiction of a Caucasian man or woman facing opposite from a Semitic profile, with the addition of a smaller skull, perhaps negroid.

These themes—so utterly removed from pre-Columbian Peru—add immeasurably to the site's controversy. But they are by no means unique. Cote shows us what appears to be a *moai*, as the great monoliths of far-off Rapa-nui are known to Pacific Ocean Easter Islanders. Another "statue" resembles Taurt, ancient Egyptian goddess of childbirth, signified by a standing hippopotamus. In Nile Valley temple art, "the Great Lady" was occasionally portrayed with Sobek, the death-god, at her back, just as the two appear at Markuwasi. Cote's computer graphics go on to match up one half of a Dynastic Egyptian king's head with the other half of a similarly pharaonic face on the Peruvian outcropping.

Hardly less anomalous than these cultural comparisons are the seeming depictions at the "Road in the Sky" of an elephant (which died out in South America no sooner than 10,000 years ago), a horse (an animal supposedly introduced into South America by 16th-century Spanish Conquistadors), plus an African lion and rhinoceros. Yet more out of place and disturbing is the representation at Markuwasi of *amphichelydia,* a species of giant turtle extinct for the last one hundred million years. If just a few such figures adorned the plateau, we might be inclined to dismiss their lookalike shapes as the haphazard handiwork of wind and rain at work with rock and time.

But to find so many—allegedly more than 200 of them—in one place, and one place only, should at least give us pause for consideration. That was the impetus for inviting Boston University geologist Robert Schoch to Markuwasi. His expert opinion was enlisted to determine once and for all if the Peruvian structures were man-made or entirely the results of erosion. Sadly, he deferred from providing a decision one way or another, leaving viewers no less uncertain than before his arrival. Schoch avows on camera that any question of the structures' cultural or natural origins seemed to him immaterial, an unusual determination for a professional geologist that must have disappointed his hosts, who went to so much trouble and expense for his personal participation.

More enlightening was the on-site research of Peruvian archaeologist Dr. Marino Sanchez, director of archaeology at the better-known Inca stronghold of Machu Picchu, who points out that the fantastic

The Old Man of Markuwasi.

shapes are not alone on the plateau. Nearby are ancient stone ruins, including irrigation canals and several *chullpas*. These are pre-Inca mortuary towers built about 800 CE and similarly found at the shores of Bolivia's Lake Titicaca. While their period does not necessarily coincide with possible creation of the Markuwasi figures, it does show they were inhabited at least 12 centuries ago.

The very existence of these ruins does suggest, however, that either some pre-Inca people did in fact sculpt the human and animal forms, or that visitors were drawn during ancient times to the plateau-top for the same cause that attracts modern researchers—namely, the evocative shapes created by the processes of erosion. Even today, native Peruvians revere *huaca*, undeniably natural configurations of trees or rocks that differ in appearance and stand out from the rest of the local environment. If the presence of chullpas further implies that the site was a necropolis, then the colossal heads may represent memorials to the honored dead, as inferred by its very name: the "Road in the Sky" (i.e., the "road" to heaven).

In any case, no one has been able to prove that the Markuwasi effigies were sculpted hundreds or thousands of years ago by prehistoric Peruvians conversant with not only Dynastic Egyptian and Easter Island cultures, but African and even long-extinct animals, or were entirely the product of overactive human imagination hard-wired to discern recognizable patterns in natural surroundings. In either case, Bill Cote's documentary takes us as far as we can go in the early 21st century toward understanding this monumental enigma. His production team, B.C. Video, in New York, won an Emmy Award 20 years ago for *The Mystery of the Sphinx*, which aired on NBC-Television, where it was seen by more than 40 million viewers. His latest effort is no less deserving of recognition.

21

Lake Michigan Stonehenge

By M.T. Bussey

Our story begins in 1985 with the discovery of Beaver Island's Stone Circle. The Beaver Island Archipelago is located in northern Lake Michigan, 280 miles almost due north of Chicago. The tract of land containing the Stone Circle is on the west side of the island below a local feature known as Angeline's Bluff. When the site was found, the area was considered isolated, with the structure sitting in an open, circular field surrounded by forest.

An old, two-track road ran through the field, used only by hunters and explorers in pickup trucks that rumbled down the trail to the end and the beautiful, pristine Lake Michigan shoreline. There were a few summer cottages along this beach, but, for the most part, it was an exquisite example of the forested dune-land that Northern Michigan offers. After the press announced that a possible "American Stonehenge" had been found, people began to search it out.

Archaeologists, historians, geologists, and world travelers began to theorize dates of construction and the importance of the Circle's location in the Northern Great Lakes. Controversy was ongoing for many years, while Native Americans from Michigan and Wisconsin began to recall venerable tribal tales of a sacred gathering place on the west side of Beaver Island, where some old "stone calendar" counted time in a medicine wheel's circle of life.

Remarkably, similar oral traditions were repeated around the world at similarly intriguing sites with their potential for rewriting history or prehistory. It's said in the academic world that sometimes more than 50 years must pass before textbooks change after the general acceptance of new evidence. So far, the Beaver Island Stone Circle has been waiting for 30 years.

The formation is elliptical in shape and therefore similar to the better-known medicine wheels of Plains Indians. These ancient astronomical observatories can be found in the northern U.S. border states and in southern Canada, located on or near the 45th Parallel, a line of latitude halfway to the Equator and halfway to the North Pole, suggesting that their builders had at least some global understanding, even 3,000 years ago. The Beaver Island Medicine Wheel is by far the largest, measuring in diameter 397 feet from north to south, its cardinal direction stones sitting at three degrees off True North. The deliberate placement of boulders indicates that this discrepancy dates the Stone Circle to be at least one thousand Years Before Present, perhaps older.

In archaeological test pit digs near the site, 3 feet of well-drained Deer Park Forested Dune Land soil sits atop white beach sand. Artifacts and stone carvings found at this beach level support the notion that occupation of the site may have preceded the high water levels of the ancient Lake Nipissing. The Nipissing Transgression was an event that made the waters of the Great Lakes slowly rise to a height of 615 to 635 feet above sea level, covering much of the current shorelines of Northern Michigan.

Nipissing levels fluctuated in a cyclic manner between six and 32 years in duration.[1] Rising water formed beach ridges from the changing lake levels. The dates of the Nipissing Transgression vary, but it is generally believed that it slowly began circa 2800 BCE and was at its height from 500 to 1000 CE. Our present understanding is that it was a slow rise, then giving the possibility that there could have been occupation of the Beaver Island site well into 1000 BCE.

Also, two levels of stones set out within the Stone Circle suggest repetitive construction of the structure through many years of occupation. In other words, with lake levels rising and falling through several thousand years after the last Ice Age (circa 10,000 BCE to 8000 BCE), someone worked to reassemble the Stone Circle, which would have been originally covered by beach sediment ridges.

Dr. Jack Eddy's research at the Bighorn Mountain Medicine Wheel, located in northern Wyoming, was a breakthrough for its Beaver Island counterpart, because of similar star alignments. Dr. Eddy observed that heliacal risings of designated stars were aligned with the placement of the cairns of the Medicine Wheel. Heliacal risings occur when a star flashes just above the horizon as it enters our atmosphere for the first time that year.

The Beaver Island Medicine Wheel features these alignments, showing a solar and lunar calendar. By looking through a western set of stones on a medicine wheel, the observer can line up the northeastern boulder with the Pleiades and watch a heliacal rising of the star Aldebaran on the Summer Solstice. Twenty-eight days later, the alignment moving to an eastern boulder then shows another heliacal rising of the star Rigel. A third star flashes a heliacal rising with the star Sirius, 28 days later. The rising and setting of the Sun on the Summer Solstice is also indicated. The Beaver Island Medicine Wheel aligns the correct boulder placements for the Summer Solstice, and these lunar flashes do occur beginning on June 21. In addition, the orientation of these three heliacal risings create 90-degree-angle triangles on both medicine wheels.

Through many years of research, the circle site itself raised many questions regarding occupation, lake levels, location, and possible connection with the ancient copper mines of the Upper Peninsula, where some 125,000 tons of the world's highest-grade copper were extracted in prehistory. The lake levels are still being researched, and definitive dates differ from the Canadian and American sides of the border.

However, if we look at the work of Dr. John Hughes, who discovered the remnants of the Au Train-Whitefish Channel that ran through the Upper Peninsula of Michigan just after the last Ice Age, we see a logical connection with the ancient copper trade. The Beaver Island archipelago was above water at that time as one solid, land-mass peninsula connected from Waugoshance Point on the Michigan mainland. The

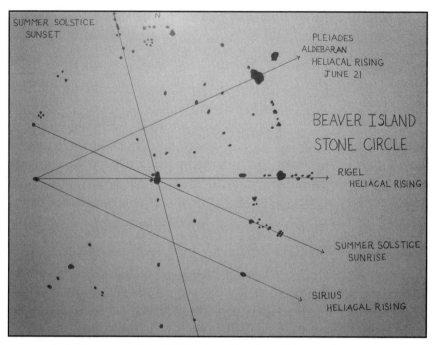

Astronomical alignments at Lake Michigan's prehistoric medicine wheel.

copper mines of the Upper Peninsula were worked circa 5,000 to 3,500 years ago, mostly between 3000 BCE and 1200 BCE.

If the site on Beaver Island was a part of that trade, as a stopover or a mining site, on the north-south water route, the stone circle complex may also be that old. In the involved and intriguing history of Beaver Island, no farming was ever recorded at the circle site below Angeline's Bluff. The medicine wheel had an original walking path that ran right through the center of the circle and past the historic Peshawbestown Native American village. The trail became a two-track road when lumbering on the island brought workers and equipment to the west side. From old photographs and recent mapping of depressions made by large stones now missing from the site, it has become clear that the elliptical circle was a megalithic structure that contained more than 150 stones and indicates a series of six concentric circles. At present, all that remains on the surface are the cardinal direction stones, large boulders just under the tree-line, which show lunar and solar alignments and the center stone.

Archaeological test pits were chosen outside the circle at the sites of carved rocks pointing through the forest floor or along alignment lines. All of the artifacts were sitting 3 feet below the surface, resting on beach sand. The first artifact discovered was a sculptured granite stone face, a circular disc, 38 inches in diameter and only 2 3/4 inches thick at the center. There is no base on this sculpture; therefore, it may have been designed to be carried, to lay flat with the face up, or to be supported by another prop.

In 2011, another carved stone head was found, only 11 feet from the previous discovery, and was amazingly similar. This second face was sculpted on a calcite boulder weighing more than 1,300 pounds. It has a rounded head and is made to sit on a flat, leveled base. Both carved faces reflect the unusual sculptural technique of pulling the facial features from the surface, while allowing the rest of the facial structure to be flat. The eyes, noses, mouths, and chins seem to be carved by the same hand in style and execution. However, the most interesting thing about these two faces is seen in the double 90-degree triangles (Pythagorean triangles) carved into the bridge of both noses, together with the anthropomorphic figure that sits under each right facing eye.

In an attempt to identify these two intentional carvings, I first focused on the elongated style of the figures. My tribal art history roots took me to Bronze Age Crete and the famous Blue Monkeys fresco found in a palace on the Minoan island of Santorini, known as Thera in the 18th century BCE. Among the Beaver Island figures, I found the same elongated, stylized forms: the long legs; arched back; the foot placed in mid-air, not standing flat on the ground; the bent arms reaching forward, and the animal head. Pythagoras, a citizen and teacher of Crete, taught the famous theorem about 555 BCE.

Though this 90-degree angle triangle is named after him, he did not invent it. The triangle was found in Babylonia on clay tablets a thousand years before his time, later surfacing in the Chinese astronomical and mathematical treatise *Chou Pei Suan*, "The Arithmetical Classic of the Gnomen [that part of a parallelogram left when a similar parallelogram has been taken from its corner] and the Circular Paths of Heaven," circa 800 BCE.[2] Some archaeo-astronomers contend that the Maya used variations of the theorem in their Long Count Calendar. All this suggests that Pythagoras became the teacher of ancient and seemingly global information that had been lost for many years. In any case, he must be credited for understanding the importance of the theorem with its connection to astronomy and navigation. But why are these 90-degree angle triangles important?

Readers may recall how their first-year high school algebra class usually started with the equation $a^2 + b^2 = c^2$. Using this equation, if the length of two sides of a 90-degree triangle is known, the length of the third can be determined. Robert and Ellen Kaplan put it very clearly in their book, *Hidden Harmonies: The Lives and Times of the Pythagorean Theorem*, when they stated, "The Pythagorean triangle is the foundation of all navigation in our world and beyond it."[3] One of the primary uses of the theorem used in navigation could have been known by ancient miners to navigate the globe looking for metal during the Bronze Age.

The stone circles, or *cromlechs*, and the rectangles of Carnac and Crucuno, located in northwestern France, circa 4500 BCE to 3300 BCE, all feature the Pythagorean Theorem. The work of Scottish engineer Alexander Thom (1894 to 1985) at these sites was a brilliant study of reasoning behind the Pythagorean triangle, as pertained at these structures. More than three thousand standing stones were prehistorically arranged at Carnac in long lines consisting of alignments, dolmens (tombs with a large flat stone laid on upright ones), tumuli (burial mounds), and single menhirs (tall, upright stones).

"Carnac," Thom pointed out, "is located at a latitude on the Earth at which the solstice sun, both summer and winter, form a perfect Pythagorean triangle relative to the parallel of the latitude; that is, to the east-west, equinoctial axis of the site."[4]

After researching the locations of these stone monuments, as well as the medicine wheels of North America, I've come to the understanding that this particular latitude, mentioned by Thom, is at or near the 45th Parallel. The Beaver Island Medicine Wheel is located directly *on* the 45th Parallel. The medicine wheels in North America, with their astronomical alignments and Pythagorean triangles, were also positioned on or close to the 45th Parallel. In consideration of the Pythagorean triangles found at stone structures in Europe, I believe it is very likely that we have this same reference in the medicine wheels of North America, especially when these solar and lunar calendars were used for the same purpose on both continents and are described by the oral histories of Native American tribal groups.

The carved stone faces on Beaver Island may contain Minoan stylized art in their full-figure, elongated forms, and also the Pythagorean triangles, which link them to an Old World Bronze Age culture. At Beaver Island, we have a concentric stone circle featuring the Pythagorean Theorem, which also appears in the stone faces found at the site. While the Minoans did not sculpt large faces in stone, Bronze Age Kelts of the Iberian Peninsula did carve large stone heads as part of their cult of the head. Their cut-stone face markers were placed at entrances to ports and towns, where some are still found in Spain and Portugal.[5] These heads imply a possible cultural connection with Iberian Kelts and Minoan Cretans, especially in light of the stone carvings of bulls, bull horns, triangles—motifs emblematic of both peoples—and a combination of Ogham and Minoan script found at the Beaver Island site.

In tribal art history terms, these carvings would be categorized as late tribal/early national. They show tribal-associated, symmetrical balance in a unique, national style. In the progression of all cultures, they begin with clan, move to band, then many bands together forming a tribe, and, if the tribe desires, they gather other tribes to become a nation. Beaver Island's carved faces, along with figures and triangles, are not produced by an early, tribal society. They are instead the transitional art form of a culture or cultures moving from tribe to nation. I would suggest that they were made by late tribal or early national cultures that had a defined religious belief system but an undefined political system.

Comparing dates and latitudes of several megalithic and medicine wheel sites in Western Europe and North America demonstrates their positional relationships:

Carnac, 4500 to 3300 BCE, latitude 47 degrees.

Majorville Medicine Wheel, 2500 BCE, latitude 50 degrees.

Bighorn Mountain Medicine Wheel, 1000 CE, latitude 44 degrees, three degrees off True North.

Beaver Island Medicine Wheel, 1000 CE, latitude 45 degrees, three degrees off True North.

Bronze Age use of the Pythagorean triangle for navigation of the globe was aided by keynotes from the stars. In the late 1800s, several British scholars undertook a study to decode the nursery rhymes of Mother Goose. They found that the earliest discoverable source for most of them lay in ancient

Greece. When, for example, the famous nonsense phrase, "Hey, Diddle Diddle," combines with particular star alignments, the outcome creates a double Pythagorean triangle in the summer night sky running east-west. The shape of this triangle is consistent with triangles found on Beaver Island's stone heads:

> *Hey diddle, diddle!*
> *The cat and the fiddle,*
> *The cow jumped over the moon.*
> *The little dog laughed*
> *To see such sport,*
> *And the dish ran away with the spoon.*

In terms of astronomy, each constellation referred to here features one bright, large star. According to Mary Stewart Adams, director of the Headland's International Dark Sky Park, the cat is Leo and the fiddle, Lyra. The cow is Taurus, which, at their appearance, is over the low-hanging moon. The little dog is Canis Minor. The dish is the Milky Way, and the spoon is the Little Dipper. Stars forming the large triangle within these constellations are:

Constellation	Star
Lyra	Vega
Ursa Minor	Polaris
Taurus	Aldebaran
Leo	Regulus

The stars which form the small triangle within the larger triangle are:

Constellation	Star
Ursa Minor	Polaris
Canis Minor	Antecanis

Lining up the largest star of each constellation produces a Pythagorean triangle and another small triangle within it. The stars Vega, Polaris, and Aldebaran can be connected by an east-west line with the other stars drawn into the triangles. Appearing in the summer night sky of the Northern Hemisphere, these star triangles are the same shapes seen on the carved noses of Beaver Island's two stone faces.

They and the medicine wheel are actually part of a large complex of sites extending west from Angeline's Bluff to the Lake Michigan shoreline. They include three small stone circles set out around the largest circle. The smaller circles are approximately 126 feet in diameter, and all share the same structural alignments.

There is also a wall of stone going north to south for three hundred eighty-one feet (defined by Brian and Matt Bussey, 2012) on the west side of the large circle. It is interrupted by the Redding Trail Road, which pushes through the wall. The further length of the wall is undetermined, because it runs into beach sediment ridges at either end. This wall is set on a slight ridge, only 2 feet beneath surface soil, and 1 to 3 feet above surface. The wall is another mystery, because no farming occurred at the site in historic times.

West of the wall is Lake Michigan's shoreline, which, since 2013, has been at its lowest in the past 75 to 100 years. As such, two spits of land have emerged with unusual boulders within them. Google Earth maps show a triangle shape in this area, as well as the images suggesting a bird and a bear. These possible geoglyphs need further research, if only because they are so large and, therefore, difficult to precisely map. The geometric shape of a perfect triangle is not, however, the work of natural wave action. Neither has any evidence of manmade docks or historic construction been found at the site.

What could be a pre-modern harbor location contains groupings of unusual boulders partially covered with man-made carvings and deliberately set in alignments similar to those discovered at the large circle of stone. Most striking is a set of large stones emblazoned with double triangle carvings. The larger of the two rests in reddish water, perhaps resulting due to high contents of iron within the milky quartz calcite. Officially recognized as "State of Michigan Archeology Site #20CX65," the Beaver Island Stone Circle is also a North American Medicine Wheel and part of a larger complex of sites, not one single structure. North America's medicine wheels compare in astronomical structure and alignment with European stone circles. The Pythagorean Theorem is found on both continents within ancient stone structures.

The Majorville Medicine Wheel, located in southern Alberta, Canada, has been carbon-dated at 2500 BCE, thanks to bone recovered

Prehistoric rock art on the Michigan mainland across Lake Michigan from Beaver Island depicts a Bronze Age ship of the type that carried ancient Old World copper miners to the Upper Peninsula.

from beneath the central cairn. After the end of the last Ice Age, some 11,700 years ago, Beaver Island and its entire archipelago was high above water and rested on a peninsula of land that extended from Waugoshance Point—today, a 2 1/2-mile-long cape or peninsula jutting into Lake Michigan from the northwest coast of Michigan's Lower Peninsula—just west of Mackinaw City. At that time, rivers cut through from Lake Huron to Lake Michigan (through the Mackinaw Straits) and from Lake Superior to Lake Michigan (Au Train-Whitefish Channel). Trading boats could have used these rivers in passage, east-west and north-south; both rivers would have brought them past Beaver Island.

Native American oral histories recount its ancient occupation and circle of stones, which, acting as a calendar for lunar and solar alignments, was revered as a sacred nexus between humans and heaven. Archaeologists, archaeo-astronomers, surveyors, and geologists continue to tramp through the region, looking for more clues that may eventually reveal the ultimate secrets of this interesting site.

22

Georgia's Ancient City of Shells

By Gary C. Daniels

Six hours, via driving, southeast of Atlanta, 7 miles off the Georgia coast, archaeologists have unearthed the remains of an ancient, walled city predating the construction of Egypt's pyramids on Sapelo Island. Known as the Sapelo Shell Ring Complex, it was an urban site constructed about 2017 BCE in three districts, or neighborhoods, each surrounded by circular walls 20 feet in height and constructed from hundreds of tons of seashells. Some of the earliest pottery ever found in North America was retrieved from the ruined city, which stood in contradiction to local, contemporaneous Native Americans unfamiliar with agriculture, generally regarded by scholars as a fundamental prerequisite for civilization.

That these simple tribal inhabitants somehow made the leap from hunting and gathering to civilization in a single bound, producing not only a walled city but also the new technology of pottery without benefit of agriculture, seems improbable. More likely, a far more advanced people already in the possession of a high culture arrived on the Georgia coast to organize their massive shell rings. But their identity and motivation for settling in Sapelo are unknown. Perhaps their enigma may be understood within the context of the period during which they flourished. At that time, Akkadian Sumer collapsed in the Middle East, and Dead Sea water levels reached their lowest point. In China, the Hongsan culture collapsed. Sediments from Greenland and Iceland show a cold peak about 2200 BCE.

The population of Finland decreased by a third between 2400 and 2000 BCE. In Turkey's Anatolia region, including the site of ancient Troy, more than 350 archaeological sites show evidence of having been burnt and deserted by the close of the 22nd-century BCE. Entire regions suddenly reverted to a nomadic way of life after thousands of years of settled, agricultural life. In fact, most locations throughout the ancient Old World that collapsed before 2100 BCE evidenced unambiguous signs of natural calamities and/or rapid abandonment. What happened then that could have caused such widespread devastation? Answers might come from the sky.

Scientists like Oxford University astrophysicist Victor Clube and William Napier, an astronomer at the Royal Observatory in Edinburgh, demonstrate how the Earth passed through a dense concentration of cosmic debris during the late 22nd century BCE, resulting in numerous air blasts equivalent to the explosion of atomic bombs that incinerated Bronze Age civilizations and instigated human mass-migrations throughout the world.[1] A more recent example occurred in 1908, when cosmic debris detonated several miles above Tunguska, flattening eighty million trees more than 2,000 square miles of Siberia.

A similar event magnified many fold into a meteoric bombardment struck the Earth before 2100 BCE. When Hernando de Soto first explored Georgia in 1540, he found it occupied by two indigenous peoples. The Timucua Indians had migrated there from South America, as indicated by their linguistic affinities with native Venezuelans. Did Timucua ancestors flee their homeland after it was devastated by a meteor swarm? Argentina's Rio Cuarto impact craters date to the period in question.

The Yuchi Indians believe their forefathers arrived in Georgia after "the old moon broke" and devastated their island homeland in the Bahamas. The abrupt appearance of a shell-ring city at Georgia's Sapelo Island shortly after these catastrophic events tends to confirm Yuchi oral tradition.

23

Mexico's Keltic Cross

By Dr. Cisco Drake

Keltic art was famous for its curvilinear designs. Human representation was largely confined to formalized heads and faces in otherwise-abstract designs. Beginning about 500 BCE, Keltic designers developed the La Tene style of art. They emphasized elaborate patterns of interwoven curves and spirals, including highly stylized plants and often distended animals that had little resemblance to anything in nature. The La Tene style lasted into the Middle Ages, eventually becoming a major element in medieval art. Keltic artists created decorative manuscripts, elaborate metal work, and sculptured stonework.

Mexico, of course, was settled by Spanish Catholics, whose Baroque styles absolutely dominated the construction of all churches and even secular buildings throughout the land from the 16th century onward. So intimate was the association between Baroque architecture and Catholic theology that, in Mexico at least, one was regarded as the expression of the other. The result was a kind of architectural propaganda for Roman Catholicism, in which any other style of building would be regarded as some kind of heresy.

Even so, there is in Mexico an example of Christian art that is decidedly un-Baroque and unquestionably Keltic. The piece in question is a 7-foot high cross before the Church of San Jacinto, located in Mexico City's San Angel neighborhood. Although its origins are completely unknown, the artwork bears no resemblance to anything Baroque. It is Keltic, without doubt. The full-face sculpture of human heads and animals is characteristic of the La Tene style. Intriguingly, some of the images appearing on the trunk of the cross are "pagan." These include the cock, famous as a fertility symbol in Ancient Greece, together with the crossed torch and sheaf of wheat emblem of the Eleusian Mystery Cult, likewise Greek.

The Cross of San Jacinto.

Other symbols are traditionally Christian: the ladder (Jacob's ladder), chalice with host, Christ's head crowned with thorns, the INRI, and "sacred heart." The head at the base is probably meant to represent Saint Jacinto, beside the "Lamb of God." The cross is not a single work of art, however. The variety of its elements suggests additional details were added over time. Compare the dark cross-bar with the light-colored "trunk"; the darker lamb's head at the base with the disparate INRI at the top. The original object appears to have been a freestanding column onto which the cross-bar was later added to perhaps de-paganize the monument by transforming it into a crucifix. In fact, the Kelts worshiped a pillar-cult as part of their forest religion, the pillar signifying the holy bough.

Is the Cross of San Jacinto a Keltic column superimposed with Christian imagery? The rather strange, atypical Latin inscription on the front of the base reads *Sta Crux dum volvitur Orbis* ("The world revolves around the Cross"). It is an apparent reference to Christians in Mexico and elsewhere. Does it somehow reflect the arrival of partially Christianized Kelts in pre-Catholic Mexico?

Dr. Gunnar Thompson convincingly demonstrates the powerful, widespread impact made on pre-Columbian North America above the Rio Grande by Keltic visitors.[1] Perhaps they also set up one of their sacred columns in what is now Mexico City. Where official history leaves off, what have been left are the carved stones which continue to speak on.

SECTION VI

THE FIRST AMERICANS

———◆◆◆———

The latest DNA testing of Native Americans demonstrates their significant genetic links to Western Europeans, connections preceding modern cross-breeding by 10,000 years. Nor were these early contacts localized to North American areas, as Patrick Chouinard explains in his description of fair-skinned peoples throughout pre-Columbian South America. A long-time contributor of original articles to *Ancient American* magazine, he is the author of *Forgotten Worlds* (2012) and *Lost Race of the Giants* (2013), both released by Bear and Company.

Just how far back in time human origins go on our continent has been firmly established by South Carolina's "Topper" site, dated to 50,000 years ago. Since then, waves of European immigration swept across the Atlantic Ocean, bringing to our shores New Stone Age culture-bearers from Britain, identified as the Beaker People by Mark R. Eddy. With training as an English teacher in the Northern Panhandle of West Virginia, he was able to personally compare Native American earthworks with their Beaker counterparts during his stay in Britain.

24

East Meets West in Ice Age America

By Dr. Cyclone Covey

For more than 20 years, *Ancient American* reporters have been pointing out that our continent was populated by Europeans millennia before Christopher Columbus dropped anchor off San Salvador. Our evidence to the contrary was shunned by mainstream scholars, because it diametrically opposed their textbook version of the past. They insist that the first humans in America could have only been Siberians migrating over a vast land-bridge into Alaska, less than 14,000 years ago, and no one else visited our shores until 1492.

Now comes word that "Native Americans are one-third European," according to geneticist Connie Mulligan of the University of Florida in Gainesville.[1] The other two-thirds of today's tribal Indians are Asian. "The west Eurasian [genetic] signatures that we very often find in today's Native Americans don't all come from post-colonial admixture," said Danish DNA expert Eske Willerslev, at the University of Copenhagen.[2]

"Some of them are ancient." He was supported by *Science Magazine* writer Michael Balter, who found that "traces of European ancestry previously detected in modern Native Americans do not come solely from mixing with European colonists, as most scientists had assumed, but have much deeper roots."[3]

These revolutionary conclusions have been forced by recent discovery of the oldest complete genome of a modern human sequenced so far. A genome is the entirety of an organism's hereditary information as encoded in its DNA. The paradigm-shattering genome was taken from the right upper arm bone of a 4-year-old Siberian boy buried beside the Belaya River near the Siberian village of Mal'ta. His bone was radiocarbon dated to 24,000 years ago.

Balter continued, "A portion of the boy's genome is shared only by today's Native Americans and no other groups, showing a close relationship. Yet, the child's Y chromosome belongs to a genetic group called Y haplogroup R and its mitochondrial DNA to a haplogroup U. Today, those haplogroups are found almost exclusively in people living in Europe and regions of Asia west of the Altai Mountains, which are near the borders of Russia, China, and Mongolia."[4]

Although Mal'ta Boy's DNA is closely tied to those of today's Native Americans and showed no connection to modern East Asians or Siberians, he was a Caucasian from Europe or Western Asia. DNA studies of living Indian tribal peoples are predominantly of East Asian origins. Balter observes, "Nearly all Native Americans from North and South America were equally related to the Mal'ta child, indicating that he represented very deep Native American roots."[5]

The boy's grave contained flint tools, pendants, and beaded necklace sprinkled with red ochre, a funeral rite practiced during the last glacial epoch by Western Europeans. Although his burial was discovered as long ago as the 1920s by Soviet archaeologists, not until Willerslev and coauthor Kelly Graf of Texas A&M University in College Station tested his remains preserved at Russia's State Hermitage Museum in St. Petersburg did the genetic significance of Mal'ta Boy come to light. Their findings had been almost identically preceded by a report published in *Genetics* during 2014, when it was ignored by conventional scholars.

Despite their reluctance to part with obsolete convictions, the impact of Ice Age Europeans on pre-Columbian American can no longer be denied.

25

The Lost White Race of Peru

By Patrick Chouinard

In the late 1990s, archaeologist Johann Reinhard (explorer-in-residence at the National Geographic Society) discovered a series of mummified remains atop Peru's Andes Mountains. Among them was a young Inca woman who was sacrificed to the ancient gods. Many of Reinhard's subsequent discoveries also included young children. These Inca were apparently given as offerings to the deities as well. Many of his human relics featured blond, reddish hair and baffling facial features, which hinted at alternative Amer-Indian origins.

The reoccurrence of Europoid or proto-Caucasoid traits in the remains of Native Americans continues to disrupt the foundation of conventional wisdom. This has generated distinct rumblings through-out the archaeological community. These finds have also generated a renewed interest in Native American and European origins. During mid-January 2015, an even greater opportunity has arisen that prom-ises to help archaeologists finally put to rest some of these questions.

The Cotahuasi Valley of Peru is dotted with pre-Columbian tombs containing an upward of forty mummies each. This immense discovery was dated to between 800 and 1000 CE, during which the Viking Age had just been launched back in Europe and the Anasazi civilization was nearing a climax. Together, these ancient burials are part of a vast,1,200-year-old ceremonial center, which has been linked to a pre-Inca civilization known as the Wari. Collectively, archaeologists have unearthed close to 117 mummies, but thousands wait to be properly retrieved and cataloged. The mummified remains include not only adults but children, infants, and even fetuses. The fetuses were placed in jars and buried together with the adults. Archaeologists have also discovered that a series of villages were founded surrounding the tombs.

Curled up, with their arms wrapped around the knees with ropes and then encased in strips of clothing, the mummies amounted to a familiar and not unusual find. Only their unique form of preservation and vast numbers remanded it as a top find of this decade. The tombs are set about short hill-tops, which the self-governing villages have then surrounded. Justin Jennings, curator of the Royal Ontario Museum, wrote regarding this find and the positioning with in the hilltops: "The dead, likely numbering thousands, towered over the living."[1]

Jennings noted that unlike our own modern society, in which death brings finality and a resting of purpose, in the Andes death was the beginning of a much more involved process. The mummies signified equality and purpose, as part of a folkish community. Unlike other finds, these persons were not sacrificed or part of any act of violence. Jennings maintains this view: "It's a period of great change and one of the ways which humans around the world deal with that is through violence. What we are suggesting is that [this find] Tenahaha was placed in part to deal with those changes, to find a way outside violence, to deal with periods of radical cultural change."[2]

26

Topper Beats Siberians to America by 36,500 Years

By Wayne N. May

Conventional scholars were surprised in November 2014 by the discovery of a campsite along South Carolina's Savannah River dated 25,000 years earlier than they believed possible. Since the mid-1930s, they have insisted that Mongolians trudged across a hypothetical "land-bridge" from Siberia into Alaska just 13,500 years ago to become the first Americans. Preached as impermeable dogma, it is the academic doctrine of mainstream science in the United States. "That has been repeated so many times in textbooks and lectures," says Dennis Stanford, curator of archaeology at the Smithsonian Institution, "it became part of the common lore. People forgot it was only an unproven hypothesis."[1]

That "unproven hypothesis" was dealt a serious blow to its credibility by the recent discovery of 50,000-year-old stone tools and other man-made material referred collectively to as *Topper*. According to its discoverer, Albert Goodyear, from the University of South Carolina of Archaeology and Anthropology, "Topper is the oldest radio-carbon dated site in North America."[2]

His more conventional colleagues wasted no time in throwing the shadow of doubt over the find. "He has a very old geologic formation," offered Michael Collins of the Texas Archeological Research Lab at the University of Texas at Austin, "but I can't agree with his interpretation of those stones being man-made."[3] Theodore Schurr, anthropology professor at the University of Pennsylvania and a curator at the school's museum, was also unimpressed with Topper. "It poses some real problems trying to explain how you have people in Central Asia almost at the same time as people in the Eastern United States," he said. "You almost have to hope for instantaneous expansion. We're talking about a very rapid movement of people around the globe."[4]

Schurr added that more confirming evidence needs to be brought forth before anyone can take the discovery seriously, although he did admit, "If dating is confirmed, then it really does have a significant impact on our previous understanding of New World colonization."[5]

Goodyear made his announcement only after excavating the Topper site since the 1980s. He would not have found it even then, had he followed established procedure. Mainstream archaeologists did not then probe beneath the Earth's surface for evidence of early man in America any deeper than levels corresponding to twelve thousand years ago. Going unconventionally 4 meters deeper, Goodyear found literally hundreds of tools made from locally obtained chert. The flint-like stone chisels and scrapers were used to skin hides, butcher meat, or carve antlers, wood, and ivory.

He speculates that the area's mild climate and abundant natural resources made it the ideal setting for an active society. Indeed, the large number of stone implements and their variety of purpose recovered from the Topper site suggests a populous community of craftsmen who already attained a hierarchy of skills.

And their presence on a major river in South Carolina, far from the imagined migration of Mongolians across a theoretical land-bridge to Alaska implies arrival by boat. As *Scientist* magazine's Marsha Walton and Michael Coren wrote in their coverage of Goodyear's finds, "These discoveries are leading archaeologists to support alternative theories—such as settlement by sea—for the Americas."[6]

Although Topper may be the oldest known human habitation site in North America above the Rio Grande, it was surely not the first. Forthcoming additional evidence is sure to further push back our understanding of Man's impact on our continent. The South Carolina revelation is all the more intriguing because it is 10,000 years older than evidence for Cro Magnon men in Europe. Just who were the Topper people and where they came from are mysteries no less engaging than their residence in America 50,000 years ago.

27

Clovis Bones of Contention

By Professor Julia Patterson

Mainstream archaeologists claim to have found "a missing link" between the first Americans and today's indigenous tribal peoples. DNA testing of a 1- to 1 1/2-year-old boy who died 12,600 to 13,000 years ago shows he was closely related to modern Indians. His bones were accidentally unearthed during construction near a central Montana rock cliff belonging to the Anzick family, hence the so-called "Anzick skeleton."

It had been deliberately interred with some 125 objects, including fluted spear points diagnostic of a culture referred to as "Clovis," where the first such artifacts were found near the New Mexico town of the same name. Conventional scholars have long insisted that Clovis hunter-gatherers were originally Siberians who wandered across a hypothetical land-bridge spanning the Bering Straits into Alaska and down into the American Southwest. Geneticists at Texas A&M University in College Station used the bones to recover the first complete genome sequence of an ancient North American.

"We found the genome of this boy is closely related to all Native Americans of today than to any other peoples around the world," stated Eske Willerslev from Denmark's University of Copenhagen. "We can also see from the genome study that this Anzick population is the direct ancestor to many Native Americans to date. As such, our study is in agreement with the view that present-day Native Americans are direct descendants of the first peoples in the Americas."[1]

He went on to say that the Anzick lineage "is directly ancestral to so many peoples in the Americas. We don't have genetic information by any means from all tribes, but a very, very broad estimate suggests eighty percent derives from the Anzick group, which is an amazing result—almost like a missing link, if you want."[2] Willerslev and his colleagues were chiefly ecstatic about the genome link because they believe it vindicates their venerable tenet of faith that the earliest inhabitants of our continent were the Asian ancestors of modern Native Americans. There was also more than a measure of triumph over the Solutrean Hypothesis upheld by critics of dominant archaeological dogma, who argue for much earlier connections with ice age Europe. The Anzick skeleton, Willerslev crowed, "has settled the long-standing debate about the origins of the Clovis. We can say the Solutrean theory suggesting Clovis originated from people in Europe doesn't fit our results."[3]

He neglected to mention, however, that the grooved workmanship so characteristic of Clovis spearheads appears nowhere throughout Siberia, the alleged homeland of all ancient Americans, but is found in abundance among the ice age Solutrean culture of Western Europe. As such, that the Anzick bones belonged to a person of Siberian descent proves nothing because not even the most extreme skeptic of mainstream archaeology doubts that some human migrations crossed into Alaska from Asia 15,000 years ago. But to ascertain that an entire people were Siberians, based on a single skeleton, flies in the face of elemental logic, suggesting an arrogant even sloppy rush to judgment.

Willerslev himself admits that perhaps 80 percent of America's native population traces back to Asian roots. His remaining unaccountable 20 percent tallies closely with the research of Dr. Theodore Schnurr at the Southwest Foundation for Biomedical Research, where he confirmed genetic trace elements among western aboriginal groups going back more than 20,000 years to Japan.

Having jumped to a preordained conclusion that present-day Indians are descended from Siberians—supposedly, the first inhabitants of North America—Willerslev, et al., are confounded by additional DNA evidence revealing "a deep genetic divergence that occurred between northern Native American groups and those from Central and South America that happened before the Clovis era. Specifically, although most South Americans and Mexicans are part of the Anzick lineage and therefore Clovis, northern Canadian groups belong to another lineage."[4]

Only the arrival of another, non-Siberian people could have caused such "a deep genetic divergence." These were the Solutreans, Western Europeans, who skirted the packed ice in a North Atlantic passage to America 18,000 years ago. Proof survives in their arrow-heads, which are indistinct from Clovis points conventional scholars still believe could have only been chipped by Siberians or their descendants in New Mexico.

There is also the problem of red ochre that covered the Anzick boy's bones. The mineral substance was employed in funeral rites to such a degree throughout eastern Canada's Marine Archaic Period that its members are known today as the "Red Paint People." Their close association, even identification with a contemporaneous Red Ochre People residing in Northern Europe during the sixth millennium BCE is generally accepted. Much earlier and prior to Clovis times, ice age Solutreans of western France likewise adorned their dead with red ochre.

Tragically, these and so many more contradictions to precedence or "proof" unjustifiably hung on the Anzick skeleton speak less to its real archaeological significance than to the insecure mentality of mainstream scientists using it as a politically correct cudgel for beating down rising opposition to their discredited notions of the past.

28

America's Stone Age Europeans

By Mark R. Eddy

In "Stonehenge and the Earthworks in the Ohio Valley: The Sacred Marriage of Earth and Sky" (*Ancient American*, No. 89), cultural diffusionist researcher, and author Fritz Zimmerman clearly demonstrates close similarities between the U or womb-like structures at Britain's Stonehenge and Ohio's Portsmouth Earthworks. He shows how two sites from vastly distant continents identically capture the summer solstice's rising sun. From this and numerous related parallels, Zimmerman concludes that prehistoric America's Adena Culture was comprised of Britain's Neolithic Beaker Culture.

The former was named by archaeologists after the Adena plantation at Chillicothe, Ohio, where the first earthwork of its kind was excavated in 1900. Native American (especially Ojibwa) oral accounts refer to this pre-Columbian people as the Alleghany (plus variations of the name: Azgens, Allewegli, Yohmkodesh, and so on). Their surviving grave goods are unlike any artifacts from other ancient earthworks; so much so, they defined an entirely distinct culture.

These Adena or Alleghany suddenly appeared on the ancient American scene in 1000 BC, their society exploding full-blown between the Atlantic seaboard and the Mississippi River. For 17 centuries, their material finesse—far superior to indigenous tribalism—ranged from massive earthworks and hill-forts to dentistry, iron works, and intricately engraved tablets. They introduced pottery making and were the first Americans to practice organized agriculture.

The Beaker Culture is likewise a pure archaeological term deriving from a singular form of pottery invented by a particular people who dominated Western Europe, especially Britain, in prehistory. Traditional academics still attribute the similarities Zimmermann observes between the Adena and Beaker cultures as recognizable, though entirely coincidental. But when we learn, for example, that the diameter of southwest England's circular monument at Avebury equals that of Newark's Great Circle in northern Ohio, explaining away such cogent comparisons as the result of mere happenstance seems less convincing. We need to understand that Britain's Beaker Culture was far more extensive in Ohio than mainstream scholars originally contended.

A site representative of these parallels is Britain's South Cadbury Hill-fort, which dominates the Somerset County plain from 500 feet above sea level. A long-standing legend has it that from this hill-top fortress, with its four rings of towering earthen ramparts, was the seat of King Arthur's realm. Today, a placard at the base of the foot path leading to South Cadbury Hill-fort informs visitors that the 18-acre plateau has been occupied since Neolithic times, beginning about 3000 BCE. As such, the general vicinity is unquestionably evocative.

During 1925, Katharine Maltwood, founder of the University of Victoria's Maltwood Gallery in Canada, was commissioned to draw a map outlining the adventures of King Arthur around Glastonbury, legendary site of the Holy Grail, when she discovered gigantic effigies of the zodiac designed in a circle on the fields of Somerset. Thereafter, she devoted the rest of her life to researching, writing, and publicizing south England's "Temple of the Stars." Much smaller but no less insightful artifacts from the area emerged in the form of New Stone Age pits filled with Beaker pottery, arrowheads, hazelnuts, and a human mandible, which could be interpreted as sacrificial offerings.

The physical resemblance of South Cadbury Hill fort to Ohio's Glenford Fort—less than 20 miles south of Newark—is striking. The latter site, reminiscent of the location's British counterpart, rises 200 feet above the plain in modestly sloping sides that ascend to a 27-acre plateau. Archaeologist Rich Moats's "A Summary of Fort Glenford: Adena Hill-Top Enclosure and Burial Mound" explains how artifacts recovered from the site confirm its Adena identity. In describing investigator James Dutcher's research at its wood-framed charnel house, Moats states, "A carbon date of 270 BCE was obtained from the charred remnants of this structure."[1] The hill-fort yielded large collections of flint, pottery shards, clay pipes, and various other artifacts: "all of this material is consistent with early to middle Adena cultural material."[2]

Britain's Maiden Castle (from the Keltic mai-dun for "great hill"), in Dorset, features eastern and western gateways virtually identical in their complexity to an Adena hill-fort in Butler County, Ohio, located near the town of Hamilton. Renowned archaeological surveyors Ephraim George Squire and Edwin H. Davis were not only the first investigators to personally research the Butler County site, but its close resemblance to Maiden Castle struck them at first sight: "In event of an attack, even though both these defenses were carried, there still remains a series of walls so complicated as inevitably to distract and bewilder the assailants, thus giving a marked advantage to the defenders."[3]

In his comprehensive *The Stone Circles of the British Isles*, Aubrey Burl writes of the Beaker People:

> Physically very different from the slighter, gracile Neolithic stock, these powerfully built foreigners first came to the country at the beginning of the second millennium and settled around the islets of eastern Britain before eventually moving inland up the rivers that offered them passage through the unknown forests. Over several centuries the intruders mingled increasingly with the natives, sometimes peacefully, sometimes as overlords, sometimes by conquest.[4]

Frank Joseph describes the Alleghany mound builders this way: "The Adena likewise stood out from North America's indigenous populations with larger skulls, higher and broader foreheads, prominent jaws, and more pronounced cheekbones."[5] The English Beaker immigrants' behavior of cautiously exploring new territories via river systems mirrors Adena penetration into America's heartland. They finally settled primarily in central Ohio because of the region's topographical resemblance to their overseas' homeland, in the south of England. Adena America and Beaker Britain share another, telling commonality: roads. A 5-mile-long "avenue" connects England's Stonehenge with Woodhenge, and portions of a wooden track in Ireland's County Longford are preserved at County Clare's Craggaunowen Museum, where its souvenir guidebook states, "In fact, the new and very exact science of dendrochronology, that is, dating wood by a study of its annual tree-rings, has established that it was built precisely in the spring or summer of the year 148 BC."[6]

In early 1970, when Mr. Ray Sweet was cutting peat, he uncovered a wooden plank that led to the discovery of the numerous plank roads that criss-crossed Somerset County, England, in the vicinity of the Glastonbury Tor. The roads connected villages to annual fairs and hunting grounds on the burtles, islands made from sandy glacial deposits. Other Beaker roads ran to Glastonbury, scene of Katharine Maltwood's colossally landscaped zodiac. "The track [near the factory and railway tracks]," write researchers Bryony and John Coles in Sweet Tracks to Glastonbury, "was found to run in a remarkably straight line. The aim of the Neolithic builders of the late fourth millennium BC was to provide a raised path across a wet reed swamp. . . . The planks were supported about forty centimeters [16 inches] above the rails, abutting end to end across eighteen hundred meters [1,969 yards] of marsh."[7] A straight road elevated above a marsh remaining intact for six thousand years is what modern highway engineers are trying to master. The Coles continue, "Most of the oak and much of the ash found along the whole length of the Sweet Track had been felled in the same year. This indicated that the track had been built in a single year."[8] The Neolithic builders obviously had at their disposal an industrious and large workforce. So did the Adena on the other side of the world. An outstanding example was "West Virginia's Ancient Highway to Nowhere," described by David Cain, past president of the state's Marion County Historical Society: "The ancient road was twelve miles in length, fourteen inches thick, and nine feet wide, extending from the mouth of the Monongahela River, following the East bank to Catawba, Marion County," and was paved with "knapped stone, crushed mussel shells, and clay tamped into a hard surface."[9]

Although not elevated, its thick base would have kept pedestrians' feet out of the mud. Due to 19th-century agricultural and industrial expansion, most of the road was obliterated, so its original full extent will never be known, but its massiveness is nonetheless consistent with similar boulevards laid out by Beaker construction engineers. In fact, the Adena highway's very straightness parallels Britain's Sweet Tracks.

Combining the physical evidence of road construction, hill-forts, and the physical makeup of their builders with shared time frames more than suggests that an extinct race remembered by Ojibwa elders as the Alleghany and categorized by modern archaeologists as the Adena were transatlantic visitors known as the Beaker People from Neolithic Europe.

SECTION VII

GIANTS

———————◆◆◆———————

A race of humans standing 7 to 9 feet tall that dominated the American Middle West 2,000 years ago was no fantasy. But who were these real-life titans? Where did they come from, and what became of them? These are some of the questions tackled by today's leading researchers in the new science of *giantology*.

After graduating with a degree in economics from the University of Massachusetts Amherst, James Vieira spent long hours searching out local stone structures resembling ancient Old World counterparts. During the course of his New England investigations, he stumbled across the account of an oversized human skeleton unearthed in the neighboring town of Deerfield, a piece of information that changed Vieira's life.

After personally examining hundreds of prehistoric earthworks throughout the Ohio Valley, Fritz Zimmerman released his findings in *The Nephilim Chronicles* (Create Space, 2010) and *The Encyclopedia of Ancient Giants* (Create Space, 2015).

Jason Jarrell and Sarah Farmer spent six years of scholarly research, including fieldwork on the ground and high in the mountains of West Virginia, Kentucky, and Ohio, searching for traces of the extinct colossi of ancient America.

29

When Giants Ruled America

By James Vieira

In 1848, then-congressman Abraham Lincoln visited Niagara Falls for the first time, thereafter writing a 500-word meditation on his experience: "The eyes of that extinct species of giant, whose bones fill the mounds of America, have gazed on Niagara, as our eyes do now."[1] As surprising as his words may seem today, Lincoln was merely repeating common knowledge of his time—namely, that a race of giants inhabited the lands of ancient America.

Forty-seven years after Lincoln's visit to Niagara Falls, George Sheldon observed in his *Town History of Deerfield, Massachusetts*:

> At the foot of Bars Long Hill, just where the meadow fence crossed the road and the bars were placed that gave the village its name, many skeletons were exposed while plowing down a bank, and weapons and implements were found in abundance. One of these skeletons was described to me by Henry Mather, who saw it as being of monstrous size—"the head as big as a peck basket, with double teeth all round." The skeleton was

examined by Dr. Stephen W. Williams, who said the owner must have been nearly eight feet high. In all the cases noted in this paragraph, the bodies were placed in a sitting posture, facing the east.[2]

Similar accounts may be found in late-19th-century and early-20th-century issues of *Scientific American, American Antiquarian*, the Smithsonian Institution, the *New York Times, Washington Post*, and local town and county histories. The widely dispersed sources commonly reported giant skeletal finds with double rows of teeth, unusually thick skulls, jawbones so large they could fit over the face of a living man, and strange writing or hieroglyphics found at the burial sites. According to *American Antiquarian*, for example, a skeleton 7 feet, 6 inches long was found during 1884 in a massive stone structure likened to a temple chamber within a mound at Kanawha County, West Virginia.[3]

Four years later, remains of seven skeletons 7 to 8 feet tall were unearthed in the Upper Midwest: "Seven skeletons placed in sitting position were uncovered from a burial mound near Clearwater, Minnesota. The highly unusual skulls had double rows of teeth in both the upper and lower jaws."[4]

Native American oral history clearly speaks of a race of giants inhabiting the Ohio Valley and beyond in prehistory, when they were at the center of widespread warfare: "Near the junction of the Hart and Missouri Rivers is an old cemetery of fully one hundred acres in extent, filled with bones of a giant race."[5] Sheldon was the first president of the Pocumtuck Valley Memorial Hall Museum, which preserves his original scrapbook of newspaper clippings about the region's giant skeletons. Until only a few years ago, giant skeletal remains were on display at the Pocumtuck Museum itself. According to the institution's 1886 catalog of curiosities and relics, they were found near the town of Gill, Massachusetts. Also displayed were the skull, jawbone, and thigh bone belonging to an "at least" 8-foot skeleton from Marion County, Ohio. All were re-interred as part of the Native American Graves Protection and Repatriation Act.

Among the items in Sheldon's scrapbook is *The Story of Martha's Vineyard*, by Charles Gilbert Hine, from 1908: "Some fifteen years ago, the skeleton of an Indian giant in almost perfect preservation was dug up in the same locality (Cedar Neck, Massachusetts). The bones indicated a man easily six feet and a half, possibly seven feet high. An unusual feature was a complete double row of teeth on both the upper and lower jaws."[6] Another report was 1907's *History of the Town of Rockingham, Vermont*, by Lyman Simpson Hayes: "When the earth was removed from the top of the ledges east of the falls, a remarkable human skeleton, unmistakably that of an Indian, was found. Those who saw it tell the writer the jaw bone was of such size that a large man could easily slip it over his face and the teeth, which were all double, were perfect."[7]

In 1906, Thomas Weston's *History of the Town of Middleboro, Massachusetts* reported: "A few years ago when the highway was straightened and repaired, remains were found. When his skeleton was measured by Dr. Morill Robinson and others, it was found that the thigh bone was four inches longer than that bone in an ordinary man, and that he had a double row of teeth in each jaw. His height must have been at least seven feet and eight inches."[8] A similar find was described by Maine's Harry Hayman Cochrane, in *History of Monmouth and Wales*: "Not many years ago, a massive Indian skeleton was exhumed at East Monmouth. By proceeding carefully, the entire frame was unearthed. It proved to be that of a giant, measuring almost seven and a half feet in height. The skull is said to be as large as a common iron tea kettle."[9]

According to volume 5 of *Gleason's Literary Companion*: "An Indian skeleton of immense size was recently discovered three feet under ground near Fort River Hadley, Massachusetts. The bones were so far decomposed that most of them crumbled upon exposure to the air. Some of the doctors think that the Indian was not less than seven feet high and one hundred years old when he died."[10] "History of Montague" told how "Indian skeletons were exhumed on L Street near the falls in 1873. And on the opposite shore Mr. Smith dug out seven skeletons buried in a sitting posture, each about seven feet in stature."[11]

The New England Magazine reported in 1897: "The spot where the village of Edgartown stands today was at that time an ancient Indian burial ground. In one case, a huge jawbone of a man was dug up out from the ground, larger than that of any man at the present time, so large that it could be placed against the face of an ordinary man and entirely surround his jaw."[12]

Tripp and Osgood explained in 1850's *Guide to the White Mountains and the Lake of New Hampshire* that "[a] skeleton was exhumed in this town (Moltonborough) some thirty years ago, of almost fabulous proportions. It was buried in a sandy soil, on the shore of the lake, near the mouth of a small river. It was apparently the skeleton of a man some seven feet high—the jaw bones passing easily over the face of a large man."[13]

According to Volume 2 of *The History of Western Massachusetts*: "Mr. J.D. Canning has in his possession a broken pipe and a copper tomahawk, which were unearthed together with the gigantic skeleton of an Indian; it doubtless belonged to a warrior renowned in his day and race and was probably brought from the region of Superior."[14]

"The skeleton of an Indian warrior at least six feet six inches," wrote *The Friends Intelligencer*, "was found in Musgongus, Maine, a few days ago by two men digging a cellar. The body had been buried in a sitting posture facing east, and about it were found iron implements and spear

Marcia R. Moore's forensic comparison of a modern, 6-foot-tall man with a representative of the Ron-nong-weto-wanca, or "Red-Haired Giant Sorcerers," as they are recalled in Ojibwa Indian oral traditions.

and arrow heads, while around the arms were copper bands covered with curious carvings."[15]

There are also reports of 8-foot skeletons from New Haven and Trumbull, Connecticut, Burrillville, Rhode Island; and giant skeletons in Northfield, Quincy, Chelmsford, Newton, and Massachusetts. Some of these remains were allegedly found with iron and copper implements. The following is remarkably similar to the Smithsonian Institution account of a Mound Builder grave opened in West Virginia: "The larger of the two skeletons represented a man conceivably approaching eight feet in height when living. All the bones were badly decayed, except those of the left wrist, which had been preserved by two heavy copper bracelets . . . a skeleton measuring seven and a half feet in length and 19 inches across the shoulders was discovered. Each wrist was encircled by six heavy copper bracelets."[16]

Warren K. Moorehead, the early 20th century's dean of American archeology, uncovered a giant skeleton covered in copper armor in Illinois and excavated a mound at Tioga Point, Pennsylvania, that yielded 68 skeletons averaging 7 feet in height. Specimens were sent to the American Investigating Museum in Philadelphia, from where they were "stolen" and never heard from again. He also unearthed two giant skeletons with massive teeth in Bridgeport, Connecticut. For having had the temerity of bringing such academically heretical finds to public notice, even Moorehead's stellar reputation could not escape censure from his conventional colleagues.

Sympathetic antiquarian Martin Doutre summarized the state of affairs in archeology at the time and thereafter:

> We have fully documented, reliable accounts of Smithsonian Institution personnel traveling to 1800s communities in middle-America to take possession of large skeletons exhumed from the mounds. In certain instances, the hand-over of remains and artifacts was done with a degree of formal ceremony, with the town mayor, local minister, or assorted dignitaries turning out and the spectacle of speeches and handshakes reported in the local newspaper.
>
> Mound researchers such as Patricia Mason of Newark, Ohio, in following up many of these reports have applied to the Smithsonian Institution for information related to the present-day whereabouts of those skeletons gifted to the museum's

collection, only to be told that the Smithsonian never received any such item. Like so many of these remains, it joined more than eighteen thousand skeletons of Mound Builder giants and Native Americans stored in their catacombs, inaccessible to the public.[17]

More recently, Thomas Kuhn's *The Structure of Scientific Revolutions* described the present climate of academic affairs relating to anomalous finds:

> Mop-up operations are what engage most scientists throughout their careers. This paradigm-based research is an attempt to force nature into the pre-formed and relatively inflexible box that the paradigm supplies. No effort is made to call forth new sorts of phenomena, no effort to discover anomalies. When anomalies pop up, they are usually discarded or ignored. Anomalies are usually not even noticed, and no effort is made to invent a new theory—and there is no tolerance for those who try.[18]

But from Abraham Lincoln's Niagara Falls visit to our times, American history is full of corroborating claims for pre-Columbian giants not easy to ignore. In 1754, George Washington was overseeing the building of a fort for his militia force at Winchester, Virginia. While digging, Washington's men uncovered multiple skeletons, which Washington stated were 7 feet long. His report matched accounts of earlier explorers, such as Louis Michelle, who was shown by local Native Americans in Virginia ancient burial mounds of warriors more than 7 feet tall. Michelle's maps and diaries are currently stored in London's Royal Archives. Washington is also said to have investigated giant skeletal remains unearthed immediately prior to a battle.

Curiously, excavation of a 9-foot 4-inch skeleton at Britain's Stonehenge was made in 1713. There seems to be a larger story here. What was this race of pre-Columbian giants, and where did they come from? Did Native Americans interbreed with them, accounting for Colonial Era reports of giants occasionally encountered in the backwoods of New England? Answers apparently lie among the mute skeletons of this vanished people.

30

The New York Giants

By Fritz Zimmerman

In 1876, a young man accompanied several of his neighbors in excavating a prehistoric burial mound that was to leave an indelible impression on him. What Charles Huntington witnessed would inspire him more than six decades later to carve a replica of the remarkable find.

County histories of the time featured prominent, local citizens whose reputations were beyond reproach. Eighteen seventy-nine's *History of Cattaraugus County, New York* was no less esteemed, as it recounted the circumstances involved in excavation of the ancient earthwork that changed the life of Charles Huntington:

> About two miles south of the village of Rutledge, in the town of Connewango, on lot No. 45, at a point about sixty rods east of Connewango Creek and near the residence of Norman E. Cowen, there was discovered by the first pioneers of this section a sepulcher mound, nearly circular in form, and having an entire circumference of one hundred seventy feet. The height of the mound was about twelve feet. Mr. Cheney spoke of this

work as "having the appearance of being constructed with the ditch outside of the mound, as in Druid barrows."[1]

A "Druid barrow" described a conical burial mound is surrounded by a ditch or earthwork, a type of burial mound found in both the British Isles and the Ohio Valley.

"Within the mound there were discovered nine human skeletons, which had been buried in a sitting posture and at regular intervals of space, in the form of a circle, and facing towards a common center. There were some slight appearance that the framework had enclosed the dead at the time of their internment. The skeletons were so far decayed as to crumble upon exposure to the atmosphere, but were all of very large size."[2]

Another set of giant remains was made not far from the Connewango Creek site and likewise described by the *History of Cattaraugus County*: "On examination, they proved to be skeletons entire, having been deposited there three or four feet in depth. A remarkable characteristic of these skeletons was their enormous proportions. Compared with my own stature and physical formation, they must have been giants indeed."[3]

Early illustrations of West Virginia's Moundsville 70-foot-tall structure made it the largest earthwork of its kind in the region. Like the Connewango location, it, too, was surrounded by a ditch, as in the manner of a "Druid barrow," and contained the skeletal remains of a 7-foot 6-inch female and of a man 8 feet in length.

On September 21, 1936, New Jersey's *Randolph Register* told its readers about efforts to recreate lifelike representations of humans interred in the pre-Columbian tombs:

> The full length model was preceded by three bust length models, two of them being reproductions based upon skeletons of a man and woman found at Moundsville, West Virginia, and the third based upon the skeletons found at the Cowan farm. Brought back from the obscurity of untold ages, a giant, nine-foot man has been modeled in wood by Charles Huntington of East Randolph. The model is based upon an image, which has been formed in Mr. Huntington's mind since the day, sixty-two years ago, when he witnessed the exhuming of the skeletons of pre-historic mound builders at the N. E. G. Cowan farm on the

Conewango Road. Measurements which he secured at that time form the basis upon which the model was constructed.

When several of the persons who saw these earlier figures expressed disbelief that such large human beings had ever roamed the woods and fields of this vicinity, Mr. Huntington wrote to Albany for verification. He received a letter from C. A. Hartnagel, assistant state geologist, giving figures reported by T. Apoleon Cheney, a Randolph man, who was present at the time the mound was opened. Mr. Cheney's figures checked with those, which Mr. Huntington had used. As an example of the remarkable size of the skeletons, the measurements of the femur, or bone between the ankle and knee, was twenty-eight inches in length. A facial angle of seventy-three degrees and the high forehead would indicate a large degree of intelligence.[4]

Establishment archaeologists would dismiss Mr. Huntington's wooden model as a fabrication, despite consistent, published reports of similar finds and confirmation of his original measurements by the assistant state geologist. Moreover, the occurrence of "druid barrows" with 8-foot skeletons at both New York's Connewango County and Moundsville in West Virginia suggest their human remains were at least related to the hundreds of similar skeletons found throughout the Ohio Valley.

31

A Giant Problem for Orthodox Scholars

By Jason Jarrell and Sarah Farmer

Recent years have seen an acceleration in the popularity of the "lost race of giants" concept, with some insightful researchers breaking new and important ground in the field. In an excellent article, Greg Little has recently debunked the notion that the very large skeletons frequently encountered in North American burial mounds is due to chance. His surveys indicated that the Smithsonian's finding of no less than 17 skeletons of 7 feet or more in height as documented in the 5th and 12th Bureau of Ethnology reports would have required the excavation of 2.5 million skeletons. In other words, the explanations that these were simply the "really tall" members of the populace or the product of gigantism—only one hundred cases of which have been documented in America's history, according to Little—are statistically impossible.

Many of the North American earthworks compared with those across the Atlantic in the late 1800s were subsequently linked to the

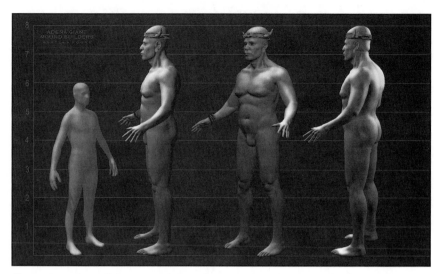

Comparison of a modern man with forensic reconstruction by Marcia R. Moore of North America's prehistoric mound builders.

Adena people. Adena enclosures are circular embankments of earth with interior or exterior ditches, featuring openings possibly referencing solar, lunar, or otherwise astrological events, usually located among mound fields. The enclosures sometimes feature timber circles incorporated into their designs. So strong are the similarities of these works to Neolithic and Bronze Age henges that mainstream archaeologists occasionally study the European examples when interpreting the Adena versions. "Henges" are prehistoric monuments consisting of a circle of stone or wooden uprights.

Archaeologists found that Adena burial mounds demonstrate an extraordinary level of variability, resulting in a bloated cultural taxonomy.

This has led their modern successors to suggest that there was no specific Adena culture *per se*. However, this ignores the fact that in the 20th century, William S. Webb and Don Dragoo identified the Adena people as a distinct group, whose anthropology evidenced a race genetically separate from other prehistoric peoples, including the supposedly later Hopewell. Both Webb and Dragoo unearthed Adena skeletons reaching 7 feet in length. Subsequent work by giantologists has identified the Adena as the primary source for most of the "gigantic" skeletons recorded in the 19th and early 20th centuries.

William S. Webb and Charles Snow devoted considerable space to analysis of the large, high-vaulted crania of the Adena people: "The forehead is typically a prominent one, bordered below by fairly sizeable brow ridges. The root of the nose is of average proportions and continues on to a prominent convex bridge that is one of the prominent features of the face. The characteristic bulge of the upper and lower jaws (alveolar prognathism) is moderate in projection. . . . Usually the cheek bones are not only of large size in themselves but they have a forward and lateral prominence. . . . "[1] The Adena are thought to have practiced artificial cranial deformation of the occipital region, enhancing their large, congenital features. Webb and Snow described the Adena cranial vault as "the highest known in the world," with an average index of 89.5, while the supposedly deformed skulls reached as high as 100.[2]

As described by the renowned physical anthropologist Carleton Stevens Coon (1904–1981), the characteristics of the Beaker People are virtually identical to Adena:

> Where Bell Beaker burials are found in central Europe, the skeletons are almost always of the same tall, brachycephalic type . . . the brow-ridges are often heavy, the general ruggedness frequently greater. The faces are characteristically narrow, the orbits medium to high, the nasal skeleton high and aquiline; the occiput frequently flat. . . . They form one of the rare groups in the world with a cranial length of one hundred eighty-four millimeters and an index of over eighty.[3]

William Boyd Dawkins described the brachycephalic Beaker crania as having "strongly marked" brow ridges, "high and broad" cheek bones, and jaws "presenting prognathism."[4]

Many of the European accounts of the skeletal remains of the "round barrow" folk are virtually identical to the frequently cited newspaper stories and local histories recording North American giants from roughly the same time period: "Those of the type . . . regarded as specifically representative of the Bronze Age were taller and much more powerfully built than the aborigines: Their skulls were comparatively short and round; they had massive jaws, strongly marked features, enormously prominent brow ridges and retreating foreheads; and their countenances must have been stern, forbidding, and sometimes almost

brutal . . . who combined harsh features and projecting brows with narrow heads, and whose stature was often great. . . . "[5]

The Beaker People are thought by anthropologist William Dawkins
to have practiced the same type of cranial deformation as Adena: "[T]
here is also generally an occipital flattening which may have been
caused by the use of an unyielding cradle board."[6]

On the south side of the Kanawha River, a tributary of the Ohio
River in West Virginia, Norris recorded two circular enclosures with
interior ditches flanking a large conical mound originally 30 to 40 feet
high, known as the Criel Mound. Enclosure Number 1 was 260 feet to
the northeast of the mound; Number 2 was 260 feet to the southwest of
the tumulus. Both of these henges were 666 feet in circuit, with outer
walls 10 feet high.

Enclosure Number 1 had an opening at the south, whereas Number
2 was open at the north, representing truly impressive samples of the
Adena "sacred circle."[7] These works were connected by a graded way
leading from Enclosure Number 1 two hundred 42 feet to the second
terrace of Kanawha River. According to its excavator, P.W. Norris, at
the bottom of the Criel Mound, the remains of a timber structure was
discovered "at least sixteen feet in diameter and six or eight feet high"
enclosing a semi-circle arrangement of ten burials situated around a
central eleventh "prominent personage."[8]

All were placed in bark coffins upon a bark floor. The conclusion
of the Bureau agents was that the 10 "attendant" burials consisted of
five women and five male warriors. In his firsthand account of the
Charleston excavations, A.R. Sines offers a description of the central
burial in the Criel mound: ". . . a most powerful man . . . the distance
from the spot where the heel bone was found to what was left of the
skull was six feet, eight feet and three-quarter inches . . . The teeth were
considerably larger than the teeth of any of the present generation."[9]

According to Norris and Sines, the cranial remnants of this figure were found with remains of a copper band or crown, which seems
to have been a type of a diadem. At the center of a level area inside
enclosure Number 1 was a small mound, 40 feet broad and 4 feet high,
the whole work being similar to a European "druid barrow" commonly
found among Western European mound fields. According to Sines,
the subsequent excavation of a nearby tumulus known as the "Wilson

Mound" revealed a female skeleton with "copper bands around the ankles and wrists and larger pieces of copper on each breast."[10]

Mound Number 11 at Charleston was 50 feet at the base and 7 feet high, beneath which Norris discovered a "human skeleton fully seven feet long" amid the "rotten traces of a bark coffin."[11]

On the north side of the Kanawha, Mound 19 was found to contain a "rude vault of angular stones" within which were the remains of a "large human skeleton" and fragments of pottery. This "vault" was a cist "eight feet in length, four wide and three feet high" built upon the natural surface of the ground. The Great Smith Mound was 35 feet high at the time of excavation. Thomas states that this mound was built in three stages, describing a primary mound 20 feet high followed by a subsequent addition of 15 more feet. After this an intrusive burial was added at a later time. According to Norris, the older 20-foot tumulus was "one of the oldest, largest, and flattest topped in this region."[12]

Built into the top of this primary mound was a large timber structure similar to that of the Criel Mound, 12 by 13 feet broad, 6 feet high, and reaching 10 feet at the ridged top. At the center of this vault, in the remains of a bark coffin, Norris discovered "a gigantic human skeleton seven feet six inches in length and nineteen inches between the shoulders."[13] This skeleton is described several times in the manuscript as "the giant" or "gigantic human skeleton."[14] The body had been wrapped in skins and encased in a type of clay, possibly for preservation.

As is fairly well recognized today, the 19th-century accounts penned by antiquarians found in township and county histories usually describe skeletons 7 to 9 feet long, with massive lower jaws and very large, thick crania. There are also a prolific number of similar reports found in newspapers from the period.

In spite of continued denial by establishment sources, the work of Webb and Snow, together with Don Dragoo, essentially corroborated the findings of the earlier antiquarians and even linked the gigantic skeletal types with a specific people and culture—namely, the Adena Mound Builders. More recently, the pioneering research of Ross Hamilton and Vine Victor Deloria, Jr. (1933–2005, Yankton Sioux historian) set a scholarly standard for giantology, synchronizing the Native and Archeological records, as outlined in Hamilton's unsurpassed work, A *Tradition of Giants*. Utilized extensively by other researchers, the little credited work of this team laid the foundation for modern giantology.[15]

And yet, in spite of this tradition of rediscovery, no satisfactory reconstruction of an Adena giant has ever been undertaken. While we are routinely reminded of the dimensions of the giants in volumes reprinting multiple hundreds of accounts of their discovery, we have been denied imagery representing their living form. Whereas numerous other anomalies (such as the Paracas and "Starchild" crania) have received due attention, the gigantic Adena have remained shrouded in mystery. In May 2015, the authors undertook a joint venture with the legendary Marcia K. Moore to remedy this situation. Marcia is best known as the premier artist re-creating the living images of the elongated crania of Peru, associated with the Paracas People. The skull used for the Adena re-creation was that of Burial 16 from the Wright Mounds, in Kentucky, described as showing "pronounced" deformation.

According to H.T.E. Hertzberg, the crania of the Wright site featured the large, prognathic lower mandibles typical of Adena, and although artificially deformed, the series demonstrated the large congenital features later noted by Webb, Snow and Dragoo: ". . . deformed as they are, these crania display a pronounced brachycrany . . . it may be noticed that four skulls . . . displaying submedium deformation, also give an average cranial index of over ninety percent. Thus the inference is that these people would have shown pronounced brachycrany even without deformation. . . ."[16] Charles Snow also felt that the Adena practice of artificial flattening of the occipital region merely enhanced congenital features: ". . . those skulls with slight or no deformation (undeformed) present similar proportions. . . . It is likely that many, if not most, of the skull characteristics so typical of Adena are of genetic nature. . . ."[17]

Carnegie Museum of Natural History archaeologist Don Dragoo described the unique traits of Adena, including the "protruding and massive chin" with "prominent bilateral protrusions," as well as "individuals approaching seven feet in height. . . . Not only were these Adena People tall, but also the massiveness of the bones indicates powerfully built individuals. The head was generally big with a large cranial capacity." [18] The postcranial dimensions of the Adena giant were derived from several sources, including the field notes of P.W. Norris, the agent of the Bureau of Ethnology who excavated the Adena mounds at Charleston, West Virginia, in 1883 and 1884.

Several mounds at Charleston yielded skeletons 7 feet long. At the Great Smith Mound, Norris encountered a house-like timber structure twelve by 13 feet broad and 6 feet high, reaching 10 feet at the ridged top. Within this structure was a "gigantic and prominent personage, surrounded by five of his (probably volunteer) warriors . . . " Norris measured the central burial *in situ* and described it as "a gigantic human skeleton seven feet six inches in length and 19 inches between the shoulders . . ."; elsewhere in the manuscript, this skeleton is regularly referred to as "the giant," or "gigantic."[19]

The measurements provided by Norris are similar to those of large skeletons from several other sources, including Warren K. Moorhead: "Six feet above these remains was found the partial skeleton of a man almost a giant in size . . . The breadth across the shoulders, with the bones correctly placed, was nineteen inches. . . ."[20] From the Bureau

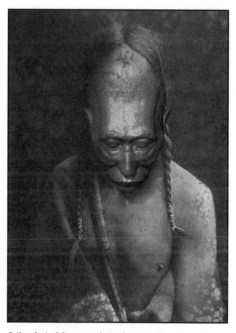

Like their Maya and Andean contemporaries, the Adena elite practiced head elongation to distinguish themselves from the lower orders. Steady pressure was applied to the soft and malleable skull of an infant between a pair of cloth-covered boards to form, over a few years, the desired shape.

of Ethnology: "The length from the base of the skull to the bones of the toes was found to be seven feet, three inches. It is probable, therefore, that this individual when living was seven feet one-half inches feet high."[21]

These details corroborate Norris's account and indicate individuals approaching 8 feet tall. Because a high frequency of reports describe skeletons reaching this height, the data was used by Marcia to formulate the likely dimensions and appearance of an 8-foot-tall Adena in the flesh. Among the artifacts buried with the giant from the Great Smith Mound were six heavy copper bracelets on each wrist, and a copper gorget was found on the chest. At the nearby Criel Mound, a central burial was found with the remnants of a copper crown or headband, possibly the remains of an antler headdress (also a trait of the Hopewell Tradition).

A similar copper head ornament was found at the Wright Mounds. It is mute but eloquent testimony to the former existence of prehistoric giants that long ago dominated our continent from its eastern seaboard to the Mississippi River, including the Great Lakes Region, where they alone would have been strong enough to wield the 40-pound stone tools that extracted 125,000 tons of copper before 1200 BCE. As such, the mysterious identity of ancient America's pit miners appears to have been solved.

32

Mexico's Lost City of Giants

By James Vieira

Over a 200-year period, thousands of newspaper reports, town and county histories, letters, photos, diaries, and scientific journals have collectively documented the existence of an ancient race of giants in North America. Extremely tall skeletons, ranging from 7 feet up to a staggering 18 feet tall, have been reportedly found in prehistoric mounds, burial chambers, caves, geometric earthworks, and ancient battlefields. Their anatomic anomalies commonly included horned skulls, jaws massive enough to fit over a modern man's head, and elongated crania often featuring multiple hyperdontia, or double rows of teeth otherwise rare in people with no associated diseases or syndromes.

Many of these discoveries were sent for professional study and evaluation to Washington, D.C., where they vanished, even though the Smithsonian Institution's own annual reports inventory at least 17 of the giant skeletons. Although curators there were mum on the subject, their Smithsonian colleagues did venture later into northwestern

Mexico, searching for a tribe of giants that supposedly ruled Yacqui country and mummified their dead.

Archaeologists would not have given Mexican giants a second thought, had they not learned of statements made by Dr. Byron Cummings, the University of Arizona's highly respected head of its archaeology department, where he was revered as the dean of Southwest Archaeology. Dr. Cummings had been contacted by a Mr. J.L. Coker, who, while mining an isolated area of Sayopa, Sonora, said he found human skeletons averaging 8 feet long; the longest example was supposedly 8 feet 3 inches.

One of their skulls measured in more than 1 foot long and 10 inches wide. The remains seemed to mirror local Yaqui Indian oral histories recalling a race of giants that inhabited the region during the deep past. Skeptical but intrigued, Dr. Cummings investigated Coker's claims and published his proposal in the December 4th, 1930, issue of Canada's *Border Cities Star* under the headline "Superstitious Natives Destroy Relics of Prehistoric Supermen," sparking the Smithsonian expedition he would eventually lead with his opening sentence: "There have been past discoveries of single skeletons measuring more than the average height of present humans, but there never has been several found together, so that the existence of a tribe or race of giants could be proven."[1]

Seven days later, a letter to the editor by a William Crocker appeared in the *Prescott Evening Courier* (Arizona):

> Nearly every issue of the papers during the last week has had something to say about an expedition going into Mexico to search for the bones of a race of giants. Why go to Mexico? Several years ago, Bill Singleton, a boss on the highway, told me while working on the road through Chino Valley [Arizona] some human bones were dug up which, when compared with those of the average man today, indicated they belonged to a race of men who measured between nine and ten feet tall. Jess Kiple at Pruchman's [?] will verify this statement. Another interesting find in this section was one made several years ago between Dewey and Humboldt, [when] a new piece of road cut into an old burial ground. Del Daves, now dead, doing some digging there, found two skeletons lying side by side, each having enormous heads. Beth Gray, a mining man of this section

who saw the skulls, said they were so big that it would take a number nine hat to fit them.[2]

Despite Crocker's accounts of giant human remains in the Grand Canyon State, University of Arizona investigators teamed up with Smithsonian researchers and Sonora scholars across the border to verify or debunk Coker's alleged discoveries. Returning several weeks later, Dr. Cummings reported in a front-page story of Dubuque, Iowa's, *Telegraph Herald and Times Journal* for December 14th:

> Five, large skeletons, the first evidences that a race of super-men once roamed this vast wasteland, were unearthed today by an international expedition of scientists. Working rapidly for two nights and a day, the little band of American and Mexican archaeologists unearthed the petrified remains of a youth six feet, eight inches tall, the skeletons of four other children of lesser stature, and several jars filled with human ashes. The importance of these discoveries was the fact that they definitely established the scene of operations as a great burial ground.[3]

But "before the expedition could get properly to work, down swooped the Yaquis, armed with rifles and knives. They fiercely bade the archaeologists quit or take the consequences. The Mexican professor [Sonora Government scientist, Manuel San Domingo] tried in vain to placate the Indians. His remonstrances were abruptly shattered by a tough Yaqui brave, who up-raised a heavy rifle butt and battered the giant remains to pieces."[4]

Years after this encounter, Dr. Cummings wrote again for *The Telegraph-Herald and Times Journal*, explaining that his finds had been corroborated by Paxson C. Hayes, Santa Barbara, California ethnologist: "Traces of a lost race of giants, who wore oriental turbans and mummified their dead in a fashion similar to that of the ancient Egyptians have been found in the Yaqui Indian country in Sonora, Mexico. Other traces of the oriental origin of the ancient giants was reported by Hayes, who declared he had found several tables buried near the mummies. These tables were of a size similar to those unearthed recently in the heart of the Gobi desert." [5] Hayes himself went on to describe the mummified giants for the *San Jose Evening News* May 22nd, 1933 issue: "They have slant eyes and sloped foreheads . . . the hair, which is black, has a peculiar auburn tinge when examined closely."[6]

Hayes had better success than his colleagues with the temperamental aboriginals, because he lived among the Yaqui for seven years, gaining their confidence. Eventually, they allowed him to freely explore the Sonora area, where he found the ruins of a lost city. The *Detroit News* broke the story, which was shortly thereafter written up at greater length by a reporter for the *Milwaukee Journal* on March 8, 1935:

> While I was in Nogales, Arizona, six weeks ago, Hayes, the discoverer of the lost city, came out of the hills long enough to re-outfit, and to present competent, factual proof of the nature of his discoveries, before returning to the site of the lost city, which is eleven days' mule-back journey southward from Hermosilla, capital of Sonora. Hayes had pictures of the mummified bodies of members of the race of giants. Thirty-four mummies have been uncovered, and the smallest measured seven feet one inch in height. He had pictures of the ruins of the buildings and samples of the burial shrouds, all in a fair state of preservation. Confirmation of the prescience of the ruins of an ancient civilization in Sonora came two years ago. Since then Hayes' party has made seven expeditions into Yaqui country.[7]

Later that year, a caption beneath his photograph that appeared in the December 31st edition of the *San Jose News* read: "Paxson Hayes, explorer, studies the head of a giant mummy discovered by him in a deep cave hitherto unexplored regions of Sonora, Mexico. The mummified remains were of a race seven and one-half feet tall and preserved in excellent condition. Corn found with the mummies has been given to scientists."[8]

Early the next month, Washington State's *Spokane Daily Chronicle* for January 9, 1936, made a surprising addition to his discovery:

> These crumbling ruins of a long-perished city, where mummified human forms revealed that seven-foot giants and three foot pygmies apparently lived together, were found by Paxson C. Hayes ethnologist, who has spent the last seven years exploring the upland wastes of northern Mexico. The architecture is of a type never-before discovered, resembling that of cliff dwellings, but with distinct Mongolian features. The strange civilization is believed to antedate that of the Mayans. Hayes plans an expedition for a thorough search of the huge caves in Sonora, four hundred miles from Hermosillo City.[9]

The story was taken up in a front-page article by California's *Berkeley Daily Gazette* on June 10, 1937:

The many reports of a race of "supermen" who once inhabited parts of the Mexican State of Sonora received new support today with the arrival of Paxson C. Hayes and Gerald C. Barnes, both of Santa Barbara, *en route* from Sonora to Washington [Gerald Barnes was an early-20th-century physical therapist and author of *Swimming and Diving* (Scribner's Sons, 1922)].

Bringing out of Sonora a Mexican boa constrictor and stories of mummified and skeletal remains of men and women from six feet and seven inches to eight feet tall, they announced they had discovered the district of "the lost city of Sonora." They planned to continue to Washington for a conference with the Mexican Ambassador, Francisco Najera [1884–1944], to seek cooperation of Mexican scientists in exploration of the discoveries.

Hayes was embroiled in a controversy with Dr. Roy Chapman Andrews [1884–1960, director of the American Museum of Natural History] in 1933, over the existence of the so-called 'supermen' or race of giants. Reports of the existence of remains of a race of giants have been recurrent throughout the Southwest since before 1930. Skeletons actually were found by a party headed by Dr. Byron Cummings of the University of Arizona, which indicated the existence of such a race, it was said. The Cummings expedition was driven out of Sonora by threats of an uprising of Yaqui Indians.

Although Smithsonian investigators had participated in the University of Arizona's 1930 Sonora expedition, the Institution quickly distanced itself from their discoveries, over which they draped a veil of silence. According to Hayes's son, Carlos, his father's funding was cut off for further explorations, which he thereafter personally underwrote. Occasionally, however, Smithsonian curators' curiosity got the better of them, as reported by the *Washington Post*:

With several dozen snakes (all alive), and the burial robe of a prehistoric giant (quite dead), packed in their trailer, they [Hayes and Barnes] stopped in Washington yesterday to promote interest in their unique fields of activity . . . the visitors then dropped in at the Smithsonian Institution with the pre-historic burial robe and a four-legged stool, both of which they unearthed in a burial cave in northern Sonora, Mexico. The Californians explained that the cave, one of eighteen they had discovered, contains well-preserved mummies of a race, which averaged over six and one-half feet in height (previously reported up to eight feet tall). The caves are scattered over an area of four hundred fifty square miles. Hayes, who has just returned from his fifth expedition to the caves, heard about their existence from the Yaqui Indians of Mexico.[10]

Public interest in Mexico's ancient giants peaked with a *Deseret News* story on November 9, 1950, that mentioned how at least some of the giant mummies had blond hair, something not cited in earlier reports:

> When the bones of the mummies were laid out properly, the various bodies measured from seven feet six inches in most cases up to the largest skeleton, which was a full eight feet. . . . The greatest mystery of Hayes' finds . . . were the saffron-colored burial robes found on the giants. There may be a great historic tale behind the powder-blue designs of latch hooks and pyramids that embellish the robes. Hayes thinks that the tiny series of white dots that recur throughout the robes are symbols of the ancient Indian time cycle. . . .[11]

The *Deseret News* went on to state that Hayes showed the burial robes to chiefs of the Seri Indians on Tiburon Island, off the west coast of Mexico, but they claimed to know nothing about the ornate garments.[12] Efforts by Cummings, Hayes, Barnes, and other professionals to make the ancient Mexican giants part of American prehistory and officially recognize Sonora's lost city were ignored to death by a majority of their colleagues.

The cause was straightforwardly spelled out by a philosopher of science, Thomas Kuhn (1922–1996), in his *Structure of Scientific Revolutions*:

> Mop-up operations are what engage most scientists throughout their careers. This paradigm-based research is an attempt to force nature into the pre-formed and relatively inflexible box that the paradigm supplies. No effort is made to

call forth new sorts of phenomena, no effort to discover anomalies. When anomalies pop up they are usually discarded or ignored. Anomalies are usually not even noticed and no effort is made to invent a new theory—and there is no tolerance for those who try.[13]

SECTION VIII

NORSE

——••◆••——

Medieval Scandinavians did not blunder their way across the North Atlantic. Nor were they hapless castaways on American shores. Negotiating the treacherous seas of a transatlantic passage, then as now, demanded not only skill, but effective navigational instruments. These the Northmen possessed at a higher level than hitherto understood, making their impact on our continent all the more extensive, as proved by recent verification of an important Norse settlement on an island off Canada. The Vikings journeyed much further inland, leaving behind rock art imagery of their redoubtable long-ship described by Jennifer Robbins-Mullin, a Pittsburgh sports writer and photographer, whose "work has been exhibited all over the United States."[1]

33

Transatlantic Navigators

By Frank Joseph

In its September/October 2009 issue, *Ancient American* reported the discovery of so-called "sun stones" used by Viking mariners to sail long distances by our star long after it set. These were pairs of calcite crystals held against the sky to generate identifiable patterns when the minerals were exposed to the polarization of sunlight's ultraviolet rays. The patterns oriented to the position of the Sun on an overcast day, or when it was below the horizon, enabling seafarers to determine the four cardinal directions.

But findings released on March 25, 2015, by Britain's Proceedings of the Royal Society A, reveal that the "sun stones" were only part of navigational systems the Norse used more than one thousand years ago. Researchers at Budapest's Eötvös Loránd University (ELU; Hungary's largest university, founded in 1635) determined that the remains of a misidentified object that came to light in an 11th-century Greenland convent belong to a compass of surprising sophistication.

Found 66 years ago, the Uunartoq Disc, formerly thought to have been a personal adornment, is actually an important navigational instrument that guided Viking mariners across their 1,600-mile-long passage from Norway to Greenland. Originally 2.8 inches in diameter, the artifact once featured a central pin that cast a shadow from the Sun, thereby indicating a particular cardinal direction.

Field tests of the re-created device conducted by the Hungarians demonstrated that it performed within four degrees of error, superior to other forms of celestial navigation and comparable to the best, modern magnetic pocket compasses. Based on its faintly visible etchings, according to ELU team leader Balzs Bernth, the Uunartoq Disc was used around the vernal equinox, when daylight and nighttime share the same number of hours, a period during which the Vikings were known to have undertaken their oceanic voyages. As some measure of their efficiency, both the Disc and its calcite crystals could function together as long as 50 minutes after sundown.

The surprisingly high maritime technology operated by medieval Scandinavian sailors puts paid to mainstream skeptics, who denigrate Norse contacts in Newfoundland as accidental and fleeting. Instead, the Uunartoq Disc and its "sun stones" are physical proof that they had the means to make regular transatlantic expeditions to Vineland, as borne out by a wealth of supporting evidence for Vikings in North America.

34

How the Northmen Colonized Canada

By Dr. Cyclone Covey

A 700-year-old Norse settlement has been positively identified in Canada, it was announced in October 2015. A research "fellow" at Scotland's University of Aberdeen, Patricia Sutherland previously led an investigative team from the Memorial University of Newfoundland (St. John's), where she is adjunct professor of archaeology, to an Atlantic coastal site high above the Arctic Circle. There, they unearthed stone remains closely resembling Viking house foundations more commonly found in Greenland.

Her discovery originated 14 years ago, while visiting Quebec's Canadian Museum of Civilization, in Gatineau, where she noticed two pieces of unusual cord that had come to light during a Baffin Island dig some decades before. Neither strand was made of animal sinew native hunters typically twisted into cordage, but yarn as characteristically woven by Viking women in medieval Greenland. Following up on this lead, Sutherland initiated her own Tanfield Valley excavation at the extreme southern end of the island in summer 2001.

Over the next 11 years, amid ruins discovered during the mid-20th century, she and her colleagues retrieved more local wools that had been turned into yarns—a practice unknown to Canadian aboriginals—together with a whalebone shovel like those fashioned by Greenland Vikings for cutting sod used as roofing material, and pelts belonging to Old World rats, plus large stones cut and shaped by someone skilled in European masonry techniques; Baffin Island natives did not work with large or cut stone.

Most decisive were whetstones used for sharpening tools according to medieval European traditional methods. When their worn grooves were examined by energy dispersive spectroscopy, the Geological Survey of Canada detected microscopic streaks of bronze, brass and smelted iron—all diagnostic of Viking Age metallurgy.

Carbon-datable materials from the Tanfield Valley centered on a mid- to late-14th-century time frame, although additional valid periods as much as 400 years earlier were also obtained. These ninth- and 10th-century dates, among other discoveries Sutherland's team made, have distressed archaeologists convinced the Norse made no lasting impact on the New World, especially as far back as 1,000 years. Although these skeptics were forced long ago to concede that a Viking base camp had operated at another Canadian site, they continue to insist that Newfoundland's L'Anse aux Meadows was nothing more than a small, failed fluke.

The Baffin Island finds contradict such a conclusion, however, because they prove not only more than a single Norse settlement occurred in North America, but that both sites operated at the same time, and at least one continued to function for four centuries. These uncomfortable revelations were exacerbated by Sutherland's decision to go public with her findings on October 7, 2015, at a meeting of the Council for Northeast Historical Archaeology in St. John's, Canada, before presenting them to her colleagues for peer review. She may have decided to preempt their traditional suppression of evidence contradicting official opinion by announcing her discovery first to the popular press. If so, she had good reason for resorting to such a maneuver.

Baffin Island's Viking sod-house.

The same stone ruins where Sutherland's team found the Viking artifacts were first excavated during the 1960s by U.S. archaeologist Moreau Maxwell. He may have held back then from identifying the foundations as Norse for fear of outraging mainstream bias against Old World contacts in pre-Columbian America. To be sure, just when Maxwell was initially investigating the Tanfield Valley location, that bias was showing its teeth to Helga and Anne Stine Ingstad. They were virtually alone in trying to make their case for a Viking outpost at L'Anse aux Meadows against the ferocious, personal vindictiveness of fellow archaeologists.

Among the structures both researchers identified was a ship-repair shop, which showed that the site was not some isolated, insignificant settlement, as reductionist scholars decreed, but identified it as a way-station for voyages abroad. This disclosure complimented Norse saga accounts of Leif Eriksson's landing at Helluland—"Stone-Slab Land," his name for Baffin Island—where he explored the shoreline on foot, then sailed south to Vineland—"Wine Land," or possibly "Meadow" or "Pasture Land"—which the Ingstads believed was the settlement at L'Anse aux Meadows.

These considerations suggest that Viking travel throughout North America was far more extensive than conventional archaeologists still argue, and lend credence to related finds, such as the Vineland

Map—its medieval authenticity verified but little publicized six years ago by Copenhagen's Royal Danish Academy of Fine Arts—and Minnesota's Kensington Rune Stone, no less recently confirmed by professional geologist Scott Wolter, as a genuine Norse artifact, likewise from the 14th century.

Travel by longship from Greenland to Baffin Island took only three days, not much of a navigation achievement by Norse standards. Mainstream shock at Sutherland's discoveries there point up the myopic historical vision of her conventional colleagues, for whom the ocean was not an open highway for traveling to distant lands, but an impassable barrier that remained officially unbroken until transgressed by Christopher Columbus. By comparison with passage from Greenland, a voyage from Helluland's Tanfield Valley to Newfoundland's L'Anse aux Meadows—which the sagas relate took place—is more than 325 miles.

Viking colonization of North America's Arctic regions was in part prompted by large populations of walrus and fox. Their ivory and furs were luxury items highly valued by our medieval European ancestors. But significant as the Baffin Island site may be, it is by no means the only one of its kind in the Norse contribution to the prehistory of our continent.

35

A Viking Longship in Ontario

By Jennifer Robbins-Mullin

Petroglyph Provincial Park is located approximately 40 miles north east of Peterborough, Ontario, Canada. In the midst of the Kawartha Lake chain, the site lies among a series of lakes formed after the last glaciated period, some 11,700 years ago. The "petro" (rock) "glyphs" (hieroglyphic symbols) were made public after their discovery in 1954 by members of a geological team scouting the area. They literally stumbled upon the images deep in the thick undergrowth of berry brambles and poison ivy beneath a scattered, reaching canopy of a large forested tract. Petroglyphs had been painstakingly etched into the bald, weathered, pale, marble face of the southeastern extreme of the Canadian Shield, some of the most ancient exposed rock surface on the planet.

The "Shield" is so-called because of its resemblance to a warrior's shield laid out in cross section. It is a flat expanse eroded to a smooth, slightly concave, surface. This is the formation that now lies exposed over much of Canada, and extends due south to underlie the younger soil strata of the north Midwestern United States. It consists of rock dating from the Precambrian Period, or roughly 550 million years of metamorphic basement rock. The Precambrian is the least-understood era of the Earth's long history, spanning from the planet's formation 4 1/2 billion to 570 million years ago, when the fossil record inexplicably exploded and ushered in the Paleozoic Era.

The account of this vast segment of geological time consists mainly of scattered episodes more sketchy and speculative than any other period. Shields and other Precambrian exposures consist of complex metamorphic rocks that in many cases have been intruded by large, igneous bodies. Some rock formations have been folded, faulted, intruded, and metamorphosed many times. Each event has lent more obscurity to the interpretation of earlier events, making Precambrian history difficult in the extreme to decipher.

So it is that the rock emblazoned with the images is no less an enigma than the petroglyphs carved into it. They were probably engraved between 1,000 and 500 years ago, and are Algonquian in origin. Indeed, a present-day Ojibwa First Nation settlement at the Curve Lake Reservation exits nearby. Although it is possible that the residents (or, as the band calls themselves, the Anishinabe, or "original people") at Curve Lake are direct descendants of the rock carvers, it cannot be definitively ascribed to any group more specifically than that of the Algonquian family of languages: Ojibwa, Ottawa, Cree, Algonquin, Nipissing, Blackduck, Selkirk, and possibly including Western Basin.

At the site dubbed *Kino-manage-wap-kong*, or the "rocks that teach," by local natives, nearly 300 glyphs are regarded as "intelligible;" another 600 seem to defy a clear cut or satisfactory definition. In conjunction with the rock carvings, 31 hammer stones made of gneiss were discovered at Peterborough. Gneiss is a much harder rock than marble, but more easily cut into the surface. Understanding of the significance and origins of the petroglyphs, however, is by no means complete. To the Algonquian, Kino-manage-wap-kong was a place where the *manitous* (spirits) resided. Here the shaman came, and through meditation, isolation, and fasting, honed a clear vision, whether in a dreamlike state of near hallucination, or pin-pointing something in daily life and bringing to it clarity of meaning or purpose.

Of course, what may have been crystal clear to the carver of a glyph a thousand years ago has lost nearly all meaning for modern investigators, apart from the lingering existence of the carving itself. This is ironic, because a specific rock was deliberately chosen for the carving, the message, the vision, simply because it does endure. Whereas people and memories fade, the petroglyphs remain true to their testament, immune to at least immediate, progressive decay. But a testament to what?

Some petroglyphs are of the totemic family clan tradition, such as heron or crane, snake, loon, and turtle. Others are spiritual, including pipe, thunderbird, and arrowhead, opening up an interpretation debate. But one rock carving among the hundreds is particularly striking. It depicts a ship like no other vessel incised on the rock face, clearly different from the other carvings of apparently common birch bark canoes. The vessel has what appears to be a rudder and a mast, and, most provocatively of all, a dragon's head on the bow.

David Kelley, septuagenarian professor emeritus of archaeology at the University of Calgary, asserts that the petroglyphs were carved by a "mixed" group of explorers, who might have wandered into the region. They may have traveled separately from Africa, Scandinavia, and the Mediterranean. Kelley's theory that the petroglyphs are the work of Europeans and Africans, and were not carved by the indigenous Algonquian tribes scattered throughout the area, has been met with incredulous disbelief by both First Nation leaders and other archaeologists. Admittedly, Kelley has never seen the Peterborough petroglyphs firsthand, nor even made a committed study of the site's history. Instead, he bases the whole of his argument and opinions on the drawings of the petroglyphs as rendered by anthropologist Joan Vastokas.

Yet, not to be daunted in the face of criticism, Kelley further postulates that the symbols are part of a script called *Tiffinagh*. This ancient written language developed in North Africa, and was later widely utilized by Scandinavians during the Viking Age. The Northmen came into contact with the script during their explorations and trade in and about the Mediterranean. Given the unearthed Viking settlement at L'anse aux Meadows on the northernmost coast of Newfoundland, there could be a shred of credence given to Kelley's theory on the originators of the petroglyphs. How valid the *Tiffinagh* script hypothesis may be hinges greatly on Kelley's belief that most of the carvings at Peterborough can be found within the *Tiffinagh* lexicon. He admits that though some could be attributed to random coincidence, he claims that, "It's highly improbable that a whole complex set of them could have independently arisen in two different places."[1]

Kelley is considered an expert in deciphering Mayan glyphs, and has steadfastly defended his Tiffinagh-Peterborough position, despite heavy dissension from both peers and First Nation Elders. Jay Johnson, Peterborough Petroglyph Park assistant superintendent and full-blooded member of the Curve Lake First Nation, respects Kelley's opinion, but quickly adds that the rock carvings are consistent with Algonquian tradition and mode of representation.

Anthropologist Joan Vastokas of Trent University is not so forgiving or kind in her view of Kelley's interpretation. "All of the images correspond with the pictography of Algonquian-speaking peoples, from the north of the Great Lakes region to the west," states Vastokas, who has extensively researched the site and has written a book about the petroglyphs.[2] But none of the critics has been able to address the mystery of the ship rock carving. This is the fuel for the fiery debate.

If it were not for the rediscovered Viking settlement at L'anse aux Meadows, there would be almost no support for Kelley's theory. Perhaps an Indian who eye-witnessed the arrival of a Viking ship etched the petroglyph, or perhaps the natives invited one of the Norse to carve it himself. Indeed, one cannot look at the petroglyph of the ship and not see a bit more than the shaman in the raft that is described by the park service at the facility.

Why would the "raft" have a keel? And a mast? And sport what appears to be a serpent's head on the bow? These are features unique to the Viking sea-faring tradition. Perhaps further investigation into the matter will yield a definitive answer, but more importantly, the debate is opening the case to Scandinavian contact and cultural exposure at a time long pre-dating the first voyage of Columbus to the New World.

SECTION IX

MAYA

———◆•◆•◆———

Though the Mayas' sudden disappearance about 900 CE is still a mystery, their origins are hardly less inexplicable. But delegates attending an international archaeology conference near the ruins of Copan, a great ceremonial city in the jungles of Honduras, followed trace evidence leading out into both the Atlantic Ocean and Pacific Ocean.

Because Maya Civilization spread over most of Mexico and Central America for more than 1,000 years, it would have been strange indeed if its representatives never ventured above the Rio Grande River. Proof of their penetration into California's Sonora Desert was not unearthed, however, until recently.

36

Atlanto-Lemurian Echoes

By Frank Joseph

Beginning July 12, 2000, the world's leading authorities on Maya civilization convened for a three-day conference near the ancient ceremonial city of Copan. Professional archaeologists and anthropologists from the United States, Mexico, El Salvador, Guatemala, Brazil, Australia, and Japan addressed an audience of 350 academic colleagues and journalists representing Public Broadcasting and *Fodors*, together with *Astronomy*, *Archaeology*, *Ancient American*, the *Los Angeles Times*, and similar publications.

Among the most interesting revelations to be made public for the first time was a new conception of the Maya that is beginning to emerge from literally decades of investigation. It now seems clear that elite bands of statesmen, military leaders, astronomers, physicians, and architects had their headquarters at the huge city of Teotihuacán, some 30 miles north of Mexico City, beginning about 200 BCE. They called themselves not Maya, but *Pilli*, a term equating to "lords," or "professionals." These aristocratic groups set out in fleets of large rafts, mostly traveling Middle America's extensive river systems, to seek out large population concentrations of native peoples.

Once found, as many locals as possible were rounded up, then converted to a bloody religion of human sacrifice of which they (the Pilli) were its high priests. Thus spiritually enslaved, the masses of preliterate Indians, known as *Mayeques*, served as a reliable labor force to build the great Maya ceremonial centers and comprise the armies, which perpetually warred in one metropolis against another. Ruled as they were by their ritual calendar, the Pilli always fixed a precise date for the abandonment of their cities.

The moment they left, the Mayeques invariably reverted to their pre-civilized lifestyles, neglecting the once-great cities to the ravages of time and the jungle. The process was repeated all across the Maya sphere of influence, with ceremonial centers rising and falling. At least part of this story was discovered at Copan itself, where a recently deciphered hieroglyphic inscription describes the city's founder and first ruler, Kinich-Yax-K'uk-Mo, arriving in 465 CE from Teotihuacán, some 800 airline miles away.

Copan was chosen as the location for 2000's international conference, because it is among the most impressive as well as the best-studied Maya sites. Sitting near a well-connected river in the tropical forest, its center alone covers 247 square acres, and Copan's hieroglyphic staircase is the single longest inscription of its kind so far discovered. Copan was built with literally millions of brick-shaped stones that went into the creation of ball-courts, step-pyramids, palaces, temples, and religious monuments. But the city's chief fascination is its collection of large, free-standing statues in the round of outstanding rulers. Here are portrayed the Pilli, the aristocrats who dominated Western Honduras for nearly four centuries.

The visitor is awestruck by their faces, which bear no resemblance to the native Indians, who still inhabit the region. Depicted dynasts are often shown sporting elaborate mustaches among a native people incapable of growing facial hair. Some of the sculpted countenances are unquestionably European; others are Chinese-like. The founder of Copan, Kinich-Yax-K'uk-Mo, appears full-face in a facade on the *Rosalila*, or Pink Pyramid, painstakingly re-created in a full-size plaster replica at the local museum. In restoring its original color scheme, the archaeologists revealed that he wore a blond mustache.

The identifiable portrait of an aged white man is repeated several times throughout the ruins of the ceremonial center. He is invariably shown with traces of facial hair, but appears to have been regarded by the Maya as a deity, not a mere mortal. Interestingly, a number of Copan's sculpted friezes depict him supporting the sky with upraised hands. This is how Atlas was conceived as a titan in Greek myth. He was the eponymous ruler of Atlantis (literally, "Daughter of Atlas") cited in two fourth-century BCE dialogues by the philosopher Plato. The *Timaeus* and *Kritias* tell how Atlantis was the capital-island of a powerful empire, until it was destroyed by a natural catastrophe. During the Atlanteans' imperial heyday, Plato said they colonized parts of the Opposite Continent, and one of their possessions was named after another daughter of Atlas, the Pleiade Maia.

The Copan figure's identification with Atlas is underscored by the Mayas' own account of a Great Flood, from which the ancestors of the Pilli arrived in the distant past. The disaster-migration theme is repeated in the Mayas' *Popol Vuh*, "The Book of Consul."[1] It tells of an ancestral race arriving by sea after the *Hun yecil* (the Aztec *Hun-Esil*, or "Drowning of the Trees"), a catastrophic deluge and earthquake, to build a temple at the Huehuhuetan River in memory of their escape. Known as the "House of Darkness" for its subterranean caverns, it was used as a depository for written records carried from the inundated homeland.

In 1691, just such an underground temple was found near the city of Saconusco, and its precious library burned on orders of church officials as the incomprehensible works of Satan. The *Popol Vuh* goes on to recount that the gods, jealous of the growing power of men over Nature, clouded their wisdom, and the Mayan monarchs had to return the keys of civilization to the great kingdom across the Sunrise Sea.

But Honduras has access to both the Atlantic Ocean and Pacific Ocean, so formative influences from the West should be no less in evidence. Indeed, they are, most graphically in the Asian faces of several portrayed rulers at Copan.

Even more striking is the recent discovery of a previously unknown Mayan hieroglyph. Pronounced "ik," it signifies "the breath of life." The glyph comprises simply a "T" at the center of an island surrounded by two concentric rings. The discovery of this image is particularly remarkable, because it was described more than 80 years ago by James Churchward.

He said it was shown to him as a young British officer serving in India by the priest of a Hindu monastery, where he learned that the T-sign was the most important emblem for the Pacific Civilization of Mu before its destruction by cataclysm. According to Churchward, the glyph represented Mu itself. Could the appearance of the "T" in glyph at Copan have been a memorial to culture-bearers from the lost Motherland of the Pacific?

Yet another overseas symbol may still be seen at the Honduran ceremonial center. On the left flank of one of its statues portraying a prominent ruler is the unmistakable representation of the ancient Egyptian sign of protection, known as the Sa. It was modeled after a stylized life preserver made of papyrus and worn by sailors, much as life vests are used today. The appearance of this sacred Egyptian symbol on one of the statuary centerpieces of Copan indicates an important sea-borne influence from the Old World at work among the Maya. None of these self-evident themes from overseas were mentioned at the conference, where only conventional scholars, who regard any hint of outside forces in pre-Columbian America as the worst heresy, were allowed to speak.

The Mayan tau glyph for "breath," or "breath of life," on a temple wall at Copan.

Despite their inter-cultural myopia, the Establishment archaeologists have made some very dramatic finds of their own in recent years.

For example, they discovered that the enormous ceremonial center of Copan sits over no less than four different levels of subterranean cities, buried each on top of themselves, several hundred feet beneath the surface. Visitors are allowed entrance to a series of tunnels exposing one of these entombed cities. The amount of human labor necessary to first build and then bury the four strata, all by hand, without the luxury of modern machinery, and under the oppressive conditions of a tropical forest, staggers the imagination. Archaeologists have also gone far in deciphering the Mayan inscriptions. Their translations have utterly shattered previously held conceptions, which depicted the Mayas as a gentle people of astronomers and architects peacefully pursuing the arts and sciences. The hieroglyphs paint a far different picture of incessant warfare between rival cities and the worst excesses of ritualized torture.

One incident tells of a captured ruler whose knuckles on both hands were broken and his head scalped before his belly was slit open and a fire kindled inside it. Decapitation for the captains of victorious ball teams and removing the heart from living victims were common sights at Copan during its Classic Phase, from the fifth to ninth centuries CE. For more than a century, archaeologists could not find any remains of military defenses at the Mayas' cities, an oversight that contributed to false interpretations of the Maya as a non-belligerent race. Beginning in the 1990s, however, satellite surveys using high-resolution and infrared photography began detecting the outline of walls around more and more of the ancient ceremonial centers.

Previously gone unnoticed because they had been laid out far beyond the cities themselves, the fortifications were usually stockades of wooden posts covered with a white-lime plaster. They had no gates, but access was through a space or gap formed by the overlapping of one wall by another. The Maya ramparts were thus precisely the same as walls raised at Cahokia, in western Illinois, and Aztalan, in southern Wisconsin, during the 10th and 13th centuries CE, respectively. They support the conclusions of some investigators, who have long contended that these Middle Western ceremonial sites were built by Maya immigrants after the contemporary collapse of their civilization in Yucatan and Central America. Honduras' First Copan Congress brought many new discoveries to light. They illuminate the dark world of the Maya as never before, revealing a people of great cultural achievement contrasted by equally great cruelty. Perhaps they were a product of their environment—the pitiless jungle, where violence is commonplace—and of their mixed, contrasting heritage from different parts of the world.

37

Mesoamericans in California

By Andrew E. Rothovious

A feature article in the *Desert Sun* tells of "brittle pieces of stone technology dating back twelve thousand years,"[1] spread over a 1,100-square-mile U.S. Marines' training facility in California's Mojave Desert. About half of more than 2,000 archaeological sites at the Twenty-Nine Palms Air Ground Combat Center have been surveyed. But the abundance of prehistoric materials so far excavated is already enough to fill a museum at the base. So far, *more than 300,000* of them have been collected, cataloged, and housed at the only facility of its kind, known as the Marine Corps Archeology and Paleontology Curation Center at the combat center.

These objects mostly comprise projectile points, milling slabs and rock art panels, some unique to the region. Although most of them belong to the Serrano Culture of hunter-gatherers that arrived in Southern California about 2,500 years ago, charred bits of ancient mesquite pods (used in the manufacture of flour), plus stone tool fragments known as *lithic scatters*, together with pictographs and rock

Twenty-Nine Palms petroglyph.

drawings found in the immediate vicinity of Dead Man Lake, pre-date the Serrano by 75 centuries at least.

They roughly date to the end of the last glacial epoch, as indicated by the inclusion among the human items of bones from extinct animals, such as those that belonged to mastodons and dwarf horses. Today's tribes of Cahuilla are descendants of the Serrano (Spanish for "highlanders" or "Mountaineers"), who still maintain a tribal existence of sorts. Nearby quarries still bear the marks prehistoric men left in their labors at removing stone for arrowheads, hammers, and defleshers. All the Twenty-Nine Palms' artifacts owe their state of preservation to an ancient lava flow more than a mile long and many football fields wide. It blanketed the area with blackish, odd-shaped volcanic rock, which was long ago baked into the ground under millennia of hot, summer suns, resulting in a hardened surface. The man-made items lie atop this "desert pavement" subsequently covered by natural deposition. Stenciled handprints in the area are identical to contemporaneous counterparts found on the subterranean walls of France and Spain, where they are associated with Magdalenian cave artists of the European ice age.

"A few of the images are pictographs," Denise Goolsby told the *Desert Sun* newspaper, "designs that were painted with pigments made from plants and minerals. This early art form had a spiritual basis."

"Petroglyphs mark portals," stated John Hale, archeologist for the National Resources and Environment Affairs Division at the combat center. "That's where the shaman saw the portal into the next world, the spirit world."

"One of the designs appeared to be Mayan-inspired," Goolsby said, a heretical observation for conventional scientists convinced the Maya never traveled outside their Yucatan homelands. Yet, official certainty is contradicted by existence of Twenty-Nine Palms' ancient rock art. Alternative scholars have, in recent years, been joined by every-growing numbers of formerly mainstream archaeologists in seriously entertaining unorthodox suspicions to the effect that the Magdalenians, and even their predecessors, the Solutreans, did, in fact, sail along the edge of North Atlantic pack ice to become the first human arrivals on our Continent. The Solutreans and Magdalenians were Ice Age cave painters who inhabited Western Europe, respectively, from circa 21,000 to 17,000 Years Before Present, and from 17,000 to 12,000 Y.B.P. The shores of Dead Man Lake appear to have been among their settlements in southern California.

Goolsby couldn't help but notice a sharp contrast between the military training grounds, where the artifacts of a bygone culture are being found, with the same area U.S. Marines are actively training Afghanistan and Iraqi soldiers for war in the Middle East: "Ironically, no prehistoric battle-related objects have been uncovered on the sprawling training grounds. All the groups living in the area at the time, many millennia ago, may have managed to coexist in peace."

"We have no evidence of warfare at all," Hale agreed to the sound of U.S. Marine machine-gun fire.

SECTION X

PRE-COLUMBIAN ASIANS

———•◆•———

Bruce Cunningham travels extensively throughout Southeast Asia, Indonesia, and the Philippines, exploring obscure but significant archaeological sites, such as the Cambodian ruins described here. He is the director of Ancient Mysteries International, which stages alternative science conferences in the United States, leads tours to lost cities across the Orient, publishes books devoted to their investigation, and hosts an online magazine, *Advanced Archaeology Review.*

Jon R. Haskell is the author of *The Fenghuang and Dragon Motifs in North America: A New Perspective of Western Hemisphere Pre-Columbian History* (Parson's Porch & Co., 2015). According to a recent five-star review, "Jon Haskel is known for his detailed research with Mesoamerican Culture."

38

Cambodia's Machu Picchu

By Bruce Cunningham

Ancient American readers are familiar with Machu Picchu, the 14th-century Lost City of the Incas situated on a Peruvian mountain ridge nearly 8,000 feet above sea level. But they are probably unaware that its counterpart has been standing at least as long on the other side of the world in northern Cambodia.

It was in that far-off land that Ancient Mysteries International fielded the first visit of its kind to the ancient temples of Angkor. Our tour included Vedic specialist Stephen Knapp, guest Paul Reno, my wife, Dixie, and myself. We spent several days exploring Angkor Wat, Angkor Thom, Bayan, and numerous other Khmer temples in the Angkor Archaeological Park near Siem Reap.

Our exploration of these marvelous sites coincided with the spring equinox, the dawning of which we witnessed at Angkor Wat on the morning of March 21st. We were joined by hundreds of other visitors waiting for the Sun to appear over the temple, as though anticipating the appearance of God. By 9:00 on the morning of March 24th, we were driving through the Cambodian countryside, stopping only once in a small town for a snack break at a Westernized convenience store. Approaching the vicinity of our destination, we saw a strange community of apparently new houses; all were on stilts, each building surrounded by about 1 acre of open land. Dixie mentioned that they resembled homes in a subdivision.

We found out later that they were accommodations for infantry, who occupied Preah Vihear in substantial numbers and embedded defensive bunkers at the archaeological site, which, they believed, the Thais wanted to recover by force.

As we arrived, the soldiers who were staging warlike exercises at the temple turned us back, so we drove to the nearby visitor center. There, we were informed that, regardless of the ongoing military situation, a 100-cc motorcycle could take us one at a time to the rear of the temple, but Stephen wanted nothing to do with such an uncertain mode of transportation, having been the veteran of too many similar experiences in India.

Instead, we negotiated for the use of a small pickup truck and piled into the back to at last begin our journey up the mountain. The road beneath us was paved, but angled with a 15-percent or more grade, against which our far-from-luxurious vehicle audibly strained, and I shuddered to think of our return trip down this same precipitous slope. Eventually, the truck stopped in a field, and our driver announced that we were on our own from then on and had to walk the rest of the way to the temple complex, which was utterly deserted save for just two other tourists. The walkway leading to it appeared to be made of granite and not composed of the various types of stone, such as sandstone, found in the Angkor temples. We finally arrived at the bottom temple, where we were treated to spectacular mountain vistas of both Thailand and Laos. I was reminded of the Verde Valley in Arizona's Sedona region.

A granite (?) walkway meandered down into Thailand, then rose to what appeared to be many more stone structures on the upward levels. The first temple we encountered appeared to have been bombed during the Indo-China wars or during the tragic times of the Khmer Rouge in the 1970s. Walking up to the next temple, the stones in the walkway were becoming exceptionally massive, weighing many tons apiece. In this they were reminiscent of those common at Angkor Wat, except the examples here had been organized into an ascending grade leading to more buildings at varying levels.

Walls of the second temple we visited were made of massive granite blocks, cyclopean in style, virtually identical to those found among the pre-Inca sites of far-off Peru. This Cambodian complex gave every indication of having been built much earlier—maybe thousands of years older—than the structures at Angkor Wat, which dated to the early 12th century. Stephen agreed, in light of his exploration of many prehistoric temples in India.

Could this site have possibly been made by the same culture-bearers responsible for the Inca or even pre-Inca cities of South America? Could Preah Vihear be the Machu Picchu of Southeast Asia? Their similar mountain setting, shared cyclopean masonry, and contemporaneity suggest at least as much. Indeed, Cambodia's ancient ceremonial center at the nebulous Thai border appears to be nothing more than another Angkor-style temple complex, but uniquely situated high in the mountains. It also shares a common time period with Angkor Wat, both of which were allegedly raised by the prehistoric Khmers. Preah Vihear evidences the same basic design, but is far more megalithic.

Continuing our close scrutiny of the site, I focused my gaze on the top of a small temple at a pair of blocks weighing more than 100 tons, far greater than the heaviest stones that went into Angkor Wat. The prodigious use of stone here might even rival that of Angkor Wat itself, which is known to have tonnage surpassing Egypt's Great Pyramid. Sculpted symbolism throughout Preah Vihear, though Vedic, differed in style and execution from the religious imagery of Angkor Wat and other related locations. These and other similarities with and differences from Angkor Wat and the distant Machu Picchu imply that Preah Vihear may have been a crossroads, a mingling of Southeast Asian and South American Andean influences in Cambodia during unrecorded history.

39

Ancient Chinese Sword Found in Georgia

By Jon R. Haskell

During July 2014, an avocational surface collector chanced across a partially exposed sword mostly concealed behind roots protruding from the eroded bank of a small stream in Georgia. The foot-long object, perhaps a one-of-a-kind discovery in North America, was carved from lizardite, a greenish, serpentine rock found in Asia and the Americas. Attempts at determining when the soil at the extraction site was last exposed to sunlight with thermo-luminescent testing procedures were thwarted because researchers determined the soil had been disturbed. There remains a small section of an unknown, stranded material still attached to the sword, which may be suitable for radiocarbon dating, together with select areas of surface accretions that may produce helpful information.

Less uncertain are the find's shape and many symbolic images, which resemble jade artifacts from the Xia (2070 BCE–1600 BCE), Shang

(1600 BCE–1046 BCE) and Zhou Dynasties (1046 BCE–256 BCE). The Georgia sword's dragon figure spanning a portion at the top of the blade is typically Shang, as is the feathered crown. Its grotesque face-mask of Taotie on the guard and handle of the sword, first appears during the Liangzhu culture (3400 BCE–2250 BCE) but it is more commonly found during the Shang and Zhou periods. The Taotie, "a gluttonous ogre-mask," is a motif commonly found on Chinese ritual articles, typically consisting of a zoomorphic mask, described as being frontal, bilaterally symmetrical, with a pair of raised eyes and no lower jaw area.

The dominant presence on the Georgia piece of Shang Era diagnostics, plus the similarity of the Taotie to depictions of the Mesoamerican Olmec were-Jaguar suggest a time frame for the sword's manufacture and when it arrived in the Peach State.

The similarity of Chinese-Olmec mythology and symbolism has been the subject of scholarly debate for more than 100 years. It is perhaps no coincidence that Mexico's Olmec culture appears about 1500 BCE during the beginning of China's Shang Dynasty. It marked the beginning of the Chinese Bronze Age, resulting in ornate metalwork, including chariots and weaponry. The first Chinese script appears at this time, along with extensive public works projects, all indicators of a sophisticated and advanced culture.

It was also a time in Chinese culture when jade was more valuable than gold to become the material of choice for exquisitely formed ceremonial goods. Likewise with the Olmec elite, who mined jade deposits

Seven views of the Chinese sword found in Georgia.

located in Honduras and Guatemala. Again, it may not be coincidental that the Olmec, during their Middle Formative period (900 BCE–300 BCE), mastered the difficulties of shaping and drilling jade (a stone so hard that it cannot be worked with steel tools), with abrasive materials into small, ornamental, and votive pieces. Chinese-Olmec art parallels are quite telling. The likely introduction of Chinese concepts concerning rulership, social stratification, together with religion and religious symbolism could have altered the cultural destiny and mythological beliefs of the Olmec and later Mesoamerican groups, perhaps even Plains Indians residing north of the Rio Grande River.

But how did the sword get to Georgia?

About 900 BCE, newly formed Olmec cultural attributes started to spread throughout east coastal Mexico. There is considerable literature indicating that they served as a foundation for other contemporaneous and subsequent cultural groups, such as the Maya. Though modified by other groups to meet local needs and with changes over time, the Olmecs' basic concepts persisted into the 16th-century Conquest Period. Interestingly, some of these ancient concepts, such as those related to the planting of maize, are still practiced today with certain Mesoamerican indigenous groups. It is generally believed this dispersal was a byproduct of the Olmec land and coastal maritime trade routes transporting basic and exotic trade goods.

An intriguing element to this cultural phenomenon, and why it is referenced, is that it started about 900 BCE, which, as mentioned previously, is just when the Olmec started making jade ceremonial objects. Examples illustrating the geographic extent of this cultural diffusion were flat and cylindrical printing seals, a technology that first appeared in the Mesoamerican artifact record with the Olmec. In China, printing seals first materialized at the same time, during the Zhou dynasty. By 800 BCE, the seals were being used throughout northern South America, some 1,700 miles south from the Olmec heartland, and an equal distance north to the Adena Culture (1000 BCE–100 CE), in the upper Ohio River Valley.

Not only did this printing technology arrive there, but so did Mesoamerican art. In an unpublished research project on the Adena tablet, this author found stylistic duplicates of the unique center vertical element representing the World Tree at the Lake Chalco region south of what is now Mexico City and at Veracruz on the Gulf coast.

Arrival of seals at the beginning of the transformational mound build-ing Adena culture, along with other evidence too numerous to include here, indicates that an influential Mesoamerican group entered the region and impacted the cultural destiny of the local population.

Returning to Georgia: In 1685, Charles de Rochefort, in his chroni-cles regarding the Apalachites, who occupied the lands of southeastern America during the 17th century, writes:

> These Apalachites boast that they had propagated certain colo-nies a great way into Mexico: And they show to this day a great road by land, by which they affirm that their forces march'd into those parts. The inhabitants of the country, upon their arrival, gave them the name of *Tlatuici*, which signifies "Mountaineers," or "High-Landers." . . . This people [Apalachites] have a com-munication with the sea of the Great Gulf of Mexico, or New Spain, by means of a river . . . the Spaniards have called this River *Riu del Spirito Santo*" [the Mississippi River].[1]

Though Rochefort's observations post-date the Conquest Period, his observations highlight a geographic fact often overlooked or mini-mized in North American history. The various cultures occupying the lands of Georgia and other states fronting the Gulf of Mexico, along with the Caribbean Islands, Mexico, and South America, were in a circum-Caribbean region where everyone knew their neighbors. One can rea-sonably assume this is the reason why ball courts and rubber balls are found in the Caribbean Islands, as well as mainland Mesoameric

The Olmec and Maya also operated fleets of large, ocean-canoes and rafts plying the Gulf region's coastal waters, while i session of a logistical organization to supply the basic needs of urban areas with population densities equal to modern, major ci example, salt, a basic requirement for survival in the tropics and eded in countless tons per month, was shipped from salt-producing facili-ties in the Yucatan to known river ports stretching from the Honduran Moskito Coast to Tampico, Mexico.

Other than being a wet and scary experience, with no life preserv-ers in rough seas off the Moskito Coast, I can personally attest based on multiple trips, the dugout log design works very well. Even today, with the exception of Yamaha outboard motors, these vessels, which have not changed in manufacture or design since the Maya, still transport tons of stacked, 50-gallon barrels of gasoline, foodstuffs, and people into the Honduran interior.

In the Greater Antilles, the impressive Taino culture, which migrated from Venezuela starting about 400 BCE, and the Caribe, who also migrated from South America, were equally adept at traversing the waters of the Gulf of Mexico. Christopher Columbus makes numerous entries in his log of large Taino canoes, measuring approximately 40 to 79 feet in length, ladened with trade goods and passengers. More noteworthy, his log entries indicate that the Taino knew of the distant Calusa in Florida and the Maya at Yucatan.

From all of this, it seems apparent that circum-Caribbean region cultures, even in more ancient times, were connected by water and land routes, thereby furnishing us a possible explanation for the arrival of the Lizardite sword and two Olmec-style pendants in Georgia. The question naturally arises: Why would anyone tote around a votive sword—which, by definition, is an object expressing a religious vow, wish, or desire, offered or performed as an expression of thanks or devotion to God—if they were not Chinese. Interestingly, this sword is not the only diagnostic Chinese artifact found nearby.

According to Siu-Leung Lee, PhD, two other ancient Chinese artifacts have been recently found within a two-hour drive of the Lizardite sword's place of discovery. Though some distance from Georgia in the American Southwest, one also needs to consider the surprising amount of Chinese artifacts found in that region. Most noteworthy is Chinese script encountered in New Mexico, dated to 1046 BCE–475 BCE.

About 90 years before Columbus first sailed into Caribbean waters aboard his 58-foot-long, Italian, three-masted carrack, the Ming Chinese dispatched flotillas under the command of Admiral Zheng He in multiple voyages to territories around the Indian Ocean for the acquisition of exotic items and materials.

His first expedition consisted of approximately 185 vessels, some of them more than 500 feet long, weighing 30,000 tons each. Such information cannot prove Georgia's serpentine sword is authentically ancient Chinese, but it does provide some supporting context for its possible provenance in pre-Columbian times. If indisputable proof is still lacking, the anomalous find urges its further study and testing.

SECTION XI

UPDATES

—•◆•—

In New Page Books' first *Ancient American* anthology (*Discovering the Mysteries of Ancient America*, 2006), Chapter 5 described Rhode Island's Newport Tower, dismissed by conventional scholars as a mill owned by Benedict Arnold, but always suspected as having been built by Vikings or Knights Templar previous to the arch-traitor's ownership of it. For example, the structure and its presumed Norse origins were together dramatized in Henry Wadsworth Longfellow's *The Skeleton in Armor*:

> Three weeks we westward bore.
> And when the storm was o'er,
> Cloud-like we saw the shore
> Stretching to leeward.
> There for my lady's bower
> Built I the lofty tower,
> Which, to this very hour,
> Stands looking seaward.[1]

Only now, however, has the old edifice been sufficiently pulled apart (figuratively speaking, that is!) by Gunnar Thompson, PhD, to settle a centuries-long debate concerning the actual identity of its builders. Recognized as perhaps the foremost authority on not only the Newport Tower, but cultural diffusion in general, he was invited by directors of the Library of Congress to give a May 2005 presentation about Marco

Polo's west coast voyages. The following March, Dr. Thompson traveled to Beijing, where he received China's Zheng He Trophy.

Rick Osmon returns with a counter-review of *The Lost Civilizations of North America,* winner of "The Best Multicultural Documentary Award" at 2010's International Cherokee Film Festival, but deplored by mainstream critics for contradicting their Columbus-Was-First doctrine.

Chapter 4 in the second volume of our collected articles told of apparent Dynastic Egyptian influences at work in the vastness of Arizona's Grand Canyon. Since the 2009 publication of *Unearthing Ancient America,* new evidence has surfaced, lending that earlier supposition new credibility. So too, prospects for King Arthur's arrival on North American shores during the first half the sixth century CE, as postulated in *Discovering the Mysteries of Ancient America,* are re-examined in the light of fresh evidence discovered by Dr. Thompson.

40

Rhode Island's 14th-Century Tower

By Gunnar Thompson, PhD

At some distant and controversial point in Newport's past, a team of experienced stone builders from the British Isles constructed a round tower in the scenic preserve known today as Touro Park. Were these renegade artisans the same Colonial philosophers who bequeathed to Rhode Island a passion for freedom of religion and justice? Were they a band of marooned Templar Masons from 14th-century Scotland? Or were they just a random gang of professional handymen Governor Benedict Arnold selected to build a more-durable stone mill as replacement for a wooden windmill that blew down in the furious Windstorm of 1673? Until now, most historians have favored the "Windmill Theory." But that enduring explanation is about to be replaced by one better suited to the facts.

In April 2014, an anonymous patron of the arts commissioned archaeologists and historians at the New World Discovery Institute to

The controversial tower.

take a fresh look at the evidence. Researchers there were asked to determine if it was possible to reconstruct a new scenario of what really happened during those murky eons long ago when the City of Newport began to rise up from the marshes along Narragansett Bay. We are pleased to announce that we have found evidence of a previously unrecognized stone structure that was hidden away for many centuries beneath the skirts and girdle of an old Colonial mansion.

Our investigation has been undertaken with the invaluable assistance of Jennifer Robinson at the Newport Historical Society and Museum, located on Touro Street—not far from the spectacular and mysterious Old Stone Tower, or, as some say, "the Old Stone Mill." Ms. Robinson's familiarity with the Museum's photographic archives enabled her to pinpoint key evidence from thousands of images, from which she identified a series of snapshots dated to 1898. They were taken by a professional photographer intrigued by the unusually grandiose stone and brick "chimney structure" that emerged from behind a cloak of plaster and lath removed when the dilapidated Sueton Grant

House was demolished and hauled away to the city dump. This incidental and fortuitous photo shoot—more than 115 years ago—was pivotal to our investigation. It was already determined by Norman Isham's research in 1895 that the same masons who built the Old Stone Tower also built the chimney foundation in the Grant House. If we could identify new clues from these old photographs, then there was a chance we could unlock the secrets to a mystery that has endured for several hundred years: Who built the Tower? It is our country's oldest monumental building erected by European masons. But whether it was built before or after the Columbus Voyage of 1492 is of pivotal importance to our understanding of American history. Hence, the origin of the Newport Tower is an enduring dilemma for historians.

It is a circular structure of stone masonry erected above an arcade level consisting of eight stone pillars. Approximate height is 28 feet (about 8.5 meters); the outside diameter varies from about 24 to 25 feet (7.3 meters); the wall thickness is about 3 feet thick (.91 meters). These walls are unusually wide for Colonial structures, and they constitute an enormous weight carried by so few columns. Part of the structure includes buried foundation stones that lie beneath each of its eight pillars. Approximate weight is about 40 tons of stone, with an additional five to eight tons of cement. Chemical testing and magnification of surface material indicates that lime used in making the mortar was obtained from burned or roasted oyster shells. This was a common source for mortar in most Colonial construction during the early 17th century, as the shells were readily available at waste dumps in nearby Native villages.

Remains of a small, 6-foot-diameter lime-kiln have been excavated at the Jamestown archaeological site in Virginia dating to the early 1600s. A kiln of this size was sufficient for producing about four 60-pound bags of lime for enough mortar (mixed with sand) to build several small ovens or a basic house chimney. However, typical kilns used by early European settlers in the 17th century were entirely inadequate for the demands of Rhode Island's Old Stone Tower. Erecting the 40-ton-plus stone structure would have required the operation of an industrial-grade lime-kiln, unknown in the state at the time.

One of Newport history's glaring problems has always been the total absence of remains from a suitable lime-kiln that would have been up to the task of providing lime mortar sufficient for building the Tower when it was supposedly erected in 1673. By then, most of lime used in

making mortar for chimney construction came from outside the community, possibly from industrial kilns operated at Providence or New
Holland (later New York City).

Furthermore, the imported lime was not made of oyster shells, but
from roasting crushed limestone (today's principal source of Portland
cement). Small, oyster-shell kilns are difficult to find in the archaeological record, because most of their small stones were reused in chimneys.
On the other hand, it is incredibly unlikely that residents of Newport
during the mid-to-late 17th century would have even used oyster-shell
lime mortar, when a supply of cheap limestone cement was readily available by ship from nearby sources.

A clue was identified in one of the 1898 Sueton Grant House demoli-
tion photographs (P9745) from the N.H.S. [Newport Historical Society]
Archive. The image shows what appears to be a medieval-style founda-
tion arch beneath the ground-floor Colonial fireplace and chimney.
This incredible photo, showing a 14th-century medieval arch under a
Colonial fireplace (built about 1650) was first published by Antoinette
Downing and Vincent Scully.

Two rectangular openings or "vents" are clearly visible right above
the medieval arch. Vents of this type were common features of medieval lime kilns in the British Isles, although they were quite rare in
Colonial and post-Colonial kilns of New England. This eclectic style of
masonry in the foundation arch, featuring a triangular keystone in the
center, was characteristic of Norman-Scottish and Irish construction in
the British Isles during the 14th century. Use of oyster-shell lime cement
was also common at the same time in Norman-Scottish construction.

As Norman Isham noted in 1895, the style of arches and composition of mortar used in the Grant House and the Old Stone Tower
are identical. Thus, we are confident in concluding that the masons
who built both structures were the same workers, and both were constructed at an identical point in time. The enduring notion among
historians that the Old Stone Tower was built in 1673—during the
Colonial era—has rested almost entirely upon a brief and casual mention in 1675's last will of Benedict Arnold to the effect that he owned
the "stone-built windmill."

He certainly owned the structure, as it was situated on his property,
and regarded the Tower as a "windmill." Indeed, the building was similar in size and shape to common, stone-built windmills in England and

Sueton Grant House, Newport
A. Colonial ground floor
B. Medieval foundation

Holland. These mills generally used a rotating turret top that housed
the wind sails (or propeller) operating the gearbox and grindstone.
However, rotating tops required special tracks and gears not available
in New England until the beginning of the 18th century.

Almost-identical masonry to that used in building the Old Stone
Tower can be seen in 14th-century Norman-Scottish ruins of the Orkney
Islands and at Greenland's Scottish-built Hvalsey Church. However, aside
from the two contemporaneous buildings at Newport—using masonry
with triangular keystones—the eclectic style with accordion-shaped
arches and triangular keystones was entirely unknown in New England
Colonial architecture. This is most certainly an intrusive design feature in Newport architecture during the 17th century. More surprises
awaited us as we examined other photographs provided by the N.H.S.
Archive Service. They showed three similar arches in the foundation of
the Sueton Grant House! Two of these had rectangular vents of the sort
found among similar lime kilns in ruins dating to the medieval British
Isles (11th to 14th centuries). Furthermore, the three foundation
arches in the Grant House were built as separate structures, although

they abutted against each other at their ends. This method of construction was not commonly encountered in the foundations designed for houses and chimneys. House foundations are typically interconnected along the entire perimeter of the superstructure they are intended to support.

However, separation of the three sections used for a kiln would not impair the function of burning or cooking oyster shells, and the presence of cracks between the three units could be explained as providing expansion-and-contraction joints in a structure that had to allow for frequent and considerable heat and cooling. An industrial kiln of this sort functioned a lot like a blast furnace: The oyster shells were baked by a continuous blast of hot air and flames over a period of three consecutive days. The Newport lime-kiln was probably fired by coal (obtained either locally or imported from Fife or Baffin Island). A single firing of oyster shells would produce several thousand pounds of lime. Thus, we have identified evidence of a structure at Newport that was suitable for "milling" adequate amounts of lime needed to build the Old Stone Tower.

Extensive Internet research regarding lime-kilns, masonry styles, and arches in Colonial America and Medieval Europe confirms the probable time of construction for the Old Stone Tower during the late 14th century. The masons were most likely Norman-Scottish—that is, they were trained in masonry traditions of Northern Scotland, at the time still regarded as a Nordic province. Between 1365 and 1410, agents of Denmark and the Kalmar Union were assisting refugees from the Eastern Settlement of Greenland.

The Settlement was a western province of Norway, and hence also of the Kalmar Union consisting of Denmark, Sweden, Norway, and the western province of Landanu, the "New Land." The Queen-Regent, Margaret Atterdag, and her successor, Erik of Pomerania, were deeply concerned about the welfare of their distant Christian subjects, whose care and protection were under the direct responsibility of the earl of the Orkney Islands, Prince Henry Sinclair. About 4,000 farmers were desperate to escape from the Arctic onslaught of the Little Ice Age then overtaking Europe.

As they had no suitable ocean-going vessels for carrying their belongings to new homes in the southern territories along the Eastern Seaboard, they were entirely dependent upon Norman-Scottish merchants or Hanseatic German sea captains for ferry service. As the owner of a merchant shipping company, Sinclair was in a position to provide ferry service, which was probably offered on the condition that farmers pay for their transport by turning over a portion of future earnings from goods—such as stockfish and turkey corn—produced for the markets of North European ports.

In fact, Mercator himself identified Narragansett Bay as the principal destination of ancient mariners and explorers. His world map in 1569 features a distinctive, south-facing bay directly west of England. The name he gave for the trading metropolis was Norombega. In Colonial times, this seafaring town became known as Newport, Rhode Island. A red dot placed beside the city of Norombega marked it as one of the eight most important cities along the Eastern seaboard. Practically everybody knew where it was and how to get there. Presumptions that Mercator's maps were "mythical in design" are entirely erroneous, if only because he was the leading scientific geographer of his age, and perhaps the greatest geographer who ever lived.

Centuries later, Newport's Nathan Isham was well aware of the close association between the Grant House on Thames Street and the Old Stone Tower in Touro Park. As a professor of architecture at Brown University, it was Isham's business to explore, uncover, and document the evolution of Colonial buildings in New England. While thus engaged in 1895, he entered the cramped cellar of the abandoned Grant House with a lantern. He was able to see the ancient vault beneath the Colonial brick chimney. It was made from slender stones of metamorphic rocks called *gneiss*.

They had been assembled in a very peculiar, fanlike manner with narrow stones of various lengths placed side-by-side. The "keystone" upon which all the other stones depended for stability was extremely bizarre. It was shaped in the form of a triangle. Isham knew that all the other foundation vaults he had seen in Colonial houses were made from standardized bricks specially designed to form perfect Romanesque arcs. However, the stone-built vault of Sueton Grant's house was badly sagging, due in part to the instability of the triangular keystone and the massive weight from the Colonial brick chimney.

In order to verify his suspicions that the masons who built Grant's house and those who built the Stone Tower were the same, Isham took samples of mortar from both structures. He also obtained a sample from the "end-wall" of the Benedict Arnold House. This end-wall had the same kind of eclectic masonry style that characterized the Old Stone Tower. Chemical analysis indicated that all of Isham's samples had the identical composition of seashell lime and sand. Many scholars believed this scientific test proved the Stone Tower was a Colonial structure dating to the 17th century.

Naturally, Viking enthusiasts disagreed with the prevailing belief among certified historians. A Swedish architectural historian, Oscar Montelius, insisted that the Tower was a 12th-century Norse church or baptistery. Danish archeologist Carl C. Rafn (1837) concurred. Similar churches, often called "Crusader Temples," were constructed by knights who returned to Europe with battle scars and gallant tales of glorious combat from the First Crusade.

More recently, Scott Wolter has identified the "Hooked-X" symbol on rune stones from Narragansett Bay to Maine. William Penhallow (New England Antiquities Research Association) noted that the Old Stone Tower was used as an observatory, and James Whittall (Early Sites Research Society) noted that the Tower was linked to a 1398 expedition by Prince Henry Sinclair, Earl of Orkney. Architectural historians Antoinette Downing and Vincent Scully acknowledged that masons who built the Old Stone Tower depended on a construction technology with roots in medieval Europe. However, they stressed that Isham's test and clues from the historical record were sufficient to identify the Tower as being "a Colonial windmill."[1]

As evidence that the Old Stone Tower didn't exist prior to 1673, Downing and Scully noted that the street passing by the hillside lot was not called "Mill Street" by local residents. Indeed, two historical documents (circa 1673) refer to the nearby street as "Carr's Lane" and "the way past Robert Griffin's House." Presumably, "Mill Street" was named right after Benedict Arnold supposedly built the "mill."

That's another problem with Downing's theory.

A British Admiralty Map of 1777 identified the roadway beside the Old Stone Tower as "Banister Street." Charles Blascowitz, the British cartographer who made the map, drew an unidentified circle to show precisely where the Old Stone Tower is located. He didn't endorse the strange notion that the enigmatic structure was a windmill. Elsewhere on his map, he indicated locations of six windmills. The road that is today called "Mill Street" was actually indicated on a Newport City map by Henry Bull in 1641. This map was drawn a decade before Arnold moved into town.

On Bull's map, the street goes all the way uphill for a quarter mile right past the site where the Old Stone Tower is located. Evidently, there was no functioning mill on the hill, so the name of the roadway east of Thames Street was problematical until after the city started issuing official maps. The impression we get from Newport City maps (from the Newport Historical Society Archives) leaves us with the principal north-south "Main Street" already in place when English renegades from Providence arrived to establish Newport by 1639.

Abandoned stone foundations might have been the legacy of unknown settlers who built the earliest log cabins along the waterfront street. Evidently, these early settlers constructed a roadway up the hill to the location where they built the Old Stone Tower. Indian wars, climate change, or disease led to abandonment of the early settlement. New English colonists identified the Old Stone Tower as a windmill because that was the only plausible term they could imagine. It certainly wasn't a church, because Colonial churches were always whitewashed wooden buildings with bells and steeples.

At a time when most medieval masons were building with uniform, polished (or "dressed") stone blocks, Scandinavians preferred "eclectic masonry." Builders assembled irregular shapes and sizes of stones that were fitted together in complex puzzles of stonework. Fanlike archways consisted of long, slender stones of irregular sizes. James Whittall (1932–1998), archaeological department director of the New England Antiquities Research Association (Rhode Island), concluded that Norse masons occasionally used "triangular" keystones in arches. These were of a signatory or symbolic nature suggesting reverence for the Divine Mother or the Divine Triad. Whittall noted two examples known from 12th-century masonry at the Orkney Islands and Shetlands, three examples in the Scottish Western Isles, two in Iceland, and two in Greenland. Triangular keystones were likewise identified on a window and on a vault inside the Newport Tower.

The foundation level of masonry beneath Sueton Grant's house, as mentioned above, included three vaults with triangular keystones. This type of keystone, combined with the fan-like eclectic stone arch, can be regarded as an architectural "fingerprint" of medieval Scandinavian masons. The triangular shape has major limitations, however. It is a suitable device only when the span is short, such as a narrow doorway or window. Use in building long spans, such as those encountered above fireplaces, was possible only when the weight above the span was very minimal.

In the Grant House foundation, where medieval masonry was situated beneath a huge Colonial chimney structure, we see evidence of a vault being pushed downward and the sides outward due to increased weight of later additions to the superstructure. Besides the obvious break between the eclectic medieval stone masonry of the foundation and the "Classical" or Colonial nature of the standardized bricks used in the superstructure, we can ascertain the presence of two distinct masonry styles: The medieval arch was never intended to uphold the weight of the later Colonial addition.

Masons who built the medieval structures were very cognizant of weight limits corresponding to foundation structures and arches. Note, for example, that the Old Stone Tower (at least four centuries old) shows no signs of sagging, whereas most of the Colonial structures in Newport have long ago been hauled away to landfills. The differing masonry styles in the Grant House suggest that the medieval masons who constructed the Old Stone Tower lived in temporary houses situated along the pre-Colonial waterfront street.

Possibly, Nordic immigrants used half-sunken log houses with turf roofs of the sort that can be seen in the medieval houses of Iceland. The end-wall vaults of these houses were simply the fireplaces that served one-story structures. Triangular keystones in these arches were suitable as a signature or symbol of the masons who built the structures. Throughout New England, the preferred device for spanning the opening of a doorway, window, or fireplace was an oak beam. As the span or the amount of weight above the span increased, so did the size of the beam. Architects who designed monumental buildings often employed archways constructed by using standardized fitted bricks, or arch-stones. Aside from the singular example of the Old Stone Tower (and the previously hidden arches in the Grant House foundation), eclectic fan-shaped arches were totally unknown in Colonial New England. Architectural historian, Hugh Morrison, noted: "The Newport Tower has little significance in the history of Colonial architecture. Nothing quite like it had been built before or was ever built afterward. Excavations undertaken during the summer of 1948 afforded no positive evidence whatever in favor of either theory [Norse church or Colonial windmill]."[2]

Protagonists of the theory that the Old Stone Tower was intended to be a windmill have noted a vague similarity to a structure that was built in Chesterton, England, around 1625. It was certainly conceived by an architect who was familiar with the Temple Church in London, and designed to serve as an exotic windmill. All the bricks that were used in building the six-pillar structure were pre-cast from ceramic molds. The building is much smaller than the Newport Tower, but just about the same size as the newer Dutch windmills of the 17th century.

These mills featured a revolving turret top that housed the rotor fan and gearwheels that powered the grinding mechanism. This type of grinding mechanism was unavailable in New England until the early 18th century, at which time turret grinders were first installed at Boston. Unlike the Newport Tower, walls of the Chesterton structure were designed with a seven-degree inward slant. These slanting walls reduced the potentially damaging effects of gale-force winds.

Certainly, most immigrants from England were familiar with stone-built windmills. The Chesterton mill was a public notoriety that appeared in a published tabloid, *Penny Magazine*. Basic similarity to the eight pillars of the Old Stone Tower in Newport might have inspired Colonial settlers to assume that the enigmatic structure on Mill Hill might just have been a windmill. Still other alternative researchers speculate Knights Templar refugees from Vatican oppression in the early 14th century built the Newport Tower.

To be sure, Crusader temples were built all over Europe. Several structures still survive in England, Scotland, the Orkney Islands, Norway, and Italy. They were designed to reflect the basic features of Emperor Constantine's Temple of the Holy Sepulcher in Jerusalem, with a central tower (circular or octagonal) that stood about three stories high. The bottom level was an arcade resting on eight pillars connected with classical Romanesque arches and oriented to the cardinal points of a compass. The central tower functioned as an oratory or as a baptismal surrounded by a circular ambulatory or galleries.

The Newport Tower's "projecting risers" on the outsides of all eight pillars clearly indicate that the builders intended to add a circular ambulatory around the structure. Archeologists identified two posthole stains in the surrounding earth located 4 meters outward of two pillars. These stains suggest that a wooden structure might have been built around the Stone Tower for use as an ambulatory. In a 1524 report, Giovanni Verrazano, an Italian explorer in the service of King Francis I of France, mentions "a white Native Tribe" and residents of Narragansett Bay who were "inclined to whiteness," which suggests that one of the destinations of refugee farmers included the shores of Narragansett Bay.[3]

Doubtless, Nordic refugees who were transplanted to this region soon lost their ethnic and racial distinctions by merging with the local Narragansett and Wampanoag People. Legends or reports concerning the presence of a hybrid Native-European colony in this region were probably a factor in the decision by Gerhard Mercator to identify "Norombega City" as the capital of a European colony alongside the shores of Narragansett Bay on his World Map of 1569.

Other new settlements included Newfoundland, Nova Scotia, New York, and the Carolinas. In fact, Colonial settlers reported numerous contacts with "White Indians"—Welsh, Irish, and Nordic residents eager to trade furs and fish for coveted iron tools and fabrics from Europe. These early European settlers in the New World provided a "cultural bridgehead" that facilitated the survival of new immigrants from the Old World. And the enduring monument they left behind still stands in Touro Park, at the top of Mill Street, surrounded by a historical residential neighborhood on a hill above modern Newport's waterfront tourist district.

41

"The Lost Civilizations of North America" Debate

By Rick Osmon

Today, a group of "independent scholars" (euphemism often used to mean writers without institutional affiliation, formal training, or archaeological experience) trumpet the evidence for these ancient settlers of the Americas, disseminating their revisionist histories—not in referenced, professional journals, but in popular books, magazines, and, perhaps most broadly, on websites and in cable TV documentaries. While it is tempting to ignore the documentary as nonsense, the high production values coupled with the selective inclusion of academically credible scholars have resulted in its gaining international attention.[1]

The foregoing statement was used by Brad Lepper, curator of archeology, Ohio History Connection, to dismiss any influence an alternative archaeology telecast may have exerted on a large, international audience. He likewise dismissed all autodidactic scholars, discerning viewers, or anybody who fails to toe the academic line held firmly in his grip. But such an outburst is only another example of Lepper expressing his perception that he is intellectually superior to the common man.

In truth, evidence for pre-Columbian transoceanic voyages is both vast and compelling, although the documentary he hated only examined a tiny portion of that huge landscape of proof. Lepper then went on to imply that all the source materials for the presence of overseas' visitors in our continent before Columbus—that is, engraved stones, out-of-place coins, maps, foodstuffs, and other commodities explained only by transoceanic voyagers—are all mere outgrowths of the Atlantis myth and no less fantastic than some of the technological wonders ascribed to that "Lost Continent."

Although Plato's fourth-century BCE account never mentioned any such high technology, he did state that Atlantis controlled the trade of metals and transported those goods by sea. The period he described, some 11,400 years ago, both metal and sailing would have certainly been "high tech." In fact, anyone who controlled that trade would have been the Bill Gates of that era. Unfortunately, there is no lab test for assessing the age of metal artifacts. Apparently, Brad read the *CliffsNotes* instead of the original.

About the same time Plato was discussing Atlantis with his students, a fellow Greek, Pytheas of Massalia, explored northwestern Europe, thereby expanding humankind's knowledge of our planet. Although his accounts were highly valued in his day, later writers discounted them for various reasons. Less than 200 years later, the Arcadian historian Polybius doubted that Pytheas could have sailed the route and distance claimed, simply because Pytheas was too poor for outfitting such expedition. Skeptics failed to discern the real position of Thule, the name of a far-northern land Pytheas supposedly visited. Some scholars have since identified Thule with Iceland, though others disagree, because Iceland, unlike the island Pytheas described, was "uninhabited" until the eighth century.

Yet third-century Roman coins have been found in Iceland (to say nothing of similar finds in Indiana, Kentucky, and Wisconsin).

Pytheas also gave the circumference of the British Isles as 40,000 *stadia*. If our current understanding of the unit length for a *stadium* is accurate [about 600 feet], then Pytheas's estimate was within 2 percent of modern measurements. He could not have accomplished such precision without a firm working knowledge of trigonometry and navigation. It stands to reason that Pytheas was not the only ancient mariner with these skills. Yet, Lepper and most academics would toss Pytheas's account in with the works of H.P. Lovecraft and Robert E. Howard as pure, heroic fantasy.

As to Polybius's logic, George Meegan, a British adventurer and alternative educator, walked from Patagonia to Alaska's north coast without a penny, a total of 19,019 miles. Leif Erickson sailed from Greenland to Norway in an open longboat without stopping at Iceland at the age of 17. Dutch 16-year-old Laura Decker circumnavigated the globe solo in a year. People who know how to sail simply know how to sail. Those who don't tend to disbelieve those who do. Humans have steered by the stars on land and sea and traded goods of all kinds for as long as they have traveled.

The only way to deny that ancient people had developed formidable skills in mathematics, astronomy, shipbuilding, and navigation is to denigrate your own ancestors' intellect. People sailed to Australia more than forty thousand years ago, but academia is loath to admit that anyone could sail to or from America before Columbus, due mainly to doctrine more than science—specifically, due to the "Powell Doctrine," named for John W. Powell, founder and first director of the Smithsonian's Bureau of American Ethnology.

This prevailing academic dogma is elucidated by a case in point: Indiana State geologist Edward T. Cox, William W. Borden, and F.W. Putnam described a stone fortress at Devil's Backbone along the Ohio River. During 1895, the Big Four Railroad used the stones to build the Big Four Rail Bridge from Jeffersonville to Louisville. They also quarried virgin stone from atop the bluff in the most inaccessible part of the site, an area of low quality stone for building. Then, in 1902, Gerard Fowke, from the Smithsonian Institution Bureau of American Ethnology, wrote a scathing counter to Cox's, et al., assertion that artificial stonewalls existed at Devil's Backbone.

Of course, in 1902, Fowke was correct. The walls and mounds were gone, destroyed, stolen, but the denigrating description of Cox was incorrect and unprofessional, somewhat like Lepper's treatment of the film's producers and viewers. Despite Fowke's effort and Powell's (and Lepper's) intent, the United States Geological Survey topographical map of the quadrant containing Devil's Backbone has a note in red, "Historic Fort Ruins." This is rather ironic in that, before founding the Bureau of American Ethnology, Powell was director of the United States Geological Survey, a federal agency for studying the landscape, its natural resources, and the natural hazards that threaten it.

Brad Lepper's article states:

In stark contrast to the elegant consensus achieved by the inter-disciplinary work of archaeologists, geologists, geneticists, and linguists (Meltzer, 2009; Goebel et al., 2008), recent issues of the diffusionist *Ancient American* magazine amply demonstrate that there is, in fact, no consensus among diffusionist research-ers concerning which African, Asian, or European cultures arrived in America to serve as the elevators of Native American savagery; when they arrived; or which cultural achievements they are supposed to have introduced or inspired.[2]

On the contrary, diffusionists contend that representatives from all those cultures traded with and contributed to the advancement of Native Americans, and that Native Americans contributed to the advancement of Old World cultures. To his credit, however, Lepper seems to admit that the Clovis-first model is heavily flawed, and that sites such as Cactus Hill, Meadowcroft, and Monte Verde are indeed evi-dence of pre-Clovis habitation. (Clovis is a prehistoric culture that first appears in the archaeological record of North America around 13,500 years ago, and named for artifacts found near Clovis, New Mexico, where the first evidence of this tool complex was excavated, in 1932. Cactus Hill [Virginia], Meadowcroft [Pennsylvania], and Monte Verde [Chile] establish human habitation in the Americas centuries before Clovis.)

He also admits that Man may have been in the Americas for as long as 30,000 years, an inadvertent admission that his "elegant consen-sus" is neither elegant nor a consensus. When, during the last century, geologist Virginia Steen McIntyre found a paradigm-breaking date for artifacts in Mexico, despite performing state-of-the-art tests on strata containing those artifacts, she was drummed completely out of her cho-sen profession. So much for the constitutional preamble right to "the pursuit of happiness"! You can pursue your profession of choice, as long as you don't upset the dogmatic apple carts.

Scientific method demands that any new evidence must become a part of consensus. But when that evidence is denied or ignored out of hand, then the method itself is broken and the advancement of the science comes to a standstill.

"Basically, archeology is assumptions based on association," observed American historian O. Ned Eddins, "with few scientific facts to back up the assumptions."[3]

The French *Ancien autorité* has several interpretations. The one that best applies to doctrinal archeologists would be that of "former." The phrase *academic archeologist* might be a euphemism for college-trained humanities students who interpret artifacts, but it does not inherently imply adherence to scientific method.

42

King Arthur's American Colony

By Gunnar Thompson, PhD

Roman legions began occupying Britain during the early first century CE. Shortly after their arrival, Gaelic farmers moved from hill-fort sanctuaries onto flat farmlands near newly built Roman cities. Safety was not a major concern, because legionnaires patrolled the shores and the countryside. Occasional attacks by Keltic Picts or Germanic Saxons were more of nuisance than serious threats to a developing Romano-Britannic civilization. After the Huns invaded Europe, however, Emperor Honorius (410 CE) ordered his legions back to the Italian Peninsula.

When Anglo-Saxon tribes invaded from the east, most Britons returned to their ancestral hill-forts. They resumed building rustic houses with wattle-and-daub mud walls and straw roofs. This, then, was the deteriorating backdrop for Artorigios, the "bear-king," who contemplated the future of his Christian subjects from the perspective of the ancient earthen ramparts of Somerset's Cadbury Castle. The omens were not very encouraging. All across Britain, farmers were losing their crops, their livestock, and their lives to Saxon raiders. It was not enough that he organized an army of archers and knights.

After fighting and winning many battles, King Arthur realized that civilized Britons would never prevail against the outnumbering barbarians. Thus, he turned his eyes toward the West. Far across the Atlantic Ocean, the mythical Avalon, "Isle of Apples," served as a beacon of hope and prosperity. His proposal for founding a colony along the shores of the Western Isles was a desperate gamble aimed at the establishment of an enduring sanctuary for Christianity. The success of King Arthur's endeavor was recorded in a little-known document from the Archives of the British Museum.

Its *Cotton Manuscript Vitellius* (C—VII, Folio 264-9), recounts the testimony of a Dutch journalist, Jacob Cnoyen, and his "Travels in the Northern Regions," about 1364. Sections from the manuscript were copied some 200 years later by Gerhard Kramer, better remembered as the famous mapmaker Gerardus Mercator (1512–1594). Cnoyen's "Travels" were transcribed by Queen Elizabeth's chief geographer, John Dee, in 1577, and subsequently preserved at London's British Museum.[1]

In a mid-16th-century letter, Mercator expressed concern regarding efforts by English authorities to gain papal approval for establishing a new colony in America. The basis of their claim was that "prior settlement" by King Arthur's colonists provided England with a divine right to settle in the New World. According to a Papal Bull issued by Alexander VI in 1493, the "Western Isles" (i.e., the Americas) were reserved for Portugal and Spain. Cnoyen claimed to have conducted interviews with pre-Columbian Americans he personally encountered at the Court of Magnus VII, King of Norway-Sweden, 118 years before Christopher Columbus arrived in the New World. According to Cnoyen's testimony, these "pilgrims" were descendants of colonists King Arthur brought to the "Northern Regions." This is what Cnoyen had to say:

> The islands adjacent to the North Pole were formerly called *Ciliae* [perhaps Thule] and are now called *Septentrionalis* ["Northern Regions"]. Among them is *Nortnorwegen* ["North Norway"]. Part of King Arthur's army that conquered the Northern Islands and made them subject to him were present. . . . Nearly four thousand persons entered the region of in-drawing seas. They remained in this region. In 1364, eight of these people came to the King's Court in Norway. Among them were two priests, one

of who had an astrolabe [an instrument used to make astronomical measurements, typically of the altitudes of celestial
bodies, and in navigation for calculating latitude.] One was a
5th generation descendant of an immigrant from Brussels. The
eight were descendants from those who had penetrated the
Northern Regions in the first ships. Arthur's great army spent
the winter of 530 in the northern islands of Scotland.

On May 3, part of the army crossed over into Iceland.
Then four ships from the said land, *Septentrionalis*, came out
of the north. They warned Arthur about the in-drawing seas.
Therefore, Arthur did not proceed farther. Instead, he settled
people in the islands between Scotland and Iceland. He also
left settlers in Groclant [Labrador]. In those four ships, there
were sailors who asserted that they knew where the Magnetic
Lands. Afterwards, Arthur loaded up a fleet of twelve ships with
about eighteen hundred men and four hundred women. They
sailed northwards on May 3rd in the following year; that is, in
the year after the former ships had departed. Of these twelve
ships, five were driven onto the rocks in a storm; but the rest of
them made their way between the high rocks on June 18, which
was forty-four days after they had set out (Taylor, 1956, 56-68).[2]

Cnoyen went on to relate that the First Contingent settled near the
"in-drawing seas," probably a reference to Newfoundland. A Second
Contingent settled in Groclant-Labrador. The Third Expedition may
have settled along the shores of Nova Scotia. This colony consisted of
about 700 settlers with numerous farm animals. Evidently, the colonists
prospered, multiplied, and spread westward, building hill-forts across
New York and deep into the Ohio Valley. Arthur's Western Colony was
variously called "Avalon," "New Albion," "Albania Magna," "Albany," or
"Great Ireland."

The key to understanding the location of King Arthur's Colony is
Cnoyen's reference to "the Magnetic Lands." William Gilbert noted in
De Magnete (circa 1600) that all the ancients were familiar with the magnetic properties of lodestone (or magnetite). It was found any place where
iron deposits of hematite or magnetite were struck by lightning, thus
rendering them magnetic. The principal source in the Mediterranean
Region was Magnesia in Anatolia (Western Turkey). Pencil-thin strips
of this ore invariably attracted iron objects. When suspended from a

cord, the "north-pointing stone" aligned itself with the earth's Magnetic North Pole. In the region of the Eastern Mediterranean, this orientation was very close to the alignment of Earth's Geographic North Pole.

During Roman times, the Magnetic North Pole was situated in Labrador, which was about 3,000 miles south of the Geographic North Pole. Classical scholars presumed that there must be a huge Magnetic Mountain at the North Pole in order for it to attract magnetized iron needles. They also believed that the North Pole was too frigid for human habitation. However, this opinion was contrary to the experience of contemporaneous mariners. Seamen who used the "north-pointer" as a navigational device sailed directly north of Britain, toward Labrador. When they arrived at their destination, they found local residents dwelling in a temperate climate with plenty of food plants (corn, beans, and squash) and plenty of game animals (deer, turkeys, and bears).

Thus, there emerged in Roman mythology the tale of a "temperate climate" near the North Pole. Meanwhile, Greek and Roman scholars dismissed tales about the Hyperboreans as unreliable. Their skepticism was the basis for today's academic refusal to consider possibilities for transoceanic travel before Columbus. The magnetic stone was a common navigational device on ships until Vatican authorities condemned magnetism as "a demonic power." After that edict came into effect, most European seafarers kept silent about using unauthorized equipment, due to the tendency of upstanding clergymen to burn parishioners suspected of questioning Church doctrine.

Practically no one in the 14th century doubted that the Northern Region (along with Arthur's colony) was at the Geographic North Pole. However, everything began to change in 1351. That was when a joint Portuguese, Florentine, and Genovese team of explorers determined that the Nordic colonies of Iceland, Greenland, Vinland, Albion (Britain), and Great Ireland were actually situated west—not north—of Norway. This breakthrough resulted from the simultaneous observation of Polaris and a religiously incorrect magnetic compass in the region of Iceland. The *Nancy Manuscript* (1427) notes that the orientation of the Magnetic North Pole was observed to be Latitude 66 degrees N; Polaris was at 0 degrees N. In other words, the astronomers realized that there were two different poles. During the interim between 1261 and 1351, the Norwegian kings claimed ownership of the so-called "Northern Isles."[3]

However, after publication of 1351's *Medici Atlas*, it became evident to practically everyone that King Arthur's "New Albion" was actually situated in the Far West. Geographers had grown accustomed to calling the colonies in the Far North by the title of *Nortnorwegen* ("North Norway"). A Spanish friar who visited this region in 1350 noted how the inhabitants of *Ibernia* (or the Colony of Great Ireland) were Keltic. Yet, he was surprised to observe that they flew the flag of the Norse king and paid taxes to the king of Norway. The friar's report was reported in *El Libro de Conocemiento* (*The Book of Knowledge*) and confirmed by 1413's *Mecia Viladestes* Map of the North Atlantic. This map showed the Isle of Ibernia (Great Ireland) north of Iceland. The Colony had been misplaced on previous maps.[4]

Modern historians have grown accustomed to ignoring these reports, testimonials, and tax records, disregarding them as "fictional" or "mythological." However, by 1577, the queen's geographer, John Dee, realized that North Norway in the West actually encompassed the ancient colony of King Arthur. This realization was confirmed by Cnoyen's interview with American pilgrims from King Arthur's colony at the Court of King Magnus VII, nearly a century before Columbus was born. Accordingly, English Kings took immediate steps to reclaim their lost colony of New Albion in the Far West.

When King Arthur's colonists came ashore along the coast of Labrador or Nova Scotia, they immediately set about constructing hill-forts with standardized perimeter earthworks, palisades, and wattle-and-daub dwellings. These were the sorts of dwelling places where they had lived in Medieval England; they naturally built similar hill-forts and farmsteads along North America's Eastern Seaboard, as part of their traditional culture. So long as the immigrants behaved in a cordial manner, local indigenes did not regard them as a threat.

Indeed, the Arthurian colonists probably showed themselves to be an asset, because they traded iron tools, textiles, and cheese for regional essentials that included cornmeal, pumpkins, bearskins, and copper nuggets. Most natives were hunter-gatherers; some cultivated maize and beans. Forest tribes lacked sufficient numbers to have posed a serious threat to the Welsh settlers. During the 19th century, pioneers and antiquarians identified 20-odd hill-forts of enormous size along the Ohio River Valley. The structures had been abandoned long before, but elders of the Shawnee Tribe made no claim on them, declaring that they were never the dwelling places of their ancestors. Nevertheless, archaeologists continue to presume that these hill-forts must have been built by the Hopewellian ancestors of local tribes.

Huge Ohio hill-forts—such as Fort Ancient, Spruce Hill, and Fort Hill—were very similar to structures used in Medieval England. Historians have identified more than 2,000 hill-forts in England, with a preponderance of 600 in the Western Counties of Wales. These forts consisted of flattened hilltops of about 20 to 30 acres; they were surrounded by perimeter earthworks and palisades. Entrances were often modified to include elaborate ramparts that gave defenders a significant advantage. Some forts had walled roadways, consisting of parallel earthen embankments. These extraordinary structures enabled shepherds to channel their flocks of sheep, goats, geese, or herds of oxen and horses, and are the kind of structures we would expect Arthurian settlers to build in North America.

Welsh settlements in this region help explain the apparent introduction of the longbow circa 600 to 700 CE into the Eastern Woodlands. They additionally elucidate the Indian adoption of wattle-and-daub mud construction, and demonstrate how native peoples acquired metal axes used to build palisades around their villages. At Ohio's Spruce Hill, for example, historian Arlington Mallery reported the presence of numerous iron-smelting furnaces. He also noted that the inhabitants had carted up thousands of tons of stones from a quarry situated 200 feet below the top of the hill.

Tests by the Battelle Laboratory showed that iron and copper tools found at or near the hill-forts were made from melted or forged metals using Old World technology. Historians generally insist that aboriginals never used cast metal tools. However, artifacts found at some abandoned native villages included cinders and scorched earth, indicating the presence of a smithy's forge. Evidently, Welsh blacksmiths took refuge at Seneca, Shawnee, and Algonquian villages when plague spread across the land during the 14th century.

During the Mississippian Era (circa 900–1300), huge indigenous urban centers—Cahokia, Kincaid, Angel Mounds, Parkin, Moundsville, and so forth—included perimeter palisades enclosing ceremonial earthworks, communal lodges, and upper-class houses. These metropolitan areas and surrounding villages were typically located on flat terraces or prairies above the floodplains of nearby rivers. Forests were cleared for farmlands, while tens of thousands of trees were felled to provide poles and stakes needed to build palisades about 15 feet tall. Native cities were situated mostly along the Mississippi River at the western fringe of the Eastern Woodlands Region. Within this sector, they provided for the needs of a transportation system that carried cargoes of maize, wool, buffalo hides, and copper axes toward Mexico's Aztec Empire.

During the 14th century, Welsh and indigenous populations rebounded from the plague, and a new type of habitation pattern developed throughout the Ohio River Valley. We see in the ancient landscape the remains of abandoned farmsteads, sheepfolds, and huge corrals. These sites are very similar to the feudal farms of Anglo-Saxon and Norman England. One example of the utilitarian farmstead is the Newark Works that Wittlesey, Squire, and Davis plotted, in 1837. Welsh-Indian villages in the Ohio Valley were typically square or octagonal in shape, surrounded by perimeters of palisades behind external trenches. The village enclosures were typically about 20 acres, although some larger villages encompassed about 50 acres. Adjacent to the village, there was typically a huge, circular enclosure that could have served as a corral for horses and other livestock.

The circular enclosures typically had a ditch running along the inside of an earthen wall. We see exactly the same types of corrals in feudal England and Ohio. The ditch would have collected rainwater that provided for the needs of livestock. The circular "corral" doubled as an entertainment arena for horse races or popular native field games, such as lacrosse. Most of the farming villages in Ohio had roadways flanked by parallel, earthen walls. These walled roadways were apparently designed to channel flocks or herds of animals between pastures, shelters, and watering holes. Farming villages were not built for defense. In the case of Ohio's Hopeton Works, in Ross County, the village site is situated directly below a nearby bluff where it would have been vulnerable to attack by arrows from above. State archeologists have found native pottery, stone arrowheads, stone mauls, copper axes, and occasional pieces of iron at nearby mounds or in the village rectangles.

Typically, there were no artifacts or remains of houses inside the corral circles. Usually, the nearest ceremonial mounds or effigy mounds were several miles away. In other words, these flatland villages were not typically ceremonial sites; they were built primarily as utilitarian farmsteads. At Rayner's Mound in Piqua, Ohio, archeologists discovered two burial tablets with enigmatic, runic writing. In this same area, antiquarians uncovered remains of rusted swords and textiles that typically disintegrated into dust upon exposure to the air. A few pieces of iron blades that were found at North Carolina's Nelson Mound were reported in publications by the Smithsonian Institution. When Italian navigator John Cabot landed along the East Coast of North America in 1497, he saw "cultivated fields" and dung that reminded him of European draft animals.

In 1535, French explorer Jacques Cartier likewise reported seeing "cultivated fields" near Montreal. What he had in mind were fields that had been gouged with furrows by plows and draft animals. The Chief of Hochelaga informed Cartier that Saguenay natives wore "woolen clothing," indicating that sheep were raised in Canada.[5] Other explorers, such as Sebastian Cabot, Giovanni Verrazano, Gaspar Corte-Real, and Samuel Champlain, all reported seeing white people living among the Indians.

There were numerous Colonial Era reports of encounters with Welsh-speaking Indians. In 1569, David Ingram told of seeing native villages with horses, cattle, and chickens in the Eastern Woodlands. Baron Lahontan (1678) stated that "plenty of horses, black cattle, fowl, and hogs" could be found at Seneca farms, in New York.[6] During 1765, frontiersman William Rogers, encountered "White Indians" who raised grain and cattle on farms situated far beyond the British Colonies.[7] The animals and feudal farming technology could have come from Greenland Norse, who moved to Canada in the 13th century, from Iberian farmers in the seventh century, or from Welsh immigrants in the 12th century.

A preponderance of such evidence not only establishes the arrival of Western Europeans in our hemisphere long before 1492, but affirms their attempts at founding a colony in Labrador, perhaps at the personal direction of ancient Britain's legendary king.

AFTERWORD:
THE LONG-AWAITED
PARADIGM SHIFT

Since 1993, *Ancient American* magazine has published more than 20 volumes of evidence clearly demonstrating that visitors from the outside world have been sailing to our continent for tens of thousands of years. Our proofs were mostly ignored, sometimes ridiculed, but not debated on their merits by conventional scholars. They never swerved from their doctrinaire insistence that America was uninhabited until the first humans to arrive here began crossing a theoretical "land-bridge" from Siberia into Alaska, no more than 13,500 years ago. But that dominant paradigm has been gradually eroded by progress in other scientific fields, until the Ivory Tower of consensus opinion is at last beginning to show some serious cracks.

"We so radically underestimated the roles of boats and water transports for all time horizons," admitted James Adovasio, director of Pennsylvania's Mercyhurst University Archaeological Institute, "not just the more recent past."[1]

His untypical statement was allowed to stand un-criticized in the September/October 2014 issue of *Archaeology* magazine, the prestigious mouthpiece of mainstream belief. He was referring to Chile's Monte Verde, Pennsylvania's Meadowcroft Rockshelter, Oregon's Paisley Caves, and at least 40 other digs filled with artifacts not only millennia older than officialdom's 12,000-year-old starting date for human habitation in South America, but brought to our shores by persons arriving by sea—persons operating a technology deemed "impossibly advanced" until now.

Though Adovasio and his colleagues seemed surprised by the—to them—"new" implications of these discoveries, the sites in question have been thoroughly described by *Ancient American* for more than 20 years. During all that time, our repeated statement that prehistoric visitors were, first of all, *sailors* was treated with contempt. But now, the latest buzzword among the professionals is *boats*, according to Nikhil Swaminathan, *Archaeology*'s contributing editor. His leading "special section" article "America: In the Beginning" was illustrated by a map of the Americas underscored by a caption reading: "Archaeologists posit several, possible routes . . . a migration from Beringia, the land-bridge that once connected Siberia and Alaska . . . travel by boat along the northern rim of the Pacific, then southward along the coast . . . human travel from the Iberian Peninsula to Newfoundland by boat, along the edge of the ice cap . . . migration, by boat, from West Africa to Brazil."[2]

Whereas the appearance of such a map purporting to show deeply prehistoric, maritime contacts with Europe and Africa often appears in the pages of our magazine, that one should be found in a current issue of *Archaeology* is more than a little unusual. More importantly, mainstream scholars' developing about-face on the whole question of cultural diffusion versus cultural isolation represents a fundamental shift in academic perspective toward the real prehistory of our world.

NOTES

Chapter 1

1. *Radiocarbon Magazine, Volume 34, Number 3*, pp. 279–291 (January /February 2015).
2. *The Wyoming Archaeologist 38* : 55–68 (April/May 2014), *www.wyoming archaeology.org/the-wyoming-archaeologist.html.*
3. Alison, Robert M. "Canada's Last Wild Horses," 2000, *http://members .shaw.ca/save-wild-horses/Research%20Paper%20-%20R.%20Alison.htm.*
4. Canadian Museum of Nature I-8581, *nature.ca/en/home.*
5. Kuchinsky, Yuri. "Did Native Americans Really Have the Horse Before Columbus?" *www.globalserve.net/~yuku/tran/thor.htm.*
6. Cohen, Jeanie. January 30, 2012, *www.history.com/news/horse-domestication-happened-across-eurasia-study-shows.*

Chapter 2

1. Steffy, J. Richard. *Wooden Ship Building and the Interpretation of Shipwrecks* (Texas A&M University Press, 2012).
2. Smith, Roff. *www.nationalgeographicexpeditions.com/experts/roff-smith /detail.*

Chapter 3

1. Grimm, David. "Ancient Bobcat Buried Like a Human Being," *http:// news.sciencemag.org/archaeology/2015/07/ancient-bobcat-buried -human-being.*
2. Ibid.

Chapter 4

1. Schmid, Randolf E. "13,000-Year-Old Bone With Mammoth or Mastodon Carving May Be First in Western Hemisphere," *www .huffingtonpost.com/2011/06/22/mammoth-mastodon-bone-carving-florida -photo_n_882177.html.*
2. Ibid.
3. Ibid.
4. Ibid.
5. Ibid.
6. Ibid.
7. *Science Magazine 192*: 756–761.
8. Corliss, William R. *Ancient Man: A Handbook of Puzzling Artifacts* (Md.: The Sourcebook Project, 1980).
9. Ibid. The NEARA Newsletter article was volume 7, pp. 16–18.
10. Ibid. He published *The Bible in Iron* (N.Y.: Ulan Press, reprint of the 1923 original, 2012) and *Ancient Carpenters' Tools* (N.Y.: Dover Publications' reprint of the 1925 original, 2000).
11. "Mammoth," *https://en.wikipedia.org/wiki/Mammoth.*
12. Corliss, op. cit.
13. Wikipedia, op. cit.
14. Corliss, op. cit.; *American Anthropology 36 (1)* (1934).
15. Ibid.; *Archaeology of Ohio* (Cincinnati: The Western Reserve Historical Society, 1879).
16. Wikipedia, op. cit.
17. Corliss, op. cit.; Ludwell H. Johnson. "Men and Elephants in America," *Scientific Monthly, No. 75* (October 1952).
18. Ibid.; *Scientific Monthly* (41:378–79).
19. Faris, Peter. "The Grand Traverse Bay, Michigan Proboscidain," *http:// rockartblog.blogspot.com/2013/03/the-grand-traverse-bay-michigan.html.*

Section II

1. Osmon, Rick. *The Graves of the Golden Bear: Ancient Fortresses and Monuments of the Ohio Valley* (Indiana: Grave Distractions Publications, 2011).

Chapter 5

1. Charles, Herbert. *History of Venango County, Pennsylvania*, Volume I (Chicago, Ill.: Brown, Runk & Co., 1890).
2. Day, Sherman. *Historical Collections of the State of Pennsylvania* (N.Y.: George W. Gorton, 1843), p. 637.

3. Thomas, J.E. "Prehistoric Petroleum Use in Pennsylvania," *Oil Field Journal* (Winter 2000–2001), p. 20.
4. Newberry, J.S. 1890, "The First Oil Well," Harper's New Monthly Magazine, number 81 (485:7232-729).
5. Day, op. cit.; Day, Sherman. *Historical Collections of the State of Pennsylvania* (Philadelphia: George W. Gorton Publishers, 1843) p. 250.
6. Ibid.
7. *Midwestern Epigraphic Society Newsletter, Volume 26, Issue 3* (2009), *www.midwesternepigraphic.org/*.
8. Newberry, op. cit.
9. Luttwak, Edward N. *The Grand Strategy of the Byzantine Empire* (N.Y.: Belknap Press, 2009).

Chapter 6

1. "Mercury (element)," *https://en.wikipedia.org/wiki/Mercury_(element)*.
2. Radka, Larry Brian. *The Electric Mirror on the Pharos Lighthouse and Other Ancient Lighting* (W.V.: The Einhorn Press, 2006).
3. Wikipedia, op. cit.

Chapter 7

1. "Cahokia Mounds State Historic Site," *http://cahokiamounds.org/*.

Chapter 8

1. Squire, E.G. *Antiquities of the State of New York* (N.Y.: G.H. Derby, 1851); Morton, Dr. Samuel George. *Crania Americana* (Philadelphia, Pa.: J. Dobson, 1840).
2. Priest, Josiah. *American Antiquities* (N.Y.: Hoffman and White, 1833).
3. "Fluorite." *Geoscience News and Information, http://geology.com/minerals/fluorite.shtml*.
4. Dartmouth Toxic Metals. "Copper: An Ancient Metal," *www.dartmouth.edu/~toxmetal/toxic-metals/more-metals/copper-history.html*.
5. Ben-Yosef, E. "A New Approach for Geomagnetic Archaeointensity Research: Insights on Ancient Metallurgy in the Southern Levant." *Journal of Archaeological Science, http://levlab.ucsd.edu/resources/ELRAP-Publications/A-new-approach-for-geomagnetic-archaeointensity-research.pdf*.
6. Clark, George Rogers. *George Rogers Clark and the War in the West* (Louisville: University Press of Kentucky, 1976).
7. Jackson, John. "The Le Moyne Brothers Lead the Way for the French, *www.rootsweb.ancestry.com/~alcbonse/history7.html*.

Chapter 9

1. All Mitchim quotes in this chapter from *Ancient American*, Volume 16, Issue 94.

Chapter 10

1. Joseph, Frank. *The Atlantis Encyclopedia* (N.J.: New Page Books, 2005).
2. *Ancient American* Volume 18, Issue 103.
3. Childress, David. *Lost Cities of North & Central America* (Ill.: Adventures Unlimited Press, 1992).

Chapter 11

1. Horning, J.D. "Mystery Walls Discovered in Foot Lake Prompt Speculation." *West Central Tribune,* July 20, 1985, front page.
2. Ibid.
3. Ibid.
4. Horning, J.D. "History Group Diver will Probe Foot Lake Walls," *West Central Tribune,* July 24, 1985, page A-1.

Chapter 12

1. All Passmore quotes in this chapter are from *Ancient American* Volume 17, Number 99.
2. Furst, Jill Leslie, and Peter T. Furst. *Pre-Columbian Art of Mexico* (N.Y.: Abbeville Press, 1980).
3. "Crystal Skull," *https://en.wikipedia.org/wiki/Crystal_skull.*
4. Furst and Furst, op. cit.

Chapter 13: Ancient Greek Coin Found in Western Missouri

1. Thompson, Dr. Gunnar. *American Discovery* (Wash.: Misty Isles Press, 1992).
2. Morgan, Pat. *Ancient American* Volume 21, Issue 103 (March/April 1999).
3. Johnston, John. *Indian Tribes of North America, quoted in Archaeologia Americana* Volume 5, (Mass.: The American Antiquarian Society, 1820), p. 273.

Chapter 14

1. Mertz, Henriette. *The Mystic Symbol: Mark of the Michigan Mound Builders* (Wisc.: Hay River Press re-publication of the original 1970 edition, 2004).
2. Deal, David Allen. *Ancient American* Volume 19, Issue 97 (May/June 1998).

3. Barton, Golden, and Wayne May. *Ancient American* Issue 31 (February 2000), p. 17.
4. Budge, E.A. Wallis. *An Egyptian Hieroglyphic Dictionary* Volume I (N.Y.: Dover Publications, 1978).

Chapter 16

1. Petrie, Flinders. *Tools and Weapons* (London: British School of Archaeology in Egypt, 1917).
2. Wakefield, J.S., and Reinoud de Jonge. *Rocks and Rows, Sailing Routes Across the Atlantic and the Copper Trade* (Tex.: MCS Inc., 2009).
3. Petrie, op. cit.
4. Ibid.

Chapter 18

1. Engberg, Gary. *www.garyengbergoutdoors.com/blog/index.php/2009/10/27 /star-gazing-event-to-be-held-at-franks-hill/.*

Chapter 19

1. Moreno-Mayar, J. Víctor, et al. "Genome-Wide Ancestry Patterns in Rapanui Suggest Pre-European Admixture with Native Americans," *Current Biology* Volume 24, Issue 21 (November 3, 2014), pp. 2518–2525.
2. Moore, Elizabeth Armstrong. "Easter Islanders Weren't as Isolated as We Thought," *www.foxnews.com/science/2014/10/26/easter-islanders -werent-as-isolated-as-thought/.*
3. Flanagan, Bob. "Landslide Unearths Moai Statue in Pitcarin Islands," *World News Daily Report, October 9, 2014, http://worldnewsdailyreport.com /landslide-unearths-easter-island-moai-statue-in-pitcairn-islands/.*
4. Ibid.

Chapter 21

1. Rusz, Theodor. *The End of the Last Ice Age* (N.Y.: Compton Publishing, 1966).
2. Firth, Alexander. *Ancient Chinese Myth* (N.Y.: Graham Press, 1934).
3. Kaplan, Robert, and Ellen Kaplan. *Hidden Harmonies: The Lives and Times of the Pythagorean Theorem* (N.Y.: Bloomsbury Press, 2012).
4. Thom, Alexander. *Megalithic Sites in Britain* (Oxford: Clarendon Press, 1967).
5. Ross, Colin. *Iberian Archaeology* (Chicago, Ill.: Henry Regnery Press, 1981).

Chapter 22

1. Clube, Victor, and Bill Napier. *The Cosmic Serpent* (London: Universe Publishing, 1982).

Chapter 23

1. Thompson, Chapter 9, "Welsh and Irish Rovers," op. cit.

Chapter 24

1. Grant, Bob. "European Roots for Native Americans?" *The Scientist,* October 29, 2013, *www.the-scientist.com/?articles.view/articleNo/38061 /title/European-Roots-for-Native-Americans-/.*
2. Ibid.
3. Balter, Michael. "Ancient DNA Links Native Americans With Europe," *Science Magazine,* October 25 2013, *www.amren.com/news/2013/10 /ancient-dna-links-native-americans-with-europe/.*
4. Ibid.
5. Ibid.

Chapter 25

1. "3,800-Year-Old Statuettes From Advanced Caral Civilization Found in Peru," Arcodabara, June 12, 2015, *https://arcodabara.wordpress.com /category/archaeology.*
2. Ibid.

Chapter 26

1. Walton, Marsha, and Michael Coren. "Scientist: Man in Americas Earlier Than Thought; Archaeologists Put Humans in North America 50,000 Years Ago," *www.cnn.com/2004/TECH/science/11/17/carolina.dig /index.html?iref=newssearch.*
2. Ibid.
3. Ibid.
4. Ibid.
5. Ibid.
6. Ibid.

Chapter 27

1. Choi, Q. "Prehistoric Boy May Be Native American Missing Link," February 12, 2014, *www.livescience.com/43329-prehistoric-boy-may-be -native-american-missing-link.html.*
2. Ibid.
3. Ibid.
4. Ibid.

Chapter 28

1. Moats, Rich. "A Summary of Fort Glenford: Adena Hill-Top Enclosure and Burial Mound," *Ancient American*, No. 96.
2. Ibid.
3. Squier, E.G., and E.H. Davis. *Ancient Monuments of the Mississippi Valley* (Washington, D.C.: Smithsonian Books, 1998).
4. Burl, Aubrey. *The Stone Circles of the British Isles* (New Haven, Ct.: Yale University Press, 1976).
5. Joseph, Frank. *The Lost Colonies of Ancient America* (N.J.: New Page Books, 2013).
6. Healy, Michael. *Britain's New Stone Age* (London: Joyce Publishing, Ltd., 1960).
7. Coles, Bryony, and John Coles. *Sweet Tracks to Glastonbury* (London: Thames & Hudson, 1986).
8. Ibid.
9. Cain, David. *Ancient American* Volume 12, Issue 69 (June/July 2005).

Chapter 29

1. Sea, Geoffrey. "The Untold History—Lincoln's Mystery Mound Tour," February 26, 2013, portcitiesreview.com/lincolns-mystery-mound -tour-by-geoffrey-sea/.
2. Sheldon, George. *Town History of Deerfield, Massachusetts* volume 1 (New Hampshire Publishing Co., 1972 reprint of the 1856 original), p. 78.
3. Thomas, Cyrus. *Report on Mound Explorations of the Bureau of Ethnology, 12th Annual Report*, Volume 6, 1884, (Smithsonian Bureau of Ethnology, 1890-91), 133f.
4. *St. Paul Pioneer Press*, June 29, 1888.
5. "A Tradition of Giants," *Scientific American* Volume 50, Issue 88 (March 1883).
6. Sheldon, op. cit.
7. Hayes, Lyman Simpson. *History of the Town of Rockingham, Vermont* (Vt.: The Town of Rockingham, 1907).
8. Weston, Thomas. *History of the Town of Middleboro, Massachusetts* (N.Y.: 2010 Nabu Press reprint of the original 1890 edition).
9. Cochrane, Harry Hayman. *History of Monmouth and Wales* (N.Y.: Facsimile Publisher, 2015 reprint of the original 1894 edition).
10. Anonymous. *Gleason's Literary Companion* Volume 5 (Calif.: Palala Press, 2016 reprint of the 1864 edition).
11. Tedorov, Richardo. "History of Montague," *The New England Magazine* Volume 16, Issue 36 (1897).

12. Ibid.

13. Tripp, Alfredm and Harold Osgood. *Guide to the White Mountains and the Lake of New Hampshire* (N.Y.: Woolshire Press, Inc, 1893).

14. Kurtz, Ephraim. *History of Montague: The New England Magazine* Volume 16 (Mass.: Wunderbaum Publishers, 1910), p. 363.

15. Cranston, Francis. *The Friends Intelligencer* Volume 52, Issue 77 (1895), p. 751.

16. Laudervale, Alphonse. *West Virginia Historian. 12th Annual Report* (Va.: Richmond Press, 1891).

17. Doutre, Martin. *Ancient Celtic New Zealand* (N.Z.: De Danann Publishers, 1999).

18. Kuhn, Thomas. *The Structure of Scientific Revolutions* (Ill.: University of Chicago Press, 2012).

Chapter 30

1. Ellis, Franklin. *History of Cattaraugus County, New York* (N.Y.: L.H. Leverts, 1879).

2. Zimmerman, Fritz. The Encyclopedia of Ancient Giants in North America. CreateSpace, 2015.

3. Ellis, op cit.

4. Cited by Dragoo, Don W. *Mounds for the Dead* (Penna.: McDonald and Woodward/Carnegie Museum, 1963).

Chapter 31

1. Snow, Charles E., and William S. Webb. *The Adena People* (University of Tennessee Press, 1974).

2. Ibid.

3. Coon, Carleton S. *The Races of Europe* (Conn.: Greenwood Press, 1972).

4. Dawkins, William Boyd. *Early Man in Britain and His Place in the Tertiary Period* (Mass.: Adamant Media Corporation, 2001).

5. Dawkins, William Boyd. *Our Earliest Ancestors in Britain* (N.Y.: Kessinger Publishing, 2010).

6. Dawkins, [*Early Man*, op cit.

7. Binkowski, Don. *Col. P.W. Norris: Yellowstone's Greatest Superintendent* (N.Y.: C & D of Warren, 1995).

8. Ibid.

9. "Criel Mound," *www.wvexp.com/index.php/Criel_Mound*.

10. Ibid.

11. Ibid.

12. Binkowski, op cit.

13. Ibid.

14. "Criel Mound."
15. Hamilton, Ross. *A Tradition of Giants: The Elite Social Hierarchy of American Prehistory, www.academia.edu/4693378/A_TRADITION_OF _GIANTS_The_Elite_Social_Hierarchy_of_American_Prehistory.*
16. Hertzberg, H.T.E., "Skeletal Material From the Wright Site," *H.T.E. Hertzberg Anthropometry Papers, www.libraries.wright.edu/special /collectionguides/files/fsc2.pdf.*
17. Snow and Webb, op. cit.
18. Dragoo, op. cit.
19. "Criel Mound," op.cit.
20. Moorehead, Warren King. *Primitive Man in Ohio* (N.Y.: G. P. Putnam's Sons, 1892).
21. Ibid.

Chapter 32

1. Cummings, Dr. Byron. "Superstitious Natives Destroy Relics of Prehistoric Supermen," *Border Cities Star* (Windsor, Ontario) Volume 12, Issue 22 (December 4, 1930).
2. Crocker, Willaim. *Prescott Evening Courier* Volume 12, Issue 33 (December 11, 1930).
3. Cummings, Dr. Byron. *Telegraph Herald and Times Journal* Volume. 8, Issue 29 (December 14, 1930).
4. Ibid.
5. Cummings, Dr. Byron. *Telegraph Herald and Times Journal* Volume 12, Issue 44 (December 9, 1934).
6. Hayes, Paxon C. *San Jose Evening Journal* Volume 38, Issue 53 (May 22, 1939).
7. Teide, Raymond. "Prehistoric 'Giants' Befuddle Experts," *Milwaukee Journal* Volume 56, Issue 210 (March 8, 1935).
8. Snow and Webb, op. cit.
9. Dragoo, op. cit.
10. "Smithsonian Amazed at Discovery of Six and One-Half-Foot Mummies in Caves," *Washington Post* (July 22, 1937).
11. "Criel Mound," op.cit.
12. Menkin, Adolf. "Who Were the Ancient Giants?" *Deseret News* Volume 78, Issue 197 (November 11, 1950).
13. Kuhn, op. cit.

Section VIII

1. *www.zhibit.org/jrobbinsmullin.*

Chapter 35

1. Kelley, David. "Bronze Age Europeans Reportedly Visited Ontario," *Toledo Blade* (August 8, 1999).
2. Vastokas, Joan. *Sacred Art of the Algonkians: A Study of the Peterborough Petroglyphs* (London: Mansard Press, Ltd., 1973).

Chapter 36

1. Tedlock, Dennis. *Popol Vuh* (N.Y.: Touchstone, 1996).

Chapter 37

1. All quotes sourced from Goolsby, Denise. "Dig at Twenty-Nine Palms Marine Base Unveils Artifacts," January 16, 2015, *www.desertsun.com /story/news/2015/01/16/marine-corps-archeological-dig/21892001/.*

Chapter 39

1. Daniels, Gary C. "On the Nature of the Apalachites," *thenewworld.us /on-the-nature-of-the-apalachites.*

Section XI

1. Longfellow, Henry Wadsworth. *The Skeleton in Armor* (N.J.: Prentice -Hall, 1963).

Chapter 40

1. Downing, Antoinette, and Vincent Scully. *The Architectural Heritage of Newport, Rhode Island 1640–1915* (N.Y.: Clarkson N. Potter, 1967), Plate 26.
2. Morrison, Hugh. *Early American Architecture: From the First Colonial Settlements to the National Period* (N.Y.: Dover Publications, 2011).
3. Carson, James Brevoort. *Verrazano the Navigator: Or Notes on Giovanni Da Verrazano and on a Planisphere of 1529, Illustrating His American Voyage in 1524* (Mont.: Kessinger Publishing, 2007).

Chapter 41

1. Feder, Kenneth, Bradley T. Lepper, Terry A. Barnhart, and Deborah A. Bolnick. "Civilizations Lost and Found: Fabricating History. Part One: An Alternate Reality," *Skeptical Inquirer* Volume 35.5 (September/October 2011).
2. Ibid.
3. Eddins, Orland Ned. *Mountains of Stone* (Va.: Council of Indian Education, 1997).

Chapter 42

1. Taylor, E.R.G. Letter dated 1577 from Mercator to John Dee, *Imago Mundi* (13) (1956).
2. *Cotton Manuscript Vitellius, www.bl.uk/manuscripts/FullDisplay.aspx?ref =cotton_ms_vitellius_a_xv.*
3. Gilbert, William. *De Magnete* (London, c. 1600). Trans. by P. Fleury Motttelay in 1893 (N.Y.: Dover Publications, 1958).
4. Markham, Clements (trans). *The Book of Knowledge* (c.1350) (London: Hakluyt Society, 1604/1880).
5. Cook, Ramsay. *The Voyages of Jacques Cartier* (University of Toronto Press, 1993).
6. De Lahontan, Baron. *New Voyages to North-America* Volume 2 (Calif.: Forgotten Books, 2016).
7. Bolton, Herbert Eugene, and Thomas Maitland Marshall. *The Colonization of North America 1492 to 1783* (N.Y.: Kessinger Publishing, 2005).

Afterword

1. *Archaeology* magazine, *www.archaeology.org/issues/144-1409.*
2. Ibid.

INDEX